SHOPPING CENT

APPRAISAL AND ANALYSIS

Readers of this text may be interested in *The Appraisal of Shopping Centers* vidoetape, which is available from the Appraisal Institute, and in these related texts: *The Appraisal of Real Estate*, tenth edition, *The Dictionary of Real Estate Appraisal*, and *Appraising Residential Properties*.

For a catalog of Appraisal Institute publications, contact the PR/ Marketing Department of the Appraisal Institute, 875 North Michigan Avenue, Chicago, Illinois 60611-1980.

SHOPPING CENTER
APPRAISAL AND ANALYSIS

James D. Vernor, MAI, PhD

Joseph Rabianski, PhD

Appraisal Institute

875 North Michigan Avenue

Chicago, Illinois 60611-1980

**APPRAISAL
INSTITUTE**

Acknowledgments

Vice President of Publications: Christopher Bettin
Manager, Book Development: Michael R. Milgrim
Editor: Stephanie Shea-Joyce
Graphic Designer: Julie Beich

For Educational Purposes

The opinions and statements set forth herein reflect the viewpoint of the Appraisal Institute at the time of publication but do not necessarily reflect the viewpoint of each individual member. While a great deal of care has been taken to provide accurate and current information, neither the Appraisal Institute nor its editors and staff assume responsibility for the accuracy of the data contained herein. Further, the general principles and conclusions presented in this text are subject to local, state and federal laws and regulations, court cases and any revisions of the same. This publication is sold for educational purposes with the understanding that the publisher is not engaged in rendering legal, accounting or any other professional service.

Nondiscrimination Policy

The Appraisal Institute advocates equal opportunity and nondiscrimination in the appraisal profession and conducts its activities without regard to race, color, sex, religion, national origin, or handicap status.

The photos appearing in this text were supplied by H. Armstrong Roberts, Inc. and The Edward J. DeBartolo Corporation.

Cover photo of Mall of America (Minneapolis) provided by Bob Perzel © 1992

Library of Congress Cataloging-in-Publication Data

Vernor, James D.
    Shopping center appraisal and analysis / James D. Vernor, Joseph Rabianski.
      p.   cm.
    Includes bibliographical references and index.
    ISBN 0-922154-10-4
    1. Shopping centers—Valuation—United States.   I. Rabianski,
Joseph. II. Title.
HF5430.3.V47   1993   92-46567
333.33'7—dc20   CIP

TABLE OF CONTENTS

FOREWORD

In many parts of the United States, the local shopping center has become the new town square, the focus of social and cultural activities as well the provider of retail needs. Some communities draw their identity from the nearby mall and its prosperity reflects the health of the entire area. Various types of shopping centers—neighborhood, community, regional, and superregional—dot the American landscape and play a major role in the everyday life of the American people.

As important as shopping centers are to the way we live, we cannot forget their original purpose, to create profits for retailers and provide goods and services to consumers. The authors of this text provide a detailed examination of the appraiser's role in the analysis and appraisal of these sophisticated real estate investments.

Appraisers contribute to the planning and development of a shopping center by examining the supply and demand factors that impact the local economy and performing market and marketability analyses. Focusing on the site and building characteristics of the specific project, they apply valuation techniques, develop income forecasts for investors and operators, and help solve allocation problems relating to property tax assessment.

The text explores how appraisers, investors, developers, operators, retailers, engineers, and attorneys work as a team, sharing their expertise and information to create a successful real estate venture.

Bernard J. Fountain, MAI, SRA
1993 President
Appraisal Institute

PREFACE

This book was written in response to a call for proposals by the Publications Committee of the Appraisal Institute. The members of this committee felt that more needed to be known and shared about the analysis and appraisal of shopping centers. As we worked on the project, we found that there were many unresolved questions about the topic. Some of the discussion in this text is prescriptive, sharing practical advice on methods and techniques that seem to be well accepted. Many aspects of shopping center valuation have not been standardized, however, and the treatment of these topics reflects the divergence and uncertainty of practitioners. Some of the discussion will seem speculative, but a profession grows through the development of new ideas.

Shopping Center Appraisal and Analysis is likely to appeal to less experienced appraisers embarking on their first shopping center valuation assignment. It is assumed that readers have some training in real estate appraisal and a basic knowledge of the three approaches to value.

To assemble material for the text, we first reviewed all that has been written on the subject. We then conducted interviews to check this information, fill in the gaps, and locate the limits of existing knowledge. We talked to appraisers, market analysts, retail experts, developers, managers, investors, and lenders, who provided insights on a variety of property types, both large and small. Primary writing responsibility for Chapters 1, 3, 4, and 5 was assigned to Joe Rabianski; Jim Vernor was chiefly responsible for Chapters 2, 6, 7, 8, and 9. We have tried to offer examples where this seemed useful. These examples were taken from different sources and describe various situations; they do not relate to a single property.

We want to thank the many industry people who took time to read our work and share their ideas. The real estate appraisal profession is indebted to: James Ahle; William M. Alexander III; Ted Anglyn, MAI; David Beal, MAI; Alvin O. Benton, Jr., MAI, CRE: Brian Benton; Ben Boyd, MAI: John W. Cherry, Jr., MAI; David W. Childers, MAI; Steven Collins, MAI; James C. Cook, MAI; Ken Gain, MAI; Roy Gordon, MAI, CRE; Kenneth P. Holmes; Bruce A. Kellogg, MAI; W. Talmage Kirkland, MAI; Peter F. Korpacz, MAI; Daryl K. Mangan; Daniel L. McCown, MAI; Thomas A. Motta, MAI; John Poole, MAI; Marlene Poole; James H. Pritchett, MAI; Glenn J. Rufrano, MAI; Denise M. Smith, MAI; Roger Tegenkamp, MAI; Kendall Thurston, MAI; Michael G. Turbyfill, MAI; and Henry J. Wise, MAI.

James D. Vernor, MAI, PhD
Joseph Rabianski, PhD

ABOUT THE AUTHORS

James D. Vernor, MAI, BBA, MBA, PhD, is an associate professor of real estate at Georgia State University, with teaching and research responsibilities in appraisal and real estate finance. He is a contributor to *The Appraisal Journal* and was a course developer for the Appraisal Institute's Capitalization Theory and Techniques courses. Vernor is editor of *Readings in Market Research for Real Estate* and a member of the Division of Curriculum of the Education Committee.

Joseph Rabianski, BA, MA, PhD, is a professor of real estate at Georgia State University in Atlanta. Rabianski teaches and conducts research in real estate appraisal and market research, urban economics, and location analysis. He has cowritten several seminars for the Appraisal Institute and is co-author of *Principles of Real Estate Decision Making* and *Real Estate Market Analysis.*

SHOPPING CENTER

APPRAISAL AND ANALYSIS

Bourse Building, Philadelphia   *D. Degnan / H. Armstrong Roberts*

Chapter One

THE NATURE OF SHOPPING CENTERS

S hopping center analysis and evaluation begins with an understand-
ing of the terminology, conditions, and criteria that are currently used in
the retail industry. With a knowledge of these definitions and concepts, an
appraiser can begin to understand the different types of shopping centers
that currently exist and can be developed. The analysis of shopping centers also requires an understanding of the economic rationale for the existence and viability of shopping center developments.

Shopping Center Definition

The Urban Land Institute has defined a shopping center as "A group of
commercial establishments planned, developed, owned, and managed as
a unit related in location, size, and type of shops to the trade area it serves;
it provides on-site parking in definite relationship to the types and sizes of
the stores."[1]

Thus, a shopping center is more than a collection of retail uses. It reflects a unified architectural design and site plan. Ample parking is
planned to facilitate a desirable flow of pedestrian traffic; delivery and

---

1. Urban Land Institute, *Dollars & Cents of Shopping
   Centers: 1990* (Washington, D.C.: Urban Land Institute,
   1990), 3.

service areas are screened from customer view. A shopping center also has sign control, landscaping, and unified management policies, usually developed through a merchants' association. Retail and service tenants are selected for merchandising balance and interplay. The entire project strives for a synergism beyond the underlying retail and service activity, with percentage leases used to capture some of the value created for the owner and operator.

The scope of the basic definition is extended when one considers the eight characteristics of shopping centers which are listed below.

1. A unified architectural treatment for the building or buildings which provide space for businesses that are selected and managed as a unit for the benefit of all tenants. A shopping center is not a miscellaneous or unplanned assemblage of separate or common-wall structures.

2. A unified site suited to the type of center demanded by the market. The site may allow for building and parking expansion if trade area growth or other factors so indicate.

3. An easily accessible location within the trade area with adequate entrances and exits for vehicular and pedestrian traffic where appropriate.

4. Sufficient onsite parking to meet the demands generated by the center's retail commercial establishments. Parking should be arranged to distribute pedestrian traffic to maximum advantage for retail shopping and to provide acceptable walking distances from parked cars to center entrances and individual stores.

5. Service facilities screened from customers for the delivery of merchandise.

6. Site improvements, such as landscaping, lighting, and signage, to create a desirable, attractive, and safe shopping environment.

7. Tenant grouping that provides merchandising interplay among stores and the widest possible range and depth of merchandise appropriate to the trade area.

8. Surroundings that are agreeable and comfortable for shopping and create a sense of identity and place.[2]

Proper development and management are crucial to a shopping center.

Throughout this entire process of planning, financing, and development the role of the developer/manager is that of an entrepreneur. The manner in which he gets commitments from the community, the land owners, the tenants, and the lenders will dictate the success or failure of the venture; it is a business undertaking. Even after development, the operation of the center through the management of its leases and its physical operation are vital to the center. In essence, the tenants and the landlord are partners in an enterprise that is either successful for both or a failure for both.[3]

Spatial Definitions for Shopping Center Analysis

The definitions and concepts set forth below are generally accepted in the industry and endorsed by the Urban Land Institute and the International Council of Shopping Centers.[4] Shopping center analysts and appraisers must understand these definitions to obtain appropriate data for analysis from published sources and interviews with shopping center developers and managers.

Gross building area (GBA). The total area contained within the exterior walls of the shopping center measured as the distance between the outer surfaces of those exterior walls.

Gross leasable area (GLA). The total floor area designed for tenants' occupancy and exclusive use, including any basements, mezzanines, or upper floors, expressed in square feet and measured from the centerline of joint partitions and from outside wall faces.

2. Urban Land Institute, *Shopping Center Development Handbook*, 2d ed. (Washington, D.C.: Urban Land Institute, 1985), 2.

3. Gregory J. Lafakis, "Valuation Concepts and Issues and the Taxpayer's Responsibilities Concerning Regional Shopping Centers," a paper presented at the International Association of Assessing Officers' Eighth Annual Legal Seminar, San Francisco, October 1988.

4. Definitions are quoted from the Urban Land Institute's *Dollars & Cents of Shopping Centers: 1990.*

GLA is all that area for which tenants pay rent; it is the area that produces income. *GLA* lends itself readily to measurement and comparison. Because of this *GLA* has been adopted by the shopping center industry as its standard for statistical comparison.

Gross leasable area of mall shops. The total floor space occupied by mall tenants for superregional and regional centers. It does not include the area of department store tenants or any other unowned areas.

Total occupancy area. The total floor space of the center. This classification includes all areas held by the center owner and any areas that are independently managed or owned but physically a part of the center.

Common area. The total area within the shopping center that is not designed for rental to tenants, but is available for common use by all tenants or groups of tenants, their invitees, and adjacent stores. Parking and its appurtenances, malls, sidewalks, landscaped areas, public toilets, truck and service facilities, and the like are included in the common area.

Parking area. The space devoted to car parking, including onsite roadways, aisles, stalls, islands, and all other features incidental to parking.

Parking area ratio. The ratio of parking area to gross building area.

Parking index. The number of car parking spaces made available per 1,000 square feet of *GLA*. The parking index is the standard comparison used to indicate the relationship between the number of parking spaces and the gross leasable area.

Almost all of the information on rents and costs of operation for shopping centers are based on gross leasable area.

Criteria for the Description of Shopping Centers

At least six criteria are used to describe the nature or type of shopping center being analyzed. These criteria differentiate a neighborhood shopping center from a community center and a community shopping center from a regional shopping center. These criteria are: the size of the center, the anchor tenant, the type of products sold, site size, distance and travel time, and the customer base.

Size of the Shopping Center

The first criterion used to describe shopping centers is size, measured in gross leasable area. As a general guideline, neighborhood shopping centers are the smallest, community shopping centers are midsize, and regional shopping centers are large. The rules of thumb associated with this criterion are shown in Table 1.1, but there is no clear-cut distinction between a large neighborhood shopping center and a small community center with regard to square foot area. For example, a large neighborhood center can exceed 100,000 square feet, which is the minimum area for a community center. Similarly, a large community center and a small regional center may have the same square foot area.

The Anchor Tenant

The second criterion for differentiating shopping centers is the anchor tenant. The anchor tenant is sometimes referred to as the *major tenant* or the *key tenant* in the shopping center. The anchor tenant is considered the traffic generator or the attracting force of a shopping center. The anchor of a shopping center generates the greatest amount of customer patronage and is usually considered strong enough to stand alone. The type of anchor tenant depends upon the shopping center; it can be a supermarket in a neighborhood center or a department store in a regional shopping center.

Type of Products Sold

Shopping centers can be differentiated by the type of products sold by the stores in the center. The two types of products typically mentioned are convenience, or low-order, goods and shopping, or high-order, goods.

Convenience goods are commodities that are needed and purchased frequently; they are purchased without extensive price or style comparison. Convenience goods are typically sold at locations most accessible to the consumer.

Convenience goods include food; prescription and nonprescription drugs; personal care products such as shampoo, razor blades, and soaps; household care products such as detergent, bleach, and paper towels; and

Table 1.1 Characteristics of Shopping Centers

Type of Center	Population Support Required	Leading Tenant (Basis for Classification)	Typical *GLA* (in Square Feet)	General Range of *GLA* (in Square Feet)	Usual Minimum Site Area (in Acres)
Neighborhood center	3,000-40,000	Supermarket	50,000	30,000-100,000	3-10
Community center	40,000-150,000	Junior department store, large variety or discount store, or full-line department store	150,000	100,000-300,000	10-30
Regional center	150,000 or more	One or more full-line department stores	400,000	300,000-900,000	10-60
Superregional center	300,000 or more	Three or more full-line department stores	800,000	500,000-1.5 million or more	15-100 or more

Source: *Shopping Center Development Handbook* (Washington, D.C.: Urban Land Institute, 1985), 6.

personal services such as laundry and dry cleaners and hair cutting and styling salons. These goods satisfy the day-to-day needs of individuals.

Shopping, or high-order, goods are relatively expensive commodities that are purchased infrequently, when the desire or need for them arises. Before purchasing these goods, consumers usually do some comparative shopping to investigate the different prices, quality, style, and design of similar products on the market. The acquisition of shopping goods requires more effort and time. Often shopping goods are divided into soft-line goods and hard-line goods. Soft-line goods, also known as *soft goods*, are nondurable products such as wearing apparel and domestic products including linen, bedding, towels, and fabric. Hard-line goods, also known as *hard goods*, are durable items such as hardware and appliances.

Site Size

The fourth criterion, site size, is directly related to the *GLA* criterion discussed previously. Neighborhood shopping centers require the smallest sites (3 to 10 acres), while superregional malls require the largest sites (typically 60 acres or more). More precise figures are shown in Table 1.1.

Distance and Travel Time

The fifth criterion is distance or travel time from customers' points of origin. The analyst uses the measure he or she considers most appropriate. Neighborhood shopping centers attract customers from nearby — i.e., the shortest distances and smallest travel times. Regional shopping centers attract customers who incur more travel time.

Customer Base

The final criterion is the customer base — the population within the distance or travel time measured above. Neighborhood centers require smaller customer bases than regional shopping centers.

Traditional Types of Shopping Centers

The Urban Land Institute and the International Council of Shopping Centers describe shopping center types based on three criteria: the anchor tenant, products sold, and gross leasable area. Their descriptions of neighborhood, community, regional, and superregional shopping centers follow.[5]

A *neighborhood center* provides for the sale of convenience goods (foods, drugs, and sundries) and personal services (laundry and dry cleaning, barbering, shoe repairing, etc.) for the day-to-day living needs of the immediate neighborhood. A supermarket is typically the anchor tenant. The neighborhood center has a typical gross leasable area that may range in size from 30,000 to 100,000 square feet depending on the size of the anchor tenant. The neighborhood center is the smallest type of shopping center.

A *community center* provides a wider range of facilities for the sale of soft lines (wearing apparel for men, women, and children) and hard lines (hardware and appliances). In addition to the convenience goods and personal services of the neighborhood center, the community center makes a greater variety of merchandise available—more sizes, styles, colors, and prices. It is built around a junior department store, variety store, or discount department store as a major tenant and usually also includes a supermarket. It does not have a full-line department store, though it may have a strong specialty store. In theory, the typical size is 150,000 square feet of gross leasable area, but in practice it may range in size from 100,000 to 300,000 square feet. The community center is the intermediate type of center and it is often difficult to estimate its size and pulling power.

A *regional center* provides general merchandise, apparel, furniture, and home furnishings in depth and variety as well as a range of services and recreational facilities. Its orientation is the provision of shopping goods with substantially less emphasis on convenience goods. It is built around one or two full-line department stores of not less than 100,000 square feet each. The typical size is 400,000 to 750,000 square feet of gross leasable area. The regional center is the second largest type of shopping center.

A *superregional center* provides an extensive array of general merchandise, apparel, furniture, and home furnishings as well as a variety of services and recreational facilities. It is built around at least three major

5. Ibid., 3.

department stores of not less than 100,000 square feet each. The typical size of a superregional center is about 800,000 or more square feet of gross leasable area. In practice, most newly constructed superregional centers contain more than one milion square feet of *GLA*.

All centers typically include as site area (i.e., the gross land area within the property lines) an area for enclosed or open customer and employee parking. The size of the parking area is determined by applying the accepted parking index to the gross leasable area.

Table 1.1 summarizes the descriptive characteristics of neighborhood, community, regional, and superregional shopping centers; Table 1.2 provides guidelines for two other criteria—distance or travel time and customer base. The information in this second table describes the trade areas of various types of shopping centers. This topic will be discussed in greater detail in subsequent sections of this text.

Table 1.2 **Primary Trade Area—General Guidelines**			
Type of Center	Minimum Population Support Needed	Radius	Driving Time
Superregional	300,000 or more	12 miles	30 minutes
Regional	150,000 or more	8 miles	20 minutes
Community	40,000-150,000	3-5 miles	10-20 minutes
Neighborhood	2,500-40,000	1.5 miles	5-10 minutes

Note: This table provides general guidelines, which must be modified to fit the characteristics of the specific shopping center being considered.

Source: *Shopping Center Development Handbook* (Washington, D.C.: Urban Land Institute, 1985), 6.

Specialty Shopping Centers

In addition to the four traditional types of shopping centers, other types, called *specialty shopping centers*, are discussed in retail trade analysis. A specialty shopping center is defined as follows:

> A shopping center that is characterized by the absence of a traditional anchor tenant. The role of the anchor might be played by another type of tenant, or by a grouping of tenants that together

might function as an anchor tenant, or by any number of other variations.[6]

Specialty centers include festival centers, fashion centers, off-price centers, outlet centers, discount centers, power centers, and hypermarkets. Before these centers are discussed, two new types of goods must be defined: impulse goods and specialty goods. The first of these, the impulse product or good, is a product that shoppers do not actively or consciously seek; it is purchased without a prior decision to shop for it. The second type of product, the specialty good, is a product that a shopper will examine more carefully and make a greater effort to purchase.[7]

Festival Shopping Centers

A *festival shopping center* is defined by many analysts as a shopping center that contains stores that sell impulse specialty goods, either exclusively or as a high percentage of their total merchandise mix. A large portion of its *GLA* is devoted to restaurants and food vendors that offer ethnic authenticity and uniqueness. Frequently there is a blend of onsite food service and specialty food retailing. A festival center may also have a strong entertainment theme featuring informal performances by street musicians, acrobats, jugglers, and mimes.[8]

Often the term *festival shopping center* is applied to any relatively small shopping center located near a major regional shopping mall. These festival shopping centers contain stores that sell typical shopping and convenience goods and services.

Fashion Shopping Centers

A fashion shopping center is typically defined as a concentration of apparel shops, boutiques, and custom shops that carry special, high-quality merchandise. A fashion center may include one or more high-quality

6. Urban Land Institute, *Shopping Center Development Handbook*, 7.

7. Ibid., 3.

8. Ibid., 8.

fashion stores such as Bloomingdale's, Saks Fifth Avenue, Neiman Marcus, and Lord and Taylor.[9]

An alternative definition is a concentration of fashion and high-quality stores in which comparison stores predominate but, in certain cases, quality convenience stores are also accommodated in a well-designed, attractively laid out atmosphere located in a trade area characterized by high income levels. The tenant mix and quality are commensurate with the economic profile of the trade area population. The center may be anchored by one or more major specialty or better-quality department stores or by a medium-sized specialty store supplemented with an appropriate array of fashion-oriented minor stores such as boutiques owned and operated by local tenants.[10]

Off-Price and Outlet Shopping Centers

A distinction must be made between off-price retailers and outlet retailers. A factory outlet store is owned and operated by the manufacturer and sells goods directly to the public. An off-price retailer is like a discount store that sells brand-name merchandise at lower prices than can be found elsewhere.[11]

Although these distinctions are made and the terms could describe two different kinds of shopping centers, the off-price center and the factory outlet center are typically combined into a single entity. Thus most outlet malls have a mixture of off-price retailers and factory outlet stores.

Discount Shopping Centers

In its simplest form, a discount shopping center is a community center anchored by a discount department store.[12] A discount shopping center generally differs from other types of shopping centers in a least two ways: 1) it is smaller than a regional mall anchored by a department store, and 2) there is a lower percentage of national or regional tenants in a discount shopping center and, therefore, a higher percentage of local tenants.

---

9. Ibid.

10. Jerome J. Michael, "Fashion-Oriented Centers" in *Market Research For Shopping Centers*, Ruben A. Roca, ed. (New York: International Council of Shopping Centers, 1980), 76.

11. Terry Dunham, "Outlet/Off-Price Malls: A New Deal of the Cards," *Shopping Center World* (March 1983), 28, 31.

12. Urban Land Institute, *Shopping Center Development Handbook*, 9, and Richard Childs, "Discount-Anchored Centers," in *Market Research For Shopping Centers*.

Discount stores can be divided into three types. First-generation discount stores are the original discounters, who opened their stores in structures built for other purposes. Second-generation discount stores such as K-Mart were the first retail units to be built as discount stores. Third-generation discount stores were developed by traditional department stores to meet the competition from second-generation discount stores that started to infringe on the department store's trade area. These third-generation discount stores tend to be more aesthetically pleasing than second-generation stores and frequently offer more customer services. Examples of third-generation discount stores are Target (Dayton-Hudson Company) and Venture (The May Company).[13]

Discount stores are now found as the principal and only anchors of discount shopping centers, but they are also being combined with supermarkets as anchor tenants in community shopping centers.

Power Centers

Power centers are defined as large community centers with more than 250,000 square feet of space anchored by at least three, but often four or more, anchor tenants that occupy approximately 75% (60%-90%) of the gross leasable area.[14] They generally are located near regional malls in suburban markets.[15]

Power centers reflect a new concept. "Since the power mall focuses on a high proportion of anchor tenants in gross leasable area, it reverses the pattern of maximizing higher rent space in a center."[16] The anchors are typically discount-oriented, specialty retailers[17] such as T.J. Maxx, Mervyn's, Marshalls, Toys R Us, Builders Square, Home Depot, Hechinger, Pier One, Phar-Mor Drug, Electric Avenue (Montgomery Ward), Cub Foods, and Circuit City. Sometimes one of the anchors is referred to

13. Childs, 124-125.
14. A precise description of a power center's characteristics does not exist. According to "The Markets In Perspective" section of *Emerging Trends in Real Estate: 1990*, published by the Real Estate Research Corporation, the power center has three or four strong anchors that occupy 60% to 80% of the space. The *Special Trends* issue of the publication (March 1990) reports that the power center has four or more anchor tenants that occupy at least 75% to 80% of the center's area. Mellow/McMahon Real Estate Advisors report that anchor tenants occupy 60% to 90% of the space.
15. Mellow/McMahon Real Estate Advisors, Inc., *Property*, vol. 1, no. 1 (Fall 1990), 7.
16. *Emerging Trends in Real Estate, 1990*, 27.
17. Mellow/McMahon Real Estate Advisors, *Property*, 1.

as a "category killer," which means that it is so strong in its line of merchandising that no competing specialty retailer in the same line can be attracted to the center.

Hypermarket

> The hypermarket is like a community center in the types and range of goods offered, but it is more like a regional center in establishing a quasi-monopoly position . . . . The hypermarket is essentially a horizontally integrated community center where the typical retailers of a community center—including the grocery, drug, apparel, and general merchandise stores—are operated by a single owner under one roof with centralized checkout for all types of goods.[18]

Because of the nature of the products sold by a hypermarket, it will draw sales from both neighborhood and community shopping centers and from freestanding retail establishments. The retail establishments least likely to be hurt by a hypermarket are regional shopping centers because they tend to carry higher fashion apparel and are more oriented to the needs of comparison shoppers. In addition, smaller neighborhood shopping centers and convenience centers may not be hurt by a hypermarket if their customers find them convenient places to shop quickly for a few items.[19]

The advantages of a hypermarket are a wide range of goods under one roof, the overall shopping experience offered by this type of establishment, and the relatively low prices of the products. The disadvantages are a large floor area that must be covered, which is inconvenient for one-stop shopping, and the hypermarket's orientation to bulk purchases.

In the United States hypermarkets are presently considered experimental. Their operating results and their impact on market areas must be

---

18. Adele M. Hayutin and Jack D. Siebald, "The Hypermarket Experiment in America" (New York: Salomon Brothers, Inc.), 8.

19. Ibid.

studied in greater detail before the success or failure of this type of shopping center can be judged.[20]

Warehouse Clubs

Although a warehouse club is not a shopping center according to accepted definitions, these facilities represent an important new form of retailing and competition for anchor stores. Warehouse club stores are 100,000 to 120,000 square feet in area and have nontraditional locations. They sell quality, brand-name merchandise at deeply discounted prices. Industry leaders are The Price Club, PACE, Costco, and Sam's Wholesale Club.[21] Customers, who become members by paying an annual membership fee, bag or box their own purchases in a no-frills environment. Warehouse clubs enjoy comparatively large sales per square foot of *GLA*. High profits result from bulk purchases of a carefully limited selection of high-turnover merchandise and little advertising. According to one analyst's estimate, the average sales per square foot for these retailers are more than double that of traditional discount store operators.[22]

Economic Rationale for Shopping Centers

The successful operation of a shopping center is based on a number of economic relationships. These relationships have been discussed in economic and planning literature since the 1950s. Knowledge of these relationships and concepts will help appraisers and analysts understand the success of some shopping centers and the failure of others. These relationships and concepts are discussed in the following sections.

Principle of Cumulative Attraction

Retail establishments that sell similar, but not identical, shopping goods tend to locate in close proximity to one another. They do this because the number of potential customers entering each retail establishment that is part of this cluster is believed to be greater than the number of potential customers that would enter each establishment if it were not near its com-

---

20. Ibid., 9.

21. Howard C. Gelbtuch, "The Warehouse Club Industry," *The Appraisal Journal* (April 1990), 153-159.

22. Ibid., 157.

petitors. This relationship between potential customers and proximity to competitors is called the *principle of cumulative attraction*.[23] This clustering can be seen in the location of auto malls around or near superregional malls and the presence of several auto dealerships within a relatively short stretch of a major street or highway. Other examples of cumulative attraction include a food court in a regional or superregional mall and a row of fast-food establishments at the intersection of two major streets.

Retail establishments that sell shopping goods also take advantage of the principle of cumulative attraction. However, their clusters are not as geographically concentrated as auto dealerships. Furniture and appliance dealerships also exhibit clustering tendencies.

The food court and fast-food rows mentioned earlier are clusters of convenience good providers. This is an unusual situation because retail establishments that sell convenience goods tend to repel, not attract, each other. Dry cleaners/laundries, drug stores, liquor stores, hardware stores, and other suppliers of convenience goods or services very seldom, if ever, locate in close proximity to one another because most consumers of these goods shop at the closest available establishment. When the number of consumers (and thus the purchasing power) in a small geographic area increases, the demand for convenience goods increases and these establishments may be found relatively close to one another, but never side by side like auto dealerships and fast-food operations.

The concept of product differentiation[24] is related to the principle of cumulative attraction. Cumulative attraction is based on the premise that the shopping goods sold by competitors are similar, but not identical, as is the case with auto dealerships. The economic concept of product differentiation is relevant because consumers can differentiate between products based not only on real differences, but also on imaginary differences and the circumstances surrounding the sale of the product or service.

Using auto dealerships as an example, a consumer may know that the automobiles for sale are really different from each other. The quality of materials and workmanship of Car A may be superior to the quality standards of Car B. Other consumers may choose among automobiles based on

23. Richard Nelson, *The Selection of Retail Locations* (New York: F. W. Dodge Corporation, 1958), 57-64.

24. Paul Samuelson and William Nordhaus, *Economics* (New York: McGraw-Hill Book Co., 1986), 508-509.

imaginary differences. A consumer may simply believe that Car A is better than Car B or choose Car A instead of Car B because it is better-looking. In this last instance, the decision is based purely on a cosmetic attribute. Finally, a consumer may choose between Car A and Car B based on the circumstances and helpfulness of the sales staff, the reputation of the service department, or the financing arrangements available.

The principle of cumulative attraction can be demonstrated by examining the tenants of a shopping center. Since the focus is on shopping goods, the regional shopping center exhibits the principle of cumulative attraction more than the neighborhood shopping center does. Analysis of the tenants in a regional center will reveal that retail establishments selling shopping goods such as women's clothing, shoes, and jewelry are located in close proximity to each other. When a department store is brought into the picture, the extent of cumulative attraction expands when each department in the department store is viewed as a separate entity. The men's department, women's department, shoe department, and jewelry department of the department store broaden the opportunity for comparative shopping beyond the retail establishments in the mall area. In addition, many of the other departments in the department store have corresponding retail establishments in the mall that provide an opportunity for comparative shopping for electronics, bedding and linen, infant wear, greeting cards, books, and other goods.

Generative, Supportive, and Suscipient Establishments

A shopping center can also be viewed as a combination of generative, supportive, and suscipient retail establishments.[25] Generative establishments are most typically anchor stores which do a great amount of advertising and attract potential customers to the shopping center. The supportive retail establishments are stores that typically do not advertise, but some may do a small amount of promotion. Supportive retail establishments provide a wide merchandise mix and the opportunity for comparative shopping. Supportive retail establishments include clothing, shoe, and jewelry stores. Suscipient retail establishments do not advertise

---

25. Nelson, 53.

and often offer convenience goods or services. Customers seldom go to a mall for the purpose of visiting one of these establishments. Once the customer is at the mall, however, he or she can take care of other needs by visiting suscipient retail establishments such as card shops, soft pretzel vendors, and fast-food restaurants.

Some establishments are not easily classified under this threefold system. For example, a bookstore may be generative if the customer is an avid reader who goes to the mall specifically to buy a book and then stops to shop. A bookstore can also be a suscipient retail establishment if a customer shopping for other goods goes into the bookstore to browse and finds something to take home. Similarly, record stores are not easy to classify. For teenagers shopping for musical recordings may be the generative activity, while for adults it may be a suscipient activity. Luggage shops and gift shops are also difficult to classify.

From one prospective, the analysis of a shopping center reflects the principle of cumulative attraction; another perspective reveals the existence of various generative, supportive, and suscipient relationships.

Retail Compatibility

Obviously a shopping center will be less successful if the retail establishments within the center are incompatible with one another. Compatibility refers to both merchandising mix and visual effect.[26] The issue of merchandise mix has been discussed; visual effect can be explained by example. Imagine a motorcycle and lawn mower repair shop situated in a regional shopping center between the High Luster Jewelry store and the Lovely Lady boutique. Would the customers entering the shopping center consider the jewelry store and the women's clothing store to be compatible? Of course they would. Would these same customers consider the motorcycle and lawn mower repair shop to be compatible? The answer is likely to be no.

When there is a great degree of retail compatibility within a shopping center, the appearance of that shopping center is more pleasing and more

26. Ibid., 65-78.

opportunities for comparison shopping are provided in those product lines that customers are seeking.

Affinity Groupings

The concept of affinity groupings is relatively new.[27] Affinity groupings identify relationships between retail establishments that sell shopping goods. In some instances the shopping goods are similar, as in the case of two women's clothing stores. In other cases the concept of affinity groupings refers to two retail establishments that sell shopping goods that are related in the minds of consumers such as a women's wear shop and a women's shoe and accessory store. Affinity groupings can also refer to two retail establishments that are related because together they satisfy the consumer's desire for one-stop shopping. This situation is reflected in the relationship between a women's wear store and the family clothing or infant wear store.

Researchers have tried to establish a statistical relationship between the location of certain stores within a shopping center. The working hypothesis is that stores in the same affinity groupings will locate either adjacent to one another or in very close proximity. Although the tenant arrangement postulated by the affinity grouping concept makes sense, a strong statistical relationship was not discovered.

Nevertheless, casual observation of a successful shopping center reveals that a spatial relationship exists among particular types of stores. Women's clothing stores are not found at one end of the mall while women's shoe stores are located at the other. Instead, a women's shoe store will often be found next to a women's clothing store or a few storefronts away.

The Anchor Tenant

The anchor tenant is the key to the success of a shopping center. It contributes enormously to the center's cumulative attraction potential and is the generative source of retail activity. It sets the stage for retail compati-

27. Arthur Getis and Judith M. Getis, "Retail Store Spatial Affinities," *Urban Studies* (November 1968). Reprinted in *Analysis and Valuation of Retail Locations*, Edwin M. Rams, ed. (Reston, Va: Reston Publishing, a Prentice-Hall company.)

bility and the creation of affinity groupings. Because the anchor is the most important component of a shopping center, this tenant is able to extract favorable rent rates. An anchor tenant's gross leasable area rent can be one-third to one-half of the rate paid by the tenants of the shopping center's speculative space. Anchor tenants argue that their expenditures for advertising, which generates customer traffic to the center, plus their reduced rent provide financial benefits equal to those provided by tenants who pay higher rents but incur little or no advertising expense.

Summary

A shopping center is a planned assemblage of commercial businesses that is developed, owned, and managed as a unit. Shopping centers are characterized by a unity of site and architecture, screened service areas, and a planned tenant mix. The major types of centers (superregional, regional, community, and neighborhood) are differentiated based on several criteria including their size in gross leasable area (*GLA*), the type of anchor, the type of merchandise offered, site size, and the customer base. Other types of centers, identified as specialty centers, include festival centers, fashion centers, off-price and outlet centers, discount centers, and power centers. The economic rationale for the shopping center draws on the principle of cumulative attraction; generative, supportive, and suscipient relationships; retail compatibility; and affinity groupings.

Rivercenter, San Antonio   *Courtesy of The Edward J. DeBartolo Corporation*

Chapter Two

SHOPPING CENTER INVESTMENT MARKETS

Because appraisers forecast investor behavior, they need to understand not only local investor behavior that affects the property being appraised, but also trends that are operating in national and regional markets. The nature of real estate investments in shopping centers can be analyzed from both historical and prospective standpoints.

Shopping Centers as Investments

Shopping centers in general, and regional and superregional malls in particular, have traditionally been considered very desirable investments.[1] Their desirability is due in part to the discipline and stability that an anchor tenant brings to a shopping center. Anchor tenants, typically department stores, are highly sophisticated retailers. Department stores have been defined as having a fashion orientation and selling most of their goods at full mark-up.[2] Based on extensive market research, they know which markets will support their stores. A shopping center anchored by a department store is one of the least speculative types of real estate devel-

---

1. This discussion draws on E. D. Wulfe's "Shopping Centers" in *Texas Real Estate Investment Guide* (College Station: Real Estate Center at Texas A&M University, 1990), 106-120.

2. Vern Tessier, CPA, "The Valuation of Regional and Super Regional Malls" *Assessment Digest* (Sept./Oct. 1991) 2-13.

opments. Regional and superregional malls create so much traffic that community and strip shopping centers are likely to be attracted to nearby locations in succeeding years.[3]

Because a developer is unlikely to begin construction of a new shopping center without a commitment from a construction lender, and construction financing is rarely available without a commitment from an anchor tenant, unwarranted construction of shopping centers is substantially reduced. Anchor tenants also ensure financial security because they lease a large block of space which constitutes a substantial portion of the shopping center for an extended period of time. Moreover, once they locate in an area, they are not likely to dilute their market share by opening another location nearby. When successful, a regional shopping center enjoys a real monopoly in its market and is nearly immune to competition from other regional centers.

Another advantage of shopping centers as investments is that they are typically rented on a net lease basis. Thus increases in operating expenses are usually passed through to tenants and the owner/operator is assured of a reasonably stable real income stream. Most leases also include percentage clauses which allow the owner/operator to share in the sales growth of tenants. A percentage clause also provides a hedge against inflation.

A third factor contributing to shopping centers' attractiveness is the opportunity to renew the retailing space periodically. By renovating space and re-leasing it to new tenants, a shopping center generates additional rental revenue, improves its image in the market, and increases its value. When there is a substantial oversupply of space, the ability to renovate and renew space provides a major opportunity for investors and developers. This recycling trend may be reinforced by the lack of acceptable alternative investments available to investors who might prefer outright disposition of their retail properties. Renovation and renewal is cheaper and safer than construction of a new shopping center that must prove itself in the marketplace.

Rehabilitation and renovation is feasible when a center is well-located and has good retailing fundamentals, but languishes because of a curable problem with its management, financing, or retailing operations. Physical

---

3. Ibid.

enhancement may be accomplished by adding a new facade or landscaping, upgrading the common areas, increasing the size of store windows, or adding food courts. Sometimes rehabilitating a mall means downsizing some of the space to attract smaller tenants. Specialty stores may be added or the space between anchors may be enclosed and modified to provide additional space.

The objective is to enhance the shopping and entertainment experience for those visiting the center. In some cases the tenant mix can be upgraded by adding more space or replacing one or more of the mall tenants; management may even buy out a tenant's remaining lease when necessary. Expansion makes sense when a center is already attracting traffic and its location has proven to be successful.[4] The program may be driven by the presence of sites available for construction by competitors.

Regional shopping centers were especially appealing at the end of the 1980s because alternative property types lacked market appeal. Office markets showed higher vacancy rates and risk levels and corporate industrial trends were unpredictable. Capitalization rates for regional and super-regional centers were generally lower than the rates applicable to other institutional real estate investments. Community and neighborhood centers with high occupancy rates were sold with slightly higher capitalization rates.

As investments shopping centers do not typically provide as much tax shelter as apartments or other types of real estate. According to E. D. Wulfe, "Unless an investor overpays, overleverages, experiences a low vacancy rate or unusually high operating expenses, there is little likelihood for generating tax shelter to offset other income."[5] Shopping centers are not considered tax shelters because they must be depreciated over a 31.5-year life and a substantial portion of the depreciable basis must be allocated to their expensive land area. Shopping centers require a great deal of land for parking.

Among real estate investments, regional malls have fared comparatively well in the past and, along with industrial property, they are ex-

4. Ronald B. Bruder, "Finding Opportunities for Profit in Problem Shopping Centers," *Urban Land* (May 1989), 2-3. An illustration of the cost of curing obsolescence in a mid-sized shopping mall is offered in the *Journal* *of Real Estate Development* (Winter 1989) published by Research Press, 210 Lincoln Street, Boston, Mass.

5. Wulfe, 120.

pected to be leading producers in the 1990s. Due to the overdevelopment of most kinds of real estate, new development is likely to decline markedly, but future opportunities can be found in the rehabilitation of retail space.

Shopping center owners have benefitted from increasing rents and have probably enjoyed better performance than many of their tenants. A recent report by the Urban Land Institute and the International Council of Shopping Centers indicates that net operating balances (i.e., net operating income) for all types of shopping centers rose 30% to 60% over the three-year period between 1986 and 1989. Tenant sales for the same period were up only 8% to 15%. While owners enjoyed steadily growing rents (up 25% to 40%), operating expenses remained fairly level for many shopping centers.[6]

With heightened investor interest, especially in regional malls, some retailing tenants are threatened with unmanageable occupancy cost increases. Some shopping center investors assume that property taxes will grow at the rate of inflation; unfortunately, property assessors are bound to increase assessed values in proportion to reported sales prices. When investors pay high prices for malls, their property tax bills are likely to be substantially higher than anticipated. When such tax bills are passed through to retailers, it may seriously impair their ability to conduct business profitably, and might increase the chances of them leaving the center when their leases expire.

Sales for shopping centers are reported in the "Annual Report of the Shopping Center Industry," published in the April issue of *Monitor*. In 1989 sales increased 6.5% over 1988. Furthermore, there were 10% more new centers than in the previous year, which compensated for a 10% decline between 1987 and 1988. *Monitor* also reports vacancy trends for various kinds of centers, which can be used as a benchmark for predicting market activity at the local level. Appraisers should also consult the *National Real Estate Investor* for periodic reports on the performance of regional malls. For example, one issue reported that buyers of regional malls in the Midwest are seeking beginning income rates of only 5%, but expecting a 12% to 13% internal rate of return over the holding period.

---

6. Urban Land Institute, *Development Trends, 1990,* a
   special issue of *Urban Land* (March 1990).

Risk

Successful investors in shopping centers must identify and manage the following real estate investment risks:

- The purchase or construction of a shopping center is frequently financed with too much mortgage indebtedness.
- During periods of excess competition, a center's operating income may be insufficient to cover debt obligations and still provide an acceptable equity yield.
- Location is critical. A shopping center must receive the support of a trade area with sufficient purchasing power and not be burdened by excessive competition.
- A center must have adequate ingress, egress, and visibility. (Other important locational factors are discussed elsewhere.)

The quality of management and proper merchandising are critical to a shopping center's success. Shopping centers foster relationships with and among the retailers who rent the space.[7] A shopping center is operated like a retail store with accounting, insurance, and merchandising responsibilities. Merchandising a shopping center means selecting the right mix of tenants, rather than accepting the first rent-paying applicant, and conducting periodic promotions to maintain community interest in the center. Management and merchandising require supervision of landscaping; maintenance of the parking lot, lighting, security, functional common areas, and service areas; and active concern for the visibility and accessibility of the center.

Through the leasing process and the lease instruments used, management can control the risks of shopping center operations. A rent abatement or offset clause may allow a major tenant to offset some or all of its percentage rent payments against its prorated share of some expense item, such as taxes. Tenants may also have a contractual right to carry out one of the landlord's obligations such as maintenance or insurance if the landlord fails, and to offset this expenditure against their pro rata obligation. A

---

7. Wulfe, 118.

major tenant's right to rent abatement can seriously affect the landlord's cash flows. It is important to determine whether there is operating harmony between all tenants, but especially between the anchor tenants and the center's owner/operator. Tenant lease provisions are discussed later in the text.

Other risks to shopping center investors include eminent domain proceedings to acquire part or all of the site; government controls; environmental conditions; and excessive competition from nearby sites. As shopping habits change, shopping center owner/operators must periodically renovate and update their space to maintain their merchandising ability and keep functional obsolescence in check. New forms of retailing such as power centers, power retailers, and warehouse clubs accelerate functional obsolescence and create external obsolescence for shopping centers.

With some exceptions, such as auto care malls and theme malls, shopping centers must fulfill the purchasing power needs of the population within their trade area. Buying power cannot be created. Shopping centers with substantial vacancies must be analyzed very carefully to determine where retail purchasing activity will originate. Communities with excessive shopping center development and no opportunity for additional residential growth face a long period of maladjustment.

The Urban Land Institute describes the shopping center industry as "an industry driven by competition." In stable population areas, one center's gains are another center's losses, often caused by a failure to renew and remerchandise space. According to the Real Estate Research Corporation, the development outlook for the 1990s is dominated by "overbuilding, fewer development opportunities, downward pressure on yields, cut-throat competition, and disappearing profit margins."[8] Despite this prediction, many investors anticipate that retail properties, especially regional malls, will continue to be popular investment vehicles and that their prices will be bid up due to the scarcity of supply. Strip shopping centers,

---

8. Real Estate Research Corporation, *Emerging Trends in Real Estate: 1990* (Chicago: Real Estate Research Corporation, 1989), 9.

however, are less able to compete for the limited number of small retailers in many markets.[9]

Who Buys and Sells

A strong demand for shopping center developments that are well-maintained and successfully leased derives from various types of investors, including major national retail shopping center developers, local shopping center developers, commercial property investors, institutional investors and pension funds, investment banking and security firms, syndications and real estate investment trusts (REITS), and foreign investors.[10] These investors have been active for several years. According to a recent report, pension funds have been attempting to withdraw capital from open-end real estate pools, which has resulted in an increased supply of investment-grade property on the market.[11] Some potential sellers who have been slow to sell because of a lack of reinvestment opportunities now seek to report good performance and selling may make more sense than continuing to operate. Thus real estate appraisers must not only be in tune with general market trends, but also attempt to investigate the conditions that affect the subject property in particular.

The Purchasing Process

Sophisticated investors perform a very thorough investigation before they purchase major assets. This process, called *due diligence* by major financial institutions, should interest appraisers because they contribute to it and may find the product of the process useful.

The investigation is conducted by a team of experts in accounting, finance, appraisal, engineering, property management, and law. It may involve both in-house staff and special counsel.[12] The accountant reviews the seller's operating statements and makes spot checks of various records. For example, the team might do a sample audit of the retailer's sales to confirm projections for percentage rent payments. To ensure that lease es-

---

9. Ibid.

10. Wulfe, 116.

11. "Pension Funds Crowd Real Estate Pool's Excess," *Wall Street Journal*, Sept. 13, 1990.

12. Michael H. Switzer, "Using Due Diligence in Shopping Center Purchasing," *Real Estate Review* (Fall 1986), 88-92.

calations are set according to contract, common area maintenance charges are reviewed. Accountants examine the quality of center earnings by comparing them to national and regional averages. Excessive profits are investigated because they can breed damaging competition and may be hard to maintain. Accountants also look for one-time, special, nonrecurring earnings; such aberrations are particularly important.

Accountants search for missed opportunities such as the sale of waste materials, the sale of utilities, or advertising costs that could be recovered. Appraisers prepare estimates and forecasts to guide investors in developing bids. Their work may precede other parts of the due diligence process, but they may also want to consider information obtained later in the process to revise any important assumptions on which the appraisal is based. Appraisers may perform a continuing role throughout the process to determine whether any new facts uncovered or judgments made might cause the investing institution to violate corporate policy or regulatory law. In this way the appraiser "confirms" his or her appraised value.

Engineers evaluate the physical components of the shopping center to identify needed repairs and to estimate their costs. If this information is available to the appraiser, it can provide the basis for estimates of obsolescence and costs to cure as well as the adjustments applied in the sales comparison approach and the expenses considered in the income capitalization approach. The property managers on the team will probably want to accompany the engineers on the inspection to help identify deferred maintenance and extraordinary maintenance costs and help determine whether a center is being undermaintained and thus generating less cash flow. The property managers and possibly the appraiser should do follow-up inspections before the closing to ensure that the property is in acceptable condition, that all major tenants are operating as expected, and that there are no problems with the personal property or equipment to be included in the sale.

Property managers confer with the shopping center tenants during this investigatory process to hear their complaints and concerns about the center. Complaints that surface during verbal discussions or in the estoppel certificates may be routine problems that are present in any center or they may be indications of serious and otherwise unknown deficiencies. Property managers can tell potential purchasers whether or not the shopping center is an effective synergistic retailing enterprise. If it is not, the tenants may simply be putting forth a minimal effort to avoid claims of breach of contract and fulfill their merchandising obligations under the lease. This situation would be indicated by operating with low inventory levels and secondary personnel.

The appraiser should study the role of the property manager and investigate his or her motivation to better understand the property and enterprise being appraised. Because managing a shopping center is a relationship business, the appraiser must also understand the behavior of the tenants and the shoppers in the center. Only by understanding market behavior in the present and past can the appraiser make a reliable forecast.

Legal counsel will review all key documents involved in a shopping center acquisition. In-house counsel for an institutional investor will probably have responsibility for monitoring the due diligence process to ensure that it complies with corporate policy as well as the regulatory statutes of the jurisdiction. When an institutional investor undertakes the purchase of a package of properties, in-house counsel may manage and coordinate the various individuals and processes within the investigation, often retaining local counsel to review important documents such as major leases, reciprocal easement agreements, and existing mortgages. Usually the leases of nonanchor store tenants are reviewed by the appraiser, and legal counsel is concerned only with the standard store lease form.

Local counsel will investigate local building and zoning codes for compliance and check for certificates of occupancy as well as compliance with parking and subdivision regulations, environmental safety and health codes, and hazardous waste regulations. All appropriate certificates, licenses, approvals, and litigation that affect the subject property must be reviewed. Local counsel is consulted concerning the impact of state and local taxes, including how to the property taxes for the subject parcel will be affected by the price to be paid. The contract document and proposed deed will be examined as well as the title insurance policy. Special concerns to be investigated by local counsel might include, for example, whether an easement that benefits the subject property will be cut off as a result of foreclosure on an abutting property or if the center operator can legally resell electricity to the center's tenants.

The shopping center appraiser should understand when the due diligence process is to begin, how his or her duties coordinate with the duties of the other team members, and what information is available for review in preparing the appraisal. These items should be discussed when the contract for the appraisal is negotiated, perhaps in a pre-authorization data request form. (See the appendix for a sample of this form.)

Before a sale is final, the investor's underwriters will scrutinize the economic representations contained in any promotional materials supplied by the seller's investment banker. The appraiser should determine whether the sales literature and the original offering document are available for inspection.

The due diligence process is concluded when the team members meet to identify and resolve problems and communicate unresolved issues to the seller; the seller then provides written responses. Several rounds of negotiations may be required to resolve all the problems uncovered in the process. Problems may be resolved through price negotiation, sharing of costs to cure, indemnification to the purchaser for some matters, sharing of specified risks, or the seller's promise to perform certain tasks after closing. The seller may agree to obtain certain approvals, zoning changes, quit claim deeds, or other documents to clear up ambiguities.

Financing

The amount and type of financing have a major impact on the cash flow stream, and hence the value, of a shopping center investment. Real estate investors use leverage to magnify the earning power of an asset and generate a higher equity yield. It is essential that appraisers understand the nature of financing and how financing techniques shape the equity cash flows and present values of comparable sales and the subject property.

Leverage may be observed and measured by comparing the capitalization rates (or income rates) of the mortgage and the property. Favorable leveraging of the income stream exists when the capitalization rate for the shopping center is higher than the capitalization rate (or annual constant) of the mortgage. Such leverage is very difficult to arrange when the popularity of shopping center investments depresses capitalization rates and mortgage interest rates generally exceed property capitalization rates. A better way to observe the use of favorable financial leverage is to compare the overall yield or internal rates of return of a property free and clear to the yield on the mortgage.

In more opportune times, shopping centers were frequently developed with little or no equity capital. Such aggressive financing strategy is rarely available during periods of overbuilding. Today equity contributions of 20% to 30% may be required of developer/investors. Some leaders also require a participation in the center's ownership and cash flows.

The distinction between debt and equity capital has become blurred. The following financing vehicles are expected to be used for future development or redevelopment:

- Straight construction loans from commercial banks.
- Combined construction/take-out loans from insurance companies.
- Forward loan commitments with participations from insurance companies and credit corporations.
- Presales of properties to pension funds directly or through their advisors and insurance companies.
- Participation and convertible mortgages structured by various financial players.[13]

Projects in the mid-price range from $2,000,000 to $5,000,000 will become more difficult to finance because savings and loan associations have lost some of their lending capacity. Larger institutions are not attracted to loans in this market because of the relatively high cost of underwriting. The largest deals are frequently financed by foreign construction lenders rather than commercial banks in the United States. Foreign lenders are subject to less regulation, have more risk-taking capability, and frequently offer lower interest rates.[14]

At the time of this writing, the commercial mortgage market is contracting. Many lenders have withdrawn from any new loans and the remainder are holding to high standards. By one account,

---

13. Real Estate Research Corporation, *Emerging Trends*, 22.   14. Ibid., 23.

Today's underwriting focuses on effective rent—net of concessions—and lease renewals. No lender wants a significant lease to terminate during the next several years when rents are under real downward pressure. Most new loans call for cash reserves to pay for future tenant improvements, leasing commissions, and expected vacancies.[15]

The traditional method for financing shopping center development and investment made use of separate construction loans and permanent loans. Construction loans generally carried more risk, necessitating a higher interest rate as well as the guarantees of the developer. Permanent financing was generally provided by a life insurance company or similar institution at a lower interest rate. The term on the permanent loan was longer than the term available from the construction lender, which was often a commercial bank. The guarantee for payment on a construction loan was made by the owning and developing entity, while the permanent loan was usually nonrecourse. The permanent mortgage might take the form of a straight mortgage or a bullet loan—i.e., a direct-reduction, regularly amortized mortgage loan with a five- or 10-year term.[16]

Outlook For Retailing

A shopping center is a joint-venture between retailers and developers,[17] so appraisers seeking to understand shopping centers should know something about the retailing business as well as shopping center development and management. In the 1960s and 1970s both shopping center development and department stores experienced significant growth. The shopping center development industry was dominated by several large companies, including The Hahn Company, Melvin Simon & Associates Inc., Homart Development Corporation, The Edward J. DeBartolo Corporation, and

15. "Current Commercial Mortgage Rates," *The Mortgage and Real Estate Executives Report*, February 1, 1991, 7. This is an excellent source for information about mortgage lending practices.

16. One subscription source of information about various kinds of loans and lenders for shopping center development and investment is *Fleets Guide*, published by Fleet Press, Inc., Alexandria, Va.

17. Daryl T. Mangan, "Consolidation of the Shopping Center Industry," *Urban Land* (June 1990), 30-31.

The Rouse Company.[18] Department stores grew in part through mergers and acquisitions, and by the end of the 1970s the industry was dominated by a few large corporations such as May Department Stores, Allied Stores, Associated Dry Goods, Carter Hawley Hale, Federated Department Stores, and R. H. Macy & Company. A few department stores joined to undertake development activities, including May Companies and May Centers; Federated Department Stores and Federated Stores Realty; Sears and Homart Development Company; and Dayton-Hudson and Center Companies. Passive joint ventures were undertaken by J. C. Penney's and R. H. Macy's Properties.

In the 1980s overexpansion and turmoil plagued retailers and developers alike. Few development opportunities remained, and by the middle of the decade there were complaints about excessive retail space.[19] Profits were declining and controlling expenses became management's paramount objective. Staffing and merchandising were reduced and retailers focused on profits rather than sales growth and market share development. Many companies were not successful in dealing with the changing demographics of their markets. By the mid-1980s, many department store companies were attractive targets for leveraged buyouts, which were popular then. This situation was partly the result of underutilized real estate assets. A number of leveraged buyouts and mergers burdened these companies with large amounts of debt, creating a need for short-term operating profits and changing the identity of many well-known retailers.

While the retail industry was restructuring, the development industry was also. At the beginning of the decade, a number of developers sold shares of stock to the public to raise capital. They soon learned, however, that stock market investors did not understand the business of developing shopping centers. Wall Street investors did not appreciate the high risk, heavy capital needs, high start-up costs, and short-term cash flow losses involved in these investments. Subsequently, some developers bought back their stock to go private, and some retailers sold their shopping center development entities. Institutional investors did understand the retail real es-

---

18. *Monitor* magazine provides descriptive statistics on shopping center construction and leasing in its November/December issue.

19. See, for example, "Merchant's Woe: Too Many Stores," *Fortune*, May 13, 1985.

tate business, however, and they appreciated the inflation hedge and growth potential it offered.

When traditional shopping center and retail development opportunities waned during the 1980s, developers turned to innovations such as off-price centers, power malls, specialty centers, and festival shopping centers. By the end of the decade, a trend appeared in which large developers were buying department store companies to control anchor tenants for future shopping centers. For example, L. J. Hooker purchased Bonwit Teller, B. Altman, Parisian, and Sakowitz. Campeau Corporation purchased the Federated and Allied Department Store chains. This vertical integration of retailing and shopping center development has caused great concern because it eliminates an important external check on the overexpansion of anchor stores. It will probably continue to concern real estate appraisers as their attempts to assess the ability of a subject shopping center to compete in a trade area are complicated by entangling alliances between some of the tenants and competing developers.

The early 1990s promise to be a period of continued turmoil and restructuring. The massive debt assumed in leveraged buyouts has caused financial distress and bankruptcy for several of the acquiring developers (e.g., L. J. Hooker and Campeau) as well as offers to sell many department stores and chains. Retailing stores and companies are moving back into the hands of those concerned with managing the merchandising instead of the operations, and there is renewed interest in meeting the needs of customers. Increased emphasis on retail mall management instead of new development opportunities indicates that shopping center management companies will become more important.

Problems for Retailing, Shopping Centers, and Department Stores

The problems confronting shopping centers and their anchor stores relate to marketing practices, the changing demographics of the U.S. market, and changing life-styles.[20] Through the end of the 1980s, construction of

---

20. The following discussion is drawn from Francesca Turchiano, "The Unmalling of America," *American Demographics* (April 1990), 37 and Nina J. Gruen, "Retailing Fundamentals, Problems, and Solutions," *Urban Land* (July 1990), 26.

retail space in the United States grew at a faster rate than disposable personal income, resulting in a surplus of retail space. This national trend is illustrated by comparing statistics on total retail space (which grew 80% from 1974 to 1984) with personal income discounted for inflation (which grew by about 30%). Of course, at the local level an appraiser can determine if there is excess retail space by observing vacancies in the trade area.

Losses due to vacancy and the resulting competition for tenants has hurt the profitability of shopping centers; some managers continue to focus on operating efficiency rather than marketing for consumer satisfaction and greater long-term profitability. Department stores and shopping centers have not maintained customer interest and have not created the right retailer mix to best meet customers needs. For example, many critics believe that fashion clothing, especially for women, has been overemphasized in many malls. Moreover, other forms of shopping are competing for customers' attention including catalog shopping, television shopping networks, power malls, and off-price outlets.

The future demographic outlook will be characterized by a greater proportion of shoppers 50 and older, a relatively smaller middle-income group, and a growing shortage of low-wage, entry-level workers for the retail industry. The product mix offered by many stores and malls is increasingly out of touch with the aging population and changes in purchasing power. The growing shortage of entry-level workers means increasing use of less trained workers who are less able to anticipate shopper needs. This situation may lead to a perception that retailers in general and shopping centers in particular are less capable of providing service and quality merchandise. Some evidence suggests a shift in consumer interest away from more material goods and toward new experiences. A growing percentage of female customers have joined the work force and are less likely to buy the high-style fashion merchandise so often offered.

Other important trends in retailing that will affect department stores and shopping centers are the increased market share of big discounters (e.g., Walmart, K-Mart) and the growth of wholesale price clubs (e.g., Sam's Warehouse, PACE) and other specialty discounters (e.g., Office Depot, Staples). Apparel makers and high-end retailers are opening their own discount outlets to compete with off-price outlets. "Everyday low pricing" has increased to compete with periodic promotional sales, leading customers to challenge the service and loyalty of companies who make use of occasional sales. Some local markets may not be affected by this trend, but appraisers should be aware of these general conditions and look for their effects in local markets.

The problems affecting department stores are also facing the smaller retailers occupying mall space.

> The explosion of mergers, acquisitions, and leveraged buyouts— typically financed by high interest-rate, short-term borrowing and junk bonds—is pervasive in retailing. In turn, it fosters the sale of prime assets; erosion of service quality; diversion of funds from store upkeep, advertising, and quality and depth of merchandise; and inability to expand in logical locations.[21]

Appraisers must recognize those retailers and shopping centers that are able to confront these problems successfully. Retailing needs to return to a customer orientation, providing a better merchandise mix and service level than competitors. Extensive training for sales personnel will mark the difference between market leaders and followers. (Home Depot is an example of this new emphasis on service.) Retailers themselves will probably need training by mall managers to help them better analyze demographic data, observe customer life-styles, and respond with the right merchandising strategies.

Controlling costs will continue to be critical, especially in light of increased employee training. Many retailers already use computer technology to keep track of purchasing and inventories and to provide timely sales and expense data to their managers. New integrated cash registers and inventory control systems using pistol-style scanning devices will be essential tools for the up-to-date retailer. The appraiser should look for such innovations. By initiating discussions with selected retailers in the subject shopping center, an appraiser can assess their awareness and response to current problems and new opportunities.

---

21. Real Estate Research Corporation, *Emerging Trends in Real Estate: 1990*, 26.

Given the changes going on in retailing and shopping centers, it is imperative that the appraiser investigate operating covenants to determine whether stores owned by developers can move out to a new mall. Anchors with expiring leases are very threatening because they can extract concessions either for renewing their leases or for relocating.

Retailing in a Shopping Center

There are a number of aspects of the retailing business that appraisers should be aware of and evaluate. One important consideration is the preferred store depth within the submarket. A depth of 80 feet is often considered most desirable by retailers, despite the fact that a shorter space may generate a higher rate of rent per square foot. The shorter space does not permit optimal use of the site. Local leasing agents will probably be able to describe the sizes, locations, and types of retail space that are currently popular.

An appraiser should analyze the percentage clause and its breakpoint in the lease. (The breakpoint is the level of sales at which the percentage clause is activated.) Some retailers may find it feasible to open another store nearby even if it diverts some of the trade area's purchasing power. This might be an attractive option because increasing sales at the original location could trigger the percentage clause and increase the total occupancy costs.

Some national retailing companies are increasing their share of local markets at the expense of local retailers. The appraiser should observe industry trends for the principal tenants in the mall to forecast their percentage sales and the probability of lease renewal.

Many retailers can be categorized as either "value- (or commodity) oriented" or "point-of-view" oriented. This distinction affects the extent to which the retailer contributes to the drawing power of the shopping center. Value- or commodity-oriented retailers feature depth of inventory and selection and a modest shopping environment; they may have only limited drawing power for the rest of the center. Toys R Us and Home Depot are value-oriented retailers. Point-of-view retailers offer greater service and unique merchandise in an expensive environment calculated to draw shopper traffic.

If mall tenants cater to a fashion market, for example, it would be useful for the appraiser to determine how well each of these retailers anticipates the tastes and demands of shoppers and gear their buying and inventory practices to take advantage of them. Admittedly this is a very difficult task, but limited interviews with retailers, sales clerks, customers, competitors, and mall managers may reveal which retailers are most successful.

Appraisers should be aware of normal promotional activities in shopping center submarkets. Many shopping center operators conduct annual marketing programs or special events to increase shopper interest. These activities are typically paid for by the manager of the shopping center out of a marketing fund to which all the shopping center tenants have contributed. The presence or absence of this kind of promotion on the part of the shopping center operator should be noted by the appraiser.

Summary

Appraisers should understand how investors view shopping centers. Large shopping centers are attractive because the presence of anchors reduces the market risk posed by competing centers. The use of net and percentage leases allows owners to pass some increases in operating expenses on to tenants and to recover part of the value created when the venture works. Percentage clauses also offer protection against inflation. Growth in the trade area around a good location may offer profitable opportunities for expansion on surplus land or remodeling of a tired building, even when new retail construction is sluggish.

Shopping centers are not without problems. Some smaller retailers and service tenants experience comparatively high occupancy costs in their shopping center locations. This is partly due to high property taxes based on assessments keyed to overly optimistic purchase prices. Investors and appraisers need to be sensitive to how occupancy costs relate to tenants' sales revenues.

The risks facing center owner/operators include construction of surplus retail space and changes in retailing techniques that can cause functional obsolescence. Appraisers of shopping centers should attempt to stay abreast of conditions in the retailing industry and the activities of major firms.

CNG Tower, New Orleans   *Courtesy of The Edward J. DeBartolo Corporation*

Chapter Three

LOCAL ECONOMIC ANALYSIS FOR SHOPPING CENTER APPRAISALS

T he economic analysis performed for a shopping center appraisal should be structured to obtain information on the variables that enter into appraisal techniques either directly or indirectly. Market rent is one such economic variable. It relates directly to the income approach, whether discounted cash flow analysis or direct capitalization is used. Market rent also has direct bearing on the sales comparison approach. The vacancy rate for shopping center space is considered in both yield and direct capitalization, but is only indirectly relevant to the sales comparison approach. The vacancy rate is a financial element of comparison in selecting comparable shopping centers and is used to adjust rent rates in gross rent multiplier applications. The number of potential retail customers and their income impact appraisal techniques indirectly because these factors establish the demand for retail space and consequently affect market rent and vacancy levels.

In performing economic analysis for a shopping center appraisal, the appraiser must first identify the key economic variables to be investigated. Market rent, the vacancy rate, the number of potential customers, and consumer income are four such variables. Then connections can be made between each of these major economic variables and shopping center appraisal techniques. Major economic variables and their relationship to appraisal techniques will be discussed more fully later. Definitions and the principal components of economic analysis will be addressed first.

Types of Studies

Three general categories of economic analysis need to be considered: local economic analysis, market analysis, and marketability analysis.

Local Economic Analysis

To perform local economic analysis, an appraiser investigates the major economic variables in the local economy that affect the supply of and demand for all types of real estate products and space. The local economy could be a large metropolitan statistical area, a mid-sized or small metropolitan statistical area, a small town, or even a county or portion of a county. The economic and geographic scope of the study must be determined and specified.

For example, the economic analysis of a small neighborhood shopping center at the eastern fringe of a large metropolitan statistical area would probably not be affected by economic changes at the western edge of that metropolitan area because the consumers to the west are not in the shopping center's trade area. Plant openings or closings and population changes on the other side of town will have little or no impact on the east-side shopping center. However, if an in-town shopping area or a downtown mall were being analyzed, economic factors affecting the western fringe of the metropolitan area could have a more significant impact. Knowledge of the local community and appraisal judgment are needed to define the scope of local economic analysis that is appropriate to the assignment and to determine the significance of any economic event.

To explore these examples further, data on market rents, vacancies, and potential customers at the western fringe of the metropolitan area may be only marginally useful in analyzing a shopping center to the east. Most of these data will require large adjustments. However, in analyzing a downtown mall geographically closer to the western fringe of the metropolitan area, market rents, vacancies, and customer profiles may be more usable and important to the assignment.

Local economic analysis has two parts: defining the scope of the analysis and identifying major economic variables.

Market Analysis

To conduct a market analysis, the appraiser considers the supply of and demand for a particular type of retail space in a predetermined geographic area. Thus a market analysis for a shopping center examines the supply and demand factors that affect all shopping centers in a predetermined area — e.g., the eastern fringe of the metropolitan area in which the subject property is located. A shopping center market analysis focuses on the retail goods and services offered for sale in the shopping center, which sells retail space. The ability to sell products affects the ability to sell or lease retail space.

The appraiser looks for variables that can be used to estimate the demand for retail goods and services and the supply of retail goods and services in the defined area. At this level, market analysis is not site-specific. In other words, the appraiser is not seeking information about the demand for retail goods and services and thus the demand for retail space at the subject site, but rather the demand generated in the defined area which contains the subject property.

It is apparent that market analysis has two component parts — demand analysis and supply analysis. Demand analysis identifies what goods and services customers want and how much they will purchase. Supply analysis focuses on the availability of goods and services to the customer by identifying and analyzing competitive facilities.

The principal task in market analysis is to gather information and form a conclusion as to the volume of retail sales that can be generated in a predetermined geographic area and how much of this retail demand is being met. This is referred to as *residual analysis* or the *vacuum technique*. In addition, the appraiser generates information on the availability and current sales of retail products and services in the area. This is accomplished by a survey of the competition, which is also known as a *competitive survey* or *competitive analysis*.

Marketability Analysis

Marketability analysis is directly linked to market analysis, but here attention is focused on a specific site, for example, the property on the northeast corner of the intersection of East Main and 55th Street. Marketability analysis can be defined as the study of supply and demand factors as they affect a specific site. The analyst's first task is to define the retail trade area that is appropriate to the subject property. In this instance it would be the geographic area adjacent to the intersection and extending away from it for an appropriately defined distance. In general the retail trade area for the subject property referenced in this discussion will be smaller than the geographic area that represents the eastern fringe of the metropolitan area.

In conclusion, economic analysis of shopping centers consists of three interrelated studies. The local economy is analyzed to identify trends and make projections concerning the major economic variables that affect the local economy. Then the scope of the analysis is tightened and these major economic variables are related to the supply and demand for particular types of retail goods and services in a smaller geographic area. Finally, a specific site in that smaller geographic area is analyzed and the major economic variables that affect the supply and demand for retail goods and services are related to that site.

This general overview of economic and market analysis for shopping centers can be considered an introduction to the discussion that follows. It serves an important purpose because it shows the interrelationships among local economic analysis, market analysis, and marketability analysis. These relationships may be obscured when greater detail is added to the discussion of local economic analysis in this chapter and the discussions of market analysis and marketability analysis in the following chapter.

Local Economic Analysis

The material presented in this section addresses three points. First the major economic and demographic variables important in analyzing a community for a shopping center appraisal are identified and discussed. Then the nature of local economic analysis is discussed and related to the market in which the subject property is located. Finally sources of data are identified and evaluated.

Major Economic and Demographic Variables

Employment

The first economic variable to be analyzed is employment. The number of available jobs, the types of jobs available, and future job prospects often provide the underlying reason why people reside in a given geographic area. Most people live in a certain place because they have a job in relatively close proximity to their residence and expect to retain that job. So employment is a very important variable in local economic analysis.

Employment data are reported in one of two ways. Census-based publications report employment by residence site. These sources identify whether people living in a residential area are employed or unemployed. The second way of reporting employment data is by job site — i.e., employment is reported as the number of people who are working and whose place of employment is located within the area.

Thus data on County A can show employment by residence site equal to 10,000 and employment by job site equal to 30,000 without contradiction. The first figure means that 10,000 of the people who live in that county are employed; the second figure means that there are 30,000 jobs currently available in that county. The 20,000 difference represents individuals who work in County A but reside elsewhere.

Both of these employment concepts are important to a shopping center appraisal. Employment by residence site is important for establishing the population of the trade area. Employment by job site is used to determine the potential customers for a shopping center, especially when major office buildings and industrial parks are located within the trade area of the shopping center. Individuals who work in the area are often referred to as the "daytime population" of that area.

Population, Households, and Families

Population refers to the total number of people living within a geographic area. Employment by residence site is related to population through the labor force participation ratio, which is defined as the percentage of people living in a geographic area who are part of the civilian labor force. The civilian labor force is the total number of individuals who are currently employed plus those who are able and willing to be employed and those currently seeking employment.

The relationship among population, employment, unemployment, and the labor force participation ratio is illustrated in the following example. Consider a geographic area in which the civilian labor force, measured using the employment by residence concept, is 11,000 people and 1,000 residents are unemployed. The unemployment rate is 8.3% (1,000/12,000). If the current population of the area is 21,000, the labor force participation ratio is 57.1% (12,000/21,000).

Now assume that the appraiser analyzing this geographic area was unable to obtain a current estimate of population, but was able to get an estimate of current employment and the unemployment rate. An estimate of the current population can be derived by analyzing the following relationships:

$$CLF = E + U$$
$$LFPR = CLF/P$$

Where CLF = civilian labor force
E = employment
U = unemployment
$LFPR$ = labor force participation rate
P = population

In our example $E=11,000$, $U=8.33\%$ of CLF, and $LFPR=57.1\%$. The population can be calculated as follows:

$$CLF = E + U$$
$$CLF = 11,000 + 0.0833\ CLF$$
$$CLF = 11,000/0.9167 = 12,000$$
$$P = 12,000/LFPR$$
$$P = 12,000/0.571 = 21,015$$

Households are a subset of population. A household is defined as one individual or a group of two or more individuals who live together, sharing a dwelling unit. These individuals may be related by blood or marriage or they may be unrelated. The census definition of a household is presented below.

> A household is a person or group of people who jointly occupy a dwelling unit and who constitute a single economic unit for purposes of meeting housing expenses. Households may be families, two or more persons living together, or individuals.

Households and population are related by a household composition variable known as *household size*, which is defined as the total number of persons, both related and unrelated, residing in a dwelling or housing unit. If population size in a geographic area is 21,000 and there are 7,500 households, the number of persons per household, or household size, is 2.8 (21,000/7,500).

Families are a subset of households. The census defines a family using the following set of standards:

1. A family is a group of people related by blood or marriage residing in a dwelling unit.
2. The family could then be two individuals related by marriage.
3. It could be two individuals related by marriage with one or more children who are related by blood or legal adoption.
4. It could also be two people related by marriage with a dependent parent.
5. It can also be a single adult living with a child who is also single.

Most typically, families can be identified with the first two descriptions.

The Employment, Population, and Household Triangle

Employment, population, and households are strongly interrelated. If employment increases, population and households also increase. If the population increases, an increase in employment opportunities is probably the underlying cause. (This may not be true in retirement areas where population can increase without a rise in employment. However, if the population of retirees in an area increases sufficiently, an increase in the employment level in the community will follow after a time.) As a population changes, the number of households will also change. This relationship will not hold if the population increase is caused by births or the return of minor children to families. It also does not apply when adult children return home during periods of economic recession, a phenomenon known as *doubling up*. To visualize the relationship, consider employment by residence site, population, and households as the three corners of a triangle. They are all part of a whole and when one changes the other two also change.

Employment and population are related by the labor force participation rate (*LFPR*), which is the civilian labor force divided by the population (*P*). If a local planning agency generates an employment forecast, it can be used in conjunction with the historic *LFPR* to generate a population forecast. For example, assume that employment for 1995 is forecast to be 1,650, unemployment is expected to remain at 4%, and the current *LFPR* is 57.1% and expected to remain level. The population forecast will be

$$P = CLF/0.571$$
$$P = (1,650/0.96)/0.571$$
$$P = 3,010$$

If, on the other hand, a population forecast is available, the *LFPR* can be used to generate an employment forecast. Using the same numerical example, the employment forecast is calculated as follows:

$$3,010 = (E/0.96)/0.571$$
$$3,010 \times 0.571 \times 0.96 = E$$
$$1,650 = E$$

The population (*P*) and the household (*H*) values are related by the household size variable (*P/H*). If a population forecast is generated for the local economy, the number of households can be determined by dividing the population forecast by the current household size. For example, if the current household size is 2.46 persons per household and is expected to remain constant in the near future, then the population of 3,010 will contain approximately 1,224 households. If the trend in household size is declining and the appraiser expects it to drop from 2.46 to 2.35 over the next five years, then the number of households forecast would be 1,281.

Income

Income is the next major economic variable to be analyzed. The income data gathered should be organized in an income distribution with accompanying descriptive statistics on the mean, medium, and per capita levels of income. An income distribution is simply a breakdown of households into various income categories. A simple example is shown in Table 3.1.

Table 3.1 **Income Distribution**		
	No. in Tract 0501	No. in Gwinnett County
Total Households	$4,116	$55,239
Income less than $5,000	494	3,471
Income $ 5,000 to $7,499	410	2,085
Income $ 7,500 to $9,999	388	2,405
Income $10,000 to $14,999	758	6,895
Income $15,000 to $19,999	661	7,755
Income $20,000 to $24,999	598	8,809
Income $25,000 to $34,999	538	13,631
Income $35,000 to $49,999	192	7,657
Income $50,000 or more	77	2,631
Median	$15,054	$22,572
Mean	$16,898	$24,578

Purchasing Power

The most important variable in analyzing a retail trade area is the purchasing power of area consumers. Purchasing power is calculated as the number of consumers multiplied by a measure of income. It is important to match the measure of consumers and the measure of income properly. Using the data presented in Table 3.1, purchasing power can be calculated as the population times the per capita income or the number of households times the mean household income.

The census data in Table 3.1 provide the number of households, mean income, median income, and per capita income for both census tract 0501 and Gwinnett County. To calculate purchasing power, demographic data are also needed. The population of census tract 0501 is 12,138 and there are 4,116 households. Population and households in Gwinnett County are 166,903 and 55,239 respectively. For census tract 0501, purchasing power based on population is $69,769,224 (12,138×$5,748); based on the number of households, the purchasing power in the census tract is $69,552,168. (4,116×$16,898). These two estimates of purchasing power are not identical, but they are close. The $200,000 difference between the two estimates represents a divergence of 0.29%.

For Gwinnett County, purchasing power based on population is estimated at $1,363,096,801 (166,903×$8,167); based on the household measure, purchasing power is $1,357,664,142 (55,239×$24,578). Once again, the estimates are not identical, but close, with a difference of $5.5 million, or 0.45%.

Population and Household Composition

In addition to information about the population and number of households in the local economy, the analyst also seeks information on the composition of the population and households. The principal compositional variables studied are the income distribution, which has already been discussed; the age structure of the population and households; and household size. Analysis of Table 3.1 provides an understanding of the distribution of households in various income categories and the mean and median household incomes for that distribution. Per capita income data are also available from the U.S. Census Bureau. By inspecting the mean and median household incomes, the analyst can tell whether the local economy is relatively prosperous, with a high percentage of households in the upper income categories, or relatively poor, with a high percentage of households in the lower income categories.

The ages of the individuals in local households are also provided in the census. As a descriptive variable, the age composition of the local economy is important in both retail trade area analysis and housing market analysis. If the local economy and housing market have relatively low mean and median ages, a high percentage of the population is young. If a large portion of the population is 20 to 29 years old, a demand for rental units is indicated. If, on the other hand, the mean and median ages are relatively high, an older population is indicated. A relatively high percentage of the population in the 40-to-50-year-old bracket may indicate a demand for move-up single-family homes. Finally, a large population of individuals 60 years and older can identify a retirement community and the potential need for various types of retirement housing.

Household size data provide another important indicator of the type of housing units that the population may desire. Four-person households require more space than one-person households. Four-bedroom homes may be sought by the former group, while two-bedroom homes are attractive to the latter. The analyst must realize, however, that household size alone does not establish demand. Households must have sufficient income to purchase the housing units they require or desire.

Retail Sales

The *Census of Retail Trade* provides information on the number of retail establishments in an area and the level of sales for various categories of establishments such as department stores, food stores, auto dealers, apparel and accessory stores (men's, women's, family, shoe, other), eating and drinking places, and drugstores. This information is provided on a county-by-county basis in the *Census of Retail Trade*. A supplemental publication provides the same information about retail establishments and sales for geographic areas, called *major retail centers*, which include central business districts and major retail nodes built around regional and superregional shopping centers. For example, the Atlanta metropolitan area is represented in this supplemental publication by 22 major retail centers, including the Atlanta central business district, the Lenox/Phipps mall area, and the Perimeter Center area.

Spatial Growth Patterns

An understanding of local employment, population, households, and income at a particular point in time is supplemented with information on the spatial distribution of these economic and demographic variables and the changes that have occurred over time. The distribution of population at a point in time is easily obtained from census publications. For example,

Census Tract A may contain 5,000 people while Census Tract B, immediately adjacent to it, contains 7,200. This is a rudimentary analysis of the spatial distribution of a population.

Spatial growth analysis is a time series study of population movements. The appraiser should discover where population is growing and where it is not. Over the past five to 10 years, for example, more population movement may have occurred in the eastern and northern sections of an area than in the western and southern sections. This observation is a rudimentary spatial growth analysis. More sophisticated analyses may be performed using tables and maps that show how population, and consequently other economic and demographic variables, have changed over time.

Once all significant variables affecting the local economy have been investigated, the appraiser can identify whether the subject property and its trade area are in a portion of the local economy that is experiencing rapid growth, slow growth, or no growth.

Local Economic Analysis: An Example

The sample local economic analysis that follows can be used as a model for this section of a narrative appraisal report. The model should be adapted to address the specialized needs of the community in which the subject property is located, or the specific requirements of the analysis. The local economic analysis described below is presented in three major sections focusing on employment, population and households, and income.

Descriptive Analysis of Employment

Local economic analysis begins with a detailed review of recent employment figures. At this initial stage, local economic analysis is purely descriptive. Table 3.2 presents historical employment data for a hypothetical local metropolitan area. Assuming the numbers in Table 3.2 are in thousands, they might relate to a large metropolitan area with a population of more than two million. If, on the other hand, the numbers were in hundreds, the metropolitan area might be a community with a population between 250,000 and 400,000.

The table describes employment in the principal industrial sectors of the local economy from 1984 through 1989. Categories of employment are identified using the standard industrial classification (SIC) system. When the table was constructed, data for 1990 were not yet available. Analysis of Table 3.2 can provide insight into the industrial composition of the metropolitan area and employment trends in the recent past. Three factors are examined:

1. Employment trends by SIC category
2. Comparative employment rates for a particular category relative to overall employment rates
3. Changes in the composition of industrial employment

A category-by-category analysis from 1984 to 1989 reveals that manufacturing employment has grown over the six-year period, but only by approximately 1.60%. When total manufacturing is divided between the production of durable and nondurable goods, employment declined by 0.34% in durable goods manufacturing and increased by 3.60% in nondurable goods manufacturing. This observation reveals that the production of nondurable goods is experiencing negligible growth, while durable goods manufacturing is declining, but only slightly. Further analysis of both durable and nondurable goods production reveals wide variation among SIC categories. For example, employment in electric machinery and electronic instrument production increased by 18.18% over these six years, while employment in transportation equipment production declined by 20.63%. Focusing on nondurable goods manufacturing, employment in printing and publishing increased by 21.21%, while employment in apparel production has declined by 26.52%.

This analysis reveals which employment sectors are growing and which are declining. When each employment classification is analyzed, the appraiser can report the pattern of employment growth or decline in each industrial category. Moreover, analysis of the total nonagricultural employment figure, given in the last two lines of Table 3.2, reveals that total employment has been growing, but the annual percentage of growth has been declining. From 1983 to 1984, employment grew by 8.9%; from 1988 to 1989, it grew by only 2.2%.

Table 3.2 **Nonagricultural Employment: Historical Data**	1984	1985	1986	1987
MANUFACTURING	175.3	185.5	191.1	188.7
Durable	89.1	97.4	100.4	98.4
Lumber & wood	3.8	4.9	5.0	5.0
Furniture & fixtures	4.6	4.7	4.4	4.3
Stone, clay & glass	8.7	9.5	9.8	9.7
Primary metal	6.4	6.9	7.0	7.0
Fabricated metal	8.8	9.3	9.5	9.6
Machinery—excluding electric	9.6	10.5	10.6	10.0
Electric & electronic	13.2	14.2	15.5	15.4
Transport equipment	28.6	31.8	33.0	31.8
Nondurable	86.2	88.1	90.7	90.3
Food & kindred	19.9	20.6	22.0	21.0
Textile mill products	8.4	7.5	7.1	7.4
Apparel	13.2	12.7	12.3	11.5
Paper & allied products	8.4	8.6	8.9	8.9
Printing & publishing	19.8	21.4	22.4	23.1
Chemicals	9.3	9.5	9.3	9.1
CONSTRUCTION	63.6	71.6	73.9	73.0
MINING	1.1	1.2	1.3	1.4
TRANSPORTATION, COMMUNICATION & PUBLIC UTILITIES (TCU)	100.4	104.8	109.4	115.2
Transportation	65.3	67.7	69.9	72.9
Communication	25.1	26.6	28.8	31.4
Public utilities	10.0	10.5	10.7	10.9
WHOLESALE TRADE	124.0	125.4	128.3	132.6
RETAIL TRADE	213.6	225.3	238.1	251.6
FINANCE, INSURANCE & REAL ESTATE (FIRE)	82.4	88.6	93.4	99.1
SERVICES	258.7	281.7	302.8	320.8
Hotel & lodging	18.7	20.5	23.0	23.5
Business services	73.8	83.1	91.2	97.7
Health services	47.4	50.6	54.2	58.8
GOVERNMENT	174.3	178.0	185.6	194.5
Federal	36.1	38.3	39.9	42.0
State & local	138.3	139.7	145.7	152.5
Total nonagricultural employment	1193.5	1262.2	1323.8	1376.7
Annual % change	8.9%	5.8%	4.9%	4.0%

As part of the analysis of employment change, Table 3.2 reveals the relative change for each SIC category. Some industrial sectors have experienced more change than the total economy, while others changed less. Total nonagricultural employment in the metropolitan area analyzed grew by

Table 3.2 **(continued)**					
	1988	**1989**	**1984-1989 % CHANGE**	**1984**	**1989% DISTR**
MANUFACTURING	184.7	178.1	+ 1.60%	14.69%	12.26%
Durable	95.5	88.8	–0.34%		
Lumber & wood	4.9	3.8	0%		
Furniture & fixtures	4.1	3.9	–15.22%		
Stone, clay & glass	9.2	8.7	0%		
Primary metal	6.5	6.7	+ 4.69%		
Fabricated metal	9.6	9.4	+ 6.76%		
Machinery—excluding electric	9.9	10.7	+ 11.46%		
Electric & electronic	15.9	15.6	+ 18.18%		
Transport equipment	28.7	22.7	–20.63%		
Nondurable	89.2	89.3	+ 3.60%		
Food & kindred	20.3	20.4	+ 2.51%		
Textile mill products	7.6	7.8	–7.14%		
Apparel	10.5	9.7	–26.52%		
Paper & allied products	9.1	9.7	+ 15.48%		
Printing & publishing	23.9	24.0	+ 21.21%		
Chemicals	9.2	9.5	+ 2.15%		
CONSTRUCTION	71.1	68.2	+ 7.23%	5.33%	4.69%
MINING	1.5	1.3	+ 18.18%	0.09%	0.09%
TRANSPORTATION, COMMUNICATION & PUBLIC UTILITIES (TCU)	120.3	120.9	+ 20.42%	8.41%	8.32%
Transportation	76.3	76.0	+ 16.39%	5.47%	5.23%
Communication	32.8	33.5	+ 33.47%	2.10%	2.31%
Public utilities	11.2	11.4	+ 14.00%	0.84%	0.78%
WHOLESALE TRADE	139.3	143.9	+ 16.05%	10.39%	9.90%
RETAIL TRADE	261.9	267.9	+ 25.42%	17.90%	18.44%
FINANCE, INSURANCE & REAL ESTATE (FIRE)	103.5	105.8	+ 28.40%	6.90%	7.28%
SERVICES	336.7	356.8	+ 37.92%	21.68%	24.55%
Hotels & lodging	23.5	23.6	+ 26.20		
Business services	98.2	99.4	+ 34.69		
Health services	62.7	66.1	+ 39.45		
GOVERNMENT	203.6	210.4	+ 20.71	14.6%	14.48%
Federal	43.5	43.1	+ 19.39		
State & local	160.2	167.4	+ 21.04		
Total nonagricultural employment	1422.5	1453.2	+ 21.76%	100.00%	100.00%
Annual % of change	3.3%	2.2%			

21.76% over the six-year period. Using 21.76% as a basis of comparison, the analyst can identify industrial sectors that experienced above-average growth—communications (33.47%); retail trade (25.42%); finance, insurance, and real estate—FIRE (28.4%); and services (37.92%).

The industrial sectors experiencing approximately average growth were electric and electronic instrument production (18.18%), printing and publishing (21.21%), paper and allied products (15.48%), transportation (16.39%), wholesale trade (16.05%), mining (18.18%) and government employment (20.71%).

Industrial sectors experiencing modest, below-average growth were public utilities (14.0%), machinery - excluding electric (11.46%), fabricated metals (6.76%), construction (7.23%), and primary metals (4.69%). Apparel and transport equipment manufacturing declined most.

The table illustrates that growth in the economy is occurring in the white-collar occupations—services, FIRE, communications, and select manufacturing industries. The appraiser can relate this information to the market area in which the subject property is located. For example, if the market area contains firms that participate in rapidly growing industries and the employees of these firms live near their jobs, then the appraiser can conclude that the economic strength or vitality of the market area is good and prospects for the future are excellent. If, on the other hand, the market area contains furniture plants, transportation equipment production facilities (i.e., auto production plants and airplane production plants), and apparel producers, the prospects for the market area may be poor.

A third aspect of employment analysis concerns the distribution of employment across industrial sectors. Facts relevant to this analysis are presented in the last two columns of Table 3.2, which reveal that manufacturing as a percentage of total employment declined from 14.69% in 1984 to 12.26% in 1989. Over the same time period, the service sector increased from 21.68% to 24.55%. Comparing just these two industries reveals that the local metropolitan area is becoming less dependent on manufacturing industries and more dependent on service industries. In other words, it has become more white collar and less blue collar.

In summary, to perform local economic analysis the analyst first concentrates on descriptive data, which are used to identify significant growth industries verses declining industries, and then studies the industrial composition of the metropolitan area. With this information he or she can start to form a conclusion about the economic vitality of the market area in which the subject property is located.

Predictive Analysis of Employment

Local economic analysis does not stop with descriptive data. Employment forecasts must be developed or obtained from economists and demographers. The following discussion assumes that employment forecasts for the local economic area are available from regional planning agencies, economic forecasting projects conducted at a state university, and/or the Department of Labor in the state in which the market area is located.[1]

To determine if local economic forecasts are available, analysts should check various local and state agencies for either employment forecasts or population forecasts. When only a population forecast is available, it can be converted into an employment forecast using the historical labor force participation ratio and an estimate of the future ratio.

Note that most employment forecasts are not as detailed as SIC code information. Usually only total employment is forecast. (See Table 3.3.)

Multiple Forecasts Available

Table 3.3 extends the information in Table 3.2 from the descriptive to the predictive. The predictive analysis presented here is based the assumption that two separate forecasts for employment in the community are available. (An analyses based on only one forecast is presented later.) This analysis is based on an employment forecast generated by an economic forecasting project conducted at a state university, using data from the Bureau of Business and Economic Research, and a second forecast generated by a regional planning agency. Actual employment data are available from 1984 through 1989; the two forecasts cover the current period, 1990, and the near future, 1991 through 1995.

The appraiser discovers that the forecast provided by the local university was prepared in 1990 and uses 1989 data as a starting point. The econometrician at the local university forecast employment statistics for 1990 (the current year), 1991, 1992, and 1995 as shown in Table 3.3.

The employment forecast from the regional planning agency was generated in 1987 using 1985 data as a base. The demographers and plan-

---

1. The development of an employment forecast is not covered in this text. For a detailed discussion of this process, readers are referred to literature on economic base analysis and economic base multipliers. One source is Neil G. Carn, Joseph Rabianski, Ronald Racster, and Maury Seldin, *Real Estate Market Analysis: Techniques and Applications* (Englewood Cliffs, N.J.: Prentice-Hall Publishing, 1988).

Table 3.3 **Employment: Historical Data & Forecasts**					
	Local University Forecast		Regional Planning Agency Forecast		Analyst's Forecast
Year	Total	Annual % of Change	Total	Annual % of Change	at 2.2% Growth
1984	1,193.5	8.9	1,193.5	8.9	
1985	1,262.2	5.8	1,262.2	5.8	
1986	1,323.8	4.9			
1987	1,376.7	4.0			
1988	1,422.5	3.3			
1989	1,453.2	2.2			1,453.2
1990(F)	1,489.3	2.5	1,630.0	5.25	1,482.3
1991(F)	1,504.3	1.0			1,511.9
1992(F)	1,537.7	2.2			1,542.1
1993					1,573.0
1994					1,604.5
1995(F)	1,682.4	3.04			1,636.5
1996					
1997					
1998					
1999					
2000(F)			2,152.0	2.82	

(F) = forecast
Source: U.S. Bureau of Labor Statistics

ners at the agency generated forecasts for the years 1990, 2000, and 2010. The forecast for 2010 has been ignored because its accuracy is extremely suspect. The regional planning agency's forecast for the year 2000 is used, but with reservations.

The appraiser is now ready to undertake the predictive portion of the economic analysis. A comparison of the two forecasts reveals that the forecast from the local university is probably more accurate. It relies on more recent data and was prepared in 1990. The inaccuracy of the forecast from the regional planning agency is revealed by simply comparing actual 1989 employment, 1,453, to the forecast of 1990 employment, 1,630. Based on this comparison, the appraiser decides that the local university's employment estimate of 1,682 is a reasonable forecast for 1995.

The appraiser can extend this simple predictive analysis by considering other facts contained in the two employment forecasts. First, the appraiser can examine the forecast from the local university in light of local economic developments during 1990. For example, the forecasted growth rate from 1989 to 1990 is 2.5%. If the appraiser has received news that the local unemployment rate has been increasing and a local employer plans to close its plant, the appraiser can evaluate the forecast generated in 1989 and adjust the forecasted values for 1990, 1991, 1992, and 1995 accordingly. Based on recent facts the appraiser may decide that a growth rate of 2% per year should be applied to the 1989 employment figure of 1,453. Using this 2% growth rate, the appraiser can forecast employment to be 1,636.5 in 1995. This figure is slightly more conservative than the 1,682 figure forecast by the local university. The appraiser's estimate is completely justified, however, because it is based on more recent information that was not available to the economist when the university forecast was made.

Single Forecast Available

Predictive analysis is more difficult when the appraiser is only able to obtain a forecast from the regional planning agency. Assume that an appraiser has only recent historical data and a three-year-old forecast on which to base his judgment. Table 3.4 shows how these data can be used to forecast employment for 1995. The simplest procedure is to apply the regional planning agency's growth rate for 1990 to 2000, which is 2.82% per year, to the known employment level of 1,453.2. This yields an employment forecast of 1,717.1 for 1995. As an alternative the analyst can apply reasoned judgment to adjust the regional planning agency's growth rate for the 1990s.

Assume that the appraiser examines the past data and determines that the actual growth in employment over the last year was less than 2.82%. Based on the historical data and the published information on rising unemployment rates and plant closings, he is convinced that a growth rate between 2.2% and 2.8% would be more appropriate. He eventually fixes on an annual growth rate of 2.4% per year, and applies this rate to generate an employment forecast of 1,675.4 for 1995.

Table 3.4 **Employment: Historical Data & Forecasts**						
	Historical Employment Data		**Regional Planning Agency Forecast**		**Analyst's Forecast**	
Year	**Total**	**Annual % of Change**	**Total**	**Annual % of Change**	**@2.82 Growth**	**@2.21 Growth**
1984	1,193.5		1,193.5	8.9		
1985	1,262.2	5.8	1,262.2	5.8		
1986	1,323.8	4.9				
1987	1,376.7	4.0				
1988	1,422.5	3.3				
1989	1,453.2				1,453.2	1,453.2
1990			1,630.0	5.25	1,494.2	1,488.1
1991					1,536.3	1,523.8
1992					1,580.0	1,560.4
1993					1,624.2	1,597.8
1994					1,670.0	1,636.2
1995					1,717.1	1,675.4
1996						
1997						
1998						
1999						
2000			2,152.0	2.82		

The analyst's forecast, which is represented in Table 3.4, is based on the judgment of other experts, but their estimates are used with caution. The appraiser realizes that the agency forecast was out of date since it was made three years ago and could not reflect the decreasing rate of employment growth over the last few years. Therefore the appraiser has to use this forecast's long-term employment growth rate of 2.82% as the ceiling value in his analysis.

Tables 3.3 and 3.4 illustrate forecasts of employment growth. Predictive analysis can also be used to forecast employment stability or decline.

Predictive Analysis of Population

Like an employment forecast, a population forecast is based on historical data. The analyst must first identify the agencies that issue population projections or forecasts. Assume that three sources of population data and forecasts are available. The local university provides descriptive data, which it obtains from the Department of Commerce, Bureau of Economic Analysis, and the university's economists and demographers prepare a short-term forecast. The regional planning agency also provides data and a forecast of population. As a third source, the appraiser can obtain population estimates and projections from a private vendor of secondary data.[2]

Population data and forecasts are presented in Table 3.5. The analysis is being performed in 1990. The local university received data from the U.S. Department of Commerce for 1988 and then estimated population for 1989, 1990, and future years — i.e., 1991, 1992, and 1995. These data appear in the second and third columns of Table 3.5

The regional planning agency also obtained its data from the U.S. Department of Commerce, Bureau of Economic Analysis, but the population forecast it used was published in early 1987, so it relies on 1985 data. Thus, using 1985 figures, a forecast is generated in 1987 for the years 1990, 2000, and 2010. The forecasts for 1990 and 2000 are relevant to the analysis, but the forecast for 2010 is too speculative to be useful. Based on the values forecast by the regional planning agency for 1990 and 2000, a forecast for 1995 can be extrapolated — i.e., the 20,884 employment figure for 1990 is increased by 2.64% per year through 1995.

Comparison of the forecasts and estimates for 1990 reveals that the three independent sources produce figures within a narrow range. There is only a 0.7% difference between the high forecast of 20,884 and the low forecast of 20,864. In this situation, the appraiser should feel comfortable with a 1990 population figure anywhere within the range established.

Comparing the forecasts for 1995 presents a slightly different picture. Here the local university's forecast of 3,182 is at the low end of the range, while the regional planning agency's forecast of 3,285.5 is at the high end of the range. The absolute difference is 103.5, or approximately 3.25%. In this situation the appraiser must use his or her judgment and consider any additional information that is available to determine an appropriate percentage of growth for the next five years. Recent information in local

---

2. Several private vendors sell demographic information — e.g., CACI, National Planning Data Corporation, National Decision Systems, Urban Decision Systems, and R.F. Donnelly. *Sales Marketing and Management* publishes a population forecast by county in the November issue of the magazine.

Table 3.5 **Population: Historical Data & Forecasts**					
	Local University Forecast*		Regional Planning Agency Forecast*		Private Vendor Data
Year	Total	Annual % of Change	Total	Annual % of Change	Total	Annual % of Change
1984	2,379.4	3.11	2,379.4	3.11		
1985	2,469.4	3.78	2,469.4	3.78		
1986	2,565.9	3.91				
1987	2,656.2	3.52				
1988	2,736.6	3.03				
1989	2,802.0(F)	2.39				
1990	2,864.0(F)	2.21	2,884.0(F)	3.15	2,872(F)	
1991	2,921.0(F)	2.00				
1992	2,975.0(F)	1.85				
1993						
1994						
1995	3,182.0	2.27	3,285.5	2.64	3,252.7	2.52
1996						
1997						
1998						
1999						
2000						

(F) = forecast

* Source of data: U.S. Department of Commerce, Bureau of Economic Analysis, *Local Area Personal Income 1983-1988.*

newspapers may reveal that employment growth is declining. The state department of industry and trade may reveal that new business starts have declined. If evidence such as this can be gathered from local sources, the appraiser can safely determine that the population growth rate estimated by the local university is the most appropriate and settle on 3,182 as the best population forecast. If, on the other hand, the appraiser finds that new business starts and employment growth both increased during 1990, he or she might decide that the population estimate of 3,250 made by the private vendor is the most appropriate.

When several population forecasts are available and all provide similar figures, the task is relatively straightforward. Based on current information and a reasoned judgment, the appraiser can pick a representative figure. If, on the other hand, the forecasted figures are very different, the appraiser must be more diligent in determining the most representative figure within the range of forecasted values. Further study will usually involve checking the reliability and accuracy of the agency making the forecast and the assumptions used in their analysis.

Income

The third major variable used in local economic analysis is income level. The appraiser considers per capita income, mean household income, and median household income as well as income distribution. Most government data sources tend to focus their analysis on per capita income. Table 3.6 shows historical and forecasted per capita income data obtained from the same three sources that provided the population estimates and forecasts analyzed earlier. However, the regional planning agency does not provide a forecast of per capita income. It merely provides historical information obtained from the Department of Commerce, Bureau of Economic Analysis.

The data provided by the local university also rely on Bureau of Economic Analysis data, but university economists use the data from 1988, the most recent available, to make forecasts for 1989, 1990, 1991, and 1992. The third source of per capita income data, the private vendor, provides an estimate of per capita income for 1990 and a forecast of per capita income for 1995.

Examination of the table reveals a substantial discrepancy between the forecasts provided by the local university and the private vendor. The local university forecast of 1990 per capita income is $19,880, while the private vendor forecasts per capita income at $16,493. This represents a difference of $3,387, or 20.5% on a base of $16,493. Unlike the population estimates which fell into a narrow, tolerable range, here there is a substantial discrepancy that must be resolved.

One way to resolve the issue is to go back to the most recent historical data. Table 3.6 shows that in 1988 the Department of Commerce, Bureau of Economic Analysis estimated per capita income to be approximately $18,400. Using this figure as an acceptable standard, the appraiser can assume that the private vendor's 1990 forecast of per capita income,

Table 3.6 **Per Capita Income**						
	Local University Forecast*		Regional Planning Agency Data*		Private Vendor Data	
Year	Total	Annual % of Change	Total	Annual % of Change	Total	Annual % of Change
1983	$12,930		$12,931			
1984	$14,325	10.77	$14,324	10.77		
1985	$15,460	7.96	$15,464	7.96		
1986	$16,397	6.16	$16,417	6.16		
1987	$17,454	6.31	$17,453	6.31		
1988	$18,398	5.43	$18,400	5.43		
1989	$19,161(F)	4.15				
1990	$19,880(F)	3.75			$16,129	NA
1991	$20,635(F)	3.80				
1992	$21,656(F)	4.95				
1993						
1994						
1995					$22,129	6.06

(F) = forecast

* Source of data: U.S. Department of Commerce, Bureau of Economic Analysis, *Local Area Personal Income 1983-1988*.

$16,493, is inaccurate. Nevertheless, the appraiser still believes that the 6.06% annual growth in per capita income is an appropriate estimate. Thus, the appraiser can construct his or her own per capita income forecast for 1995 using the following estimates:

1. Per capita income of $18,400 in 1988
2. The income growth rates for 1989 through 1992 established by the local university
3. The 6.06% annual growth rate for 1993 to 1995 established by the private vendor.

These figures will produce an acceptable, conservative estimate of per capita income into the future. The results of the appraiser's calculations are show in Table 3.7. The appraiser's forecast, derived from the expert opinion of economists and demographers at the local university and the professionals employed by the private vendor, indicates a per capita income estimate of $19,880 for 1990 and a forecasted per capita income of $25,850 for 1995. This forecast was generated using the growth rates for 1989 to 1992 established by the local university and the private vendor's growth rate of 6.06% for subsequent years.

Table 3.7 **Appraiser's Forecast of Per Capita Income**		
Year	**Annual % of Growth**	**Per Capita Income**
1988		$18,398
1989	4.15%	$19,162
1990	3.75%	$19,880
1991	3.80%	$20,636
1992	4.95%	$21,657
1993	6.06%	$22,969
1994	6.06%	$24,361
1995	6.06%	$25,838
		say $25,850

If, in light of current information, a more conservative estimate is warranted, the appraiser could have selected a 3.75% growth rate for the entire period. (This is the lowest growth rate estimated by the local university's economists.) Under this assumption the per capita income of $18,398 in 1988 would grow to $23,806 in 1992.

Data Sources for Local Economic Analysis

The appraiser's first responsibility in performing local economic analysis for a shopping center appraisal is to find data on the economy in the area where the shopping center is located. The major economic variables to be analyzed are employment, population, and income.

Employment data on major metropolitan areas are generally easy to find; it is more difficult to find information on smaller urban areas. Descriptive or historical employment data compiled on a countywide basis are generally available in every state. Each state Department of Labor has a bureau or division that collects employment data by job site on a quarterly or annual basis. These data are usually free or available for a modest fee to cover the cost of processing the request or reproducing the master file. The Bureau of Labor Statistics of the U.S. Department of Labor provides employment data for the nation's largest metropolitan areas.

Population estimates for all metropolitan areas are compiled every 10 years and limited data are available for intervening years. A regional planning agency or the research department of the local electric power company can provide these data. Private vendors of census data are a very convenient sources of population estimates for the aggregate local economy and for smaller geographic areas such as census tracts. Information on one-, three-, and five-mile rings around the subject property or irregularly shaped areas around the subject property can be obtained.

Income estimates are also available from private vendors of census data. These companies tailor their research to pinpoint a particular geographic area. In addition, annual income estimates for larger metropolitan areas are available from the census and from local regional planning agencies.

Employment, population, and income forecasts are more difficult to obtain than historical data. Their availability depends on the existence of an economic forecasting center or bureau of economics and business research at a state or local university that has undertaken the task of forecasting demographic and economic variables. The cooperation of the professional staff at the regional planning agency is also needed to obtain forecasts. Private vendors of data are often the best source of population and income forecasts by census tracts, counties, and specialty areas.

Accuracy of Data

When secondary data are used, their accuracy should be evaluated. This evaluation will either support the appraiser's confidence in the data or prove that the data are inaccurate and should not be used. Verification is especially important when the appraiser is using population and employment forecasts provided by public agencies and private vendors.

A simple, straightforward way to assess accuracy is to evaluate the internal consistency and accuracy of the forecasts made by a specific entity over an extended period. For example, if a private vendor of census-based data provides a population estimate for 1990 and a forecast for 1995, an appraiser who has been using this vendor for several years can check the vendor's past population estimates going back, say, from 1989 through 1984.

Table 3.8 **Internal Accuracy of Population Forecasts**		
Year	**Estimated Population**	**Forecasted Population**
1981	5,200	
1982	5,400	
1983	5,600	
1984	5,700	
1985	5,800	
1986	6,000	6,400
1987	6,200	6,700
1988	6,300	6,900
1989	6,400	7,100
1990	6,600	7,300
1991	6,800	7,600
1992	6,700*	7,800
1993		8,100
1994		8,400
1995		8,500
1996		8,700
1997		7,900*

* Adjusted

Consider the case of a private vendor that has provided an appraiser with population estimates and forecasts over a ten-year period.[3] Historical and forecasted data are shown in Table 3.8. Note that this accuracy check requires the continued and consistent use of the same data source.

In 1981 the data vendor provided the appraiser with a 1981 population estimate and a population forecast for 1986. In 1982 the appraiser obtained a current population estimate and a forecast of population in the same geographic area. These data were obtained and saved for 10 years, from 1981 through 1991. Displaying the data as shown in Table 3.8 allows the appraiser to make an initial observation and to calculate a coefficient of determination (R^2). Observation reveals that the forecasted populations of recent years have been consistently higher than the esti-

---

3. Most private vendors cannot supply historical estimates and forecasts because they do not store old databases. Once the database is updated with the most recent information, the outdated database is dropped. Thus any check for accuracy must be performed on data that the appraiser has stored in his or her own files.

mated populations, by 400 to 800 individuals. Armed with this information, the appraiser can evaluate the accuracy of this private vendor's population forecast for 1996. It is relatively safe to say that the 8,700 figure forecast for 1996 is an overestimate. A more accurate, appropriate range would be 7,900 to 8,300, given the historical discrepancy characteristic of this vendor.

When the 1990 population figures are released by the Bureau of the Census late in 1991 or early in 1992, this private vendor will incorporate these data into its database. For example, if the appraiser requests data for this same geographic area in 1992, he may discover that the population estimate for 1990 is 6,500. This information supports the belief that this vendor has been slightly too high on its current period estimates and substantially too high on its population forecasts. At this time the vendor will recalculate its estimate of population for 1992 and the population forecast for 1997. Based on the new data, the population forecast for 1997 could very well drop to 7,900 and the 1992 estimate of population could drop to 6,700. These inconsistencies in the data will be evident to the appraiser who is keeping a historical record, but would not be apparent to the appraiser who bought 1992 data and did not see the 1991 population estimate and forecast.

In addition to examining the accuracy and consistency of a single source, the appraiser should also try to establish a procedure to judge the population estimates and, if possible, population forecasts produced by different data sources. For example, consider the data provided in Table 3.9. Simple observation reveals that the two population estimates are not identical, but are moving in the same direction and by approximately the same amount. This will suggest to the appraiser that a population estimate of 6,400 to 6,600 for 1990 is substantially accurate. The accuracy of this range can be checked when the 1990 population estimate is released by the census bureau in 1992. If that number is 6,500, then the private vendor's estimate is slightly high while the public agency's is slightly low.

Table 3.9 Comparison of Population Estimates To Check for Accuracy		
Year	Private Vendor Population Estimates	Public Agency Population Estimates
1981	5,200	5,150
1982	5,400	5,350
1983	5,600	5,500
1984	5,700	5,600
1985	5,800	5,700
1986	6,000	5,800
1987	6,200	5,950
1988	6,300	6,100
1989	6,400	6,200
1990	6,600	6,400
1991	6,800	6,600

The appraiser will never know the true population parameter because even the decennial census counts are not perfectly accurate. However, a standard for the community must be established to judge the estimates. The appraiser must discover the appropriate standard for the market relevant to the assignment. In one market the public agency may set the standard, while in another market area a private vendor's estimates could be more appropriate.

Horton Plaza Inner-City-Mall, San Diego　　　　*P. Buddle / H. Armstrong Roberts*

Chapter Four

MARKET AND MARKETABILITY ANALYSIS
FOR SHOPPING CENTER APPRAISALS

Introduction

Market analysis for a shopping center appraisal focuses on the economic vitality of the market area in which the subject property is located. The central question is whether the consumers' ability to buy retail products and the availability of retail products are in balance. The total square footage of retail space is used as a measure of the availability of retail products. Marketability analysis, which is a site-specific extension of market analysis, focuses on the economics of the subject property's retail trade area. To assess supply in a marketability analysis, the appraiser surveys the competition in the trade area. To identify demand in a marketability analysis, the appraiser estimates the subject property's ability to capture purchasing power in its retail trade area and forecasts future purchasing power to judge the continued vitality of the subject property with regard to rent levels and vacancies.

The first section of this chapter concentrates on definitions and concepts; the second presents a discussion of market analysis in the form of residual analysis; and the third discusses the demand and supply components of marketability analysis.

Definitions and Concepts

Market Analysis

Market analysis considers the demand for and supply of a particular type of property in a predetermined geographic area.[1] Market analysis for a shopping center, therefore, is an analysis of the demand and supply factors that affect all shopping centers in a specific geographic area.

Demand analysis investigates the variables that affect consumers' willingness and ability to buy retail goods and services, which create a demand for retail space. Supply analysis focuses on the availability of retail goods and services in the predetermined geographic area. At this level, the analysis is not site-specific. The demand and supply information gathered does not related to a particular site. Rather, the appraiser seeks information about the demand for and supply of retail goods and, consequently, the demand for and supply of retail space in the general area that contains the subject property.

The principal task that the appraiser undertakes in market analysis is to gather information to reach an understanding of the volume of retail sales that can be generated in a predetermined geographic area (demand analysis) and the portion of those retail needs that are being met (supply analysis). The two components are then compared to determine if there is excess supply or unmet demand. This procedure is referred to as *residual analysis*. As part of supply analysis, the appraiser performs a survey of the competition, which is known as a *competitive survey* or *competitive analysis*.

Marketability Analysis

Marketability analysis is the study of demand and supply factors that affect a specific site. It is directly linked to market analysis. The first task is to define the retail trade area that is appropriate to the subject property. For a shopping center, the trade area would be the geographic area adjacent to the site and extending away from it for an appropriately defined distance.

---

1. Much of this discussion is drawn from Neil G. Carn, Joseph Rabianski, Ronald Racster, and Maury Seldin, *Real Estate Market Analysis: Techniques and Applications*, (Englewood Cliffs, N.J.: Prentice-Hall, 1988). See also Edwin Rams, *Analysis and Valuation of Retail Locations* (Reston, Va.: Reston Publishing Company, Inc., a Prentice-Hall Company Inc., 1976) and *Market Research for Shopping Centers*, Ruben Roca, ed. (New York: International Council of Shopping Centers, 1980).

In general, the retail trade area for the subject property will be smaller than the geographic area that represents the market area.

Market Area and Retail Trade Area Compared

The geographic focus of a market analysis is the market area immediately adjacent to the subject property and extending a sufficient distance away to include all of the subject property's competition. When a regional mall is analyzed, the market area includes at least the first ring of competing regional malls. From a distance perspective, the market area for a regional mall could be a geographic area with a radius of 30 miles around the subject property. The market area for a neighborhood shopping center would include at least the first ring of neighborhood shopping centers around the subject property and should probably extend beyond the first ring. In terms of distance, the market area for a neighborhood shopping center could be the area within a three- to five-mile radius around the subject property. The market identified must be broad enough to include all of the subject property's competitors.

Retail trade area is a marketability concept. It is the geographic area immediately adjacent to the subject property from which it draws its customers. As mentioned in Chapter 1, a major concept related to the retail trade area is the time/distance criteria for defining a particular type of shopping center. According to the Urban Land Institute, the primary trade area for a neighborhood shopping center has a radius of one and one-half miles and a travel time of five to 10 minutes. A community shopping center has a primary trade area of three to five miles and a travel time of 10 to 20 minutes. A regional shopping center has a primary trade area of eight miles and a travel time of 20 minutes, while a superregional shopping center has a radius of 12 miles and a travel time of 30 minutes.

Primary and Secondary Trade Areas

Real estate market analysts commonly refer to a primary trade area and a secondary trade area, but the definitions offered for these two terms are not precise. The primary trade area can be defined in three ways.

1. The primary trade area is the geographic area immediately adjacent to the subject property and extending out to a travel time of a

certain duration. Different maximum driving times are used to establish the primary trade area of different retail establishments. For supermarkets, a travel time of five minutes may determine the primary trade area; for regional shopping centers, the primary trade area may be identified with a travel time of 20 minutes or more.

2. The primary trade area is the geographic area immediately adjacent to the property from which the retail establishment obtains 60% to 70% of its total customers.

3. The primary trade area is the geographic area immediately adjacent to the property that generates 60% to 70% of the retail establishment's total sales.

Three important variables are specified in these definitions of the primary trade area—travel time, percentage of total customers, and percentage of total sales. There may be no direct correlation among these three variables or between pairs of variables. For example, the closest 60% of a retail establishment's customers may be responsible for more or less than 60% of that establishment's sales. And, if the retail establishment is a neighborhood shopping center, neither 60% of the customers nor 60% of the sales may match up with the five-minute travel time. Thus the definitions provided must be considered guidelines that the analyst can use to define a primary trade area, not precise standards of measure.

Secondary trade area is also defined in several ways.

1. The secondary trade area is the geographic area adjacent to the primary trade area and extending away from the subject property for a predetermined driving time. For a supermarket, the secondary trade area could be the area within a driving time of five to 12 minutes from the subject property. For a regional shopping center, the secondary trade area could be the geographic area within 20 to 40 minutes of driving time.

2. The secondary trade area is the geographic area from which the retail establishment is able to obtain an additional 20% of its total customers.

3. The secondary trade area is the geographic area from which the retail establishment is able to obtain an additional 20% to 30% of its total sales.

Once again, these definitions are not precise and should only be considered guidelines.

Demand Analysis

For retail market and marketability studies, demand analysis is primarily a study of the purchasing power in either the market area or the retail trade area. Purchasing power is the product of two variables—population and income—and is calculated as population times per capita income or the number of households times the average or mean household income. Purchasing power is used in numerical analysis.

Other demand variables that play a role in the analysis of a market area or a retail trade area are consumer tastes and preferences as they relate to the merchandise mix offered by the subject property and its competitors; the physical image of both the subject property and its competitors; and the price and quality of the products and services offered by the competition. The appraiser must consider these additional variables and not simply rely on the results generated from an analysis of purchasing power.

Supply Analysis—Survey of the Competition

Supply analysis for both market and marketability studies begins with a survey of the competition, which is essentially an analysis of comparable properties. In this analysis the appraiser identifies the physical characteristics of the site and the structure, the center's financial characteristics, and the locational characteristics of the subject property and the competitive properties. On the supply side of market analysis, competitors are studied to determine their gross leasable area and average sales per gross leasable area, from which an estimate of total retail sales is obtained. Physical, financial, and locational characteristics play a secondary role in supply analysis.

In a marketability study, the characteristics of the competitors located closest to the subject property are studied in greater detail. A marketability study is site-specific and thus a highly detailed analysis is needed to assess the financial feasibility of the subject property in its retail trade area. A more detailed discussion of market analysis and marketability analysis follows.

Market Analysis for Shopping Centers

Market analysis has three components—demand analysis, supply analysis, and residual analysis. First the geographic area is established. Then the demand for retail products (and thus retail space) and the supply of retail space are analyzed. Finally, the demand and the supply components are combined to form an economic picture of the market.

Delineation of the Market Area

There are two geographic areas that the analyst must consider when analyzing the market for a shopping center. The first is the subject property's market area—i.e., the geographic area in which the subject property and its most proximate competition are located. A diagram of a subject property's market area is shown in Figure 4.1. The subject property, identified as N_S, is an existing neighborhood shopping center located in the center of the market area. An inspection of the geographic area reveals the existence of eight other neighborhood shopping centers, identified as N_1 through N_8, and six community shopping centers, identified as C_1 through C_6. The solid lines represent the street system and the geometric sections represent Census Tracts *A* through *J*.

The second geographic area studied is the subject property's retail trade area. This is the area from which the subject property will draw its customers. It is a smaller geographic area than the market area. For the present, the subject property's retail trade area is identified as the geographic area that is immediately adjacent to the subject but does not extend beyond any of its nearest surrounding competitors. Estimating a subject property's retail trade area is discussed in relation to marketability analysis later in the chapter.

Figure 4.1 Market Area and the Retail Trade Area

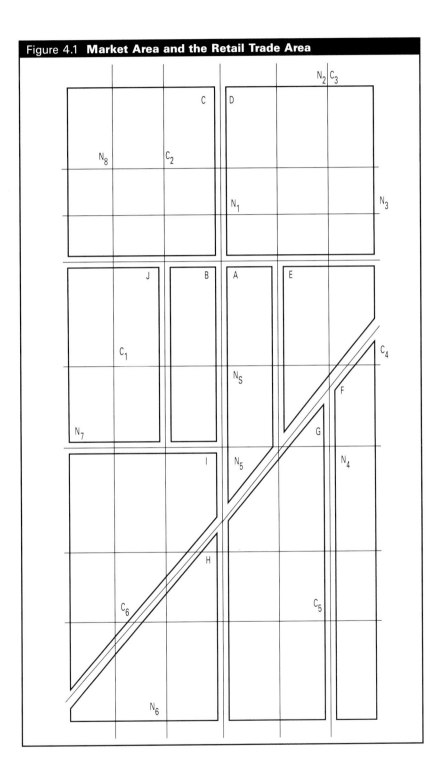

Demand Analysis

The next task is to estimate the purchasing power in the market area. The calculations are shown in Table 4.1. The census tracts within the market area are identified and population and per capita income statistics are obtained for each tract. Multiplying the population of each census tract by its per capita income yields a purchasing power estimate for each tract, which is provided in the fourth column of the table. (A similar estimate could have been calculated by multiplying the number of households by the mean household income for each census tract.) Adding the purchasing power estimates together indicates that the total purchasing power in the market area is $615,250,000.

Table 4.1 **Purchasing Power Estimation**			
Census Tract	Population	Per Capita Income	Purchasing Power (in millions)
A	7,000	$12,000	$84.00
B	6,600	$12,000	79.20
C	5,500	$10,000	55.00
D	6,400	$11,000	70.40
E	5,200	$11,000	57.20
F	5,400	$11,000	59.40
G	4,800	$10,500	50.40
H	4,600	$11,250	51.75
I	5,200	$10,250	53.30
J	5,200	$10,500	54.60
Total purchasing power			$615.25
Times percentage spent for retail goods & services			× 0.41
			252.25 million
			or $252,250,000

Now the appraiser must estimate the percentage of purchasing power that is directed towards retail expenditures. To do this the appraiser needs to identify the major categories of expenditures incurred by individuals. A breakdown of these expenditures is provided below:

Housing (shelter)	27.9%
Fuel and utilities	7.3%
Transportation	17.0%

Medical care	6.7%
Retail expenditures	41.1%

100.00% of disposable income

Percentage breakdowns like this one can be obtained from a U.S. government publication titled *The Relative Importance of Components in the Consumer Price Index*. The percentages shown were obtained from the 1991 edition of this publication. These figures reveal that approximately 41% of disposable income can be directed toward retail expenditures. Using this percentage, the subject property's market area possesses $252,250,000 ($615,250,000 × 0.41) that can be directed toward retail expenditures.

Data Availability

Much of the information used in market analysis is available from published sources and on-line computer databases. For example, information on consumer expenditure distributions published by the federal government can also be found in the "Survey of Buying Power" published in *Sales and Marketing Management* magazine. Such information is also available in Trinet Business Data, which can be accessed through the National Planning Data Corporation.[2]

Supply Analysis

The principal task of market supply analysis is to estimate the current amount of retail expenditure in the market area. To do this the appraiser must obtain square foot estimates of all the competitive facilities that exist in the market area. These data are provided in Table 4.2, which shows the four operations performed. First each neighborhood and community center in the subject property's market area is identified by number and its square footage is recorded. Square foot measurements are provided for the anchor and major tenants and for speculative space. The table identifies the amount of space occupied by supermarkets, drugstores, and dis-

2. For a listing of data sources, see Waldo L. Born, *Real Estate Market Research On-line Databases* (College Station: Real Estate Center at Texas A & M University, 1988).

Table 4.2 Market Supply Analysis—Square Foot Estimation

Neighborhood Centers	Supermarket	Drugstore	Discount Store	Total Speculative	Occupied Speculative
Subject	32,000	10,000	0	18,000	16,000
1	35,000	8,000	0	16,000	12,000
2	28,000	6,000	0	12,000	10,500
3	34,000	9,000	0	15,000	14,000
4	40,000	10,000	0	22,000	20,000
5	28,000	7,000	0	9,000	8,000
6	35,000	11,000	0	16,000	16,000
7	40,000	9,000	0	20,000	16,000
8	30,000	7,000	0	14,000	12,000
	302,000	77,000	0	142,000	124,500
Community Centers					
1	35,000	8,000	30,000	22,000	20,000
2	40,000	8,000	40,000	20,000	18,000
3	36,000	8,000	40,000	20,000	18,000
4	30,000	6,000	25,000	15,000	14,000
5	40,000	8,000	50,000	20,000	20,000
6	42,000	8,000	48,000	24,000	22,000
	223,000	46,000	233,000	121,000	112,000
Total by store	525,000	123,000	233,000	263,000	236,500
Freestanding space	+ 9,000	+ 6,000	+ 0		× 1.20
Adjusted total sq. ft.	534,000	129,000	233,000		283,800
Estimated sales per sq. ft.	× $280	× $140	× $110		× $150
Estimated sales	$149,520,000	$18,060,000	$25,630,000		$42,570,000

GRAND TOTAL = $235,780,000

count stores, and the amount of speculative space. The total gross leasable area in each of these four categories is calculated.

Second, vacant space is considered. The table makes a distinction between occupied and unoccupied space. A facility-by-facility investigation of the shopping centers reveals that there are no vacancies in supermarkets, drugstores, and discount stores, but relatively high vacancies in speculative space. Note the difference between total speculative and occupied speculative space in the two right-hand columns of the table. Because the analysis focuses on occupied space only, the square footage figures for supermarkets, drugstores, discount stores, occupied speculative space are used.[3]

Third, after vacancies are considered, the square footage of space by category must be increased to account for any freestanding retail establishments operating in the market area. In this geographic area, there are no freestanding grocery stores or supermarkets, but there is approximately 9,000 square feet of space in freestanding convenience stores; 6,000 square feet of freestanding drugstore space; no freestanding discount store space; and an additional 20% of speculative space in the form of fast-food restaurants, dry cleaners, laundries, and miscellaneous retail activity not associated with shopping centers in the market area.

The adjusted total square footage by retail establishment for major tenants is obtained by adding the freestanding space to the space in shopping centers. For speculative space it is calculated by multiplying the total square footage of speculative space by a factor that represents the freestanding tenants that compete with the tenants in speculative shopping center space.

As the fourth step in supply analysis, the adjusted total square footage of each category of space is multiplied by an estimate of sales per square foot of *GLA*. In Table 4.2 supermarket sales are estimated at $280 per

---

3. Another way to handle vacancies in the analysis is to use the total square foot figures as shown in the first five columns of the table and ignore the right-hand column, making no site-specific distinction between occupied and unoccupied space by facility. Then a vacancy line is inserted into the table and the appraiser uses overall rates of vacancy for each facility obtained from the market. For example, the appraiser might discover that vacancies for supermarkets, drugstores and discount stores are 0% in the market, while an overall vacancy of 12% exists for speculative space. This finding could be reflected by showing that 12% vacancy rate just below the figures for the total square footage by store. The appraiser would then continue with the subsequent steps in the analysis. If vacancies are handled in this manner, however, site-by-site distinctions concerning vacancies will be lost, which may adversely affect the analysis.

square foot of *GLA*, drugstore sales at $140, discount store sales at $110, and speculative space in general at $150 per square foot. These sales-per-square-foot figures must represent sales activity in the local market area, so they should be based on information gathered from knowledgeable market sources such as shopping center managers and retail property brokers. A benchmark estimate for these sales can be obtained from *Dollars & Cents of Shopping Centers*, which is published every three years by the Urban Land Institute.

Multiplying the adjusted total square footage by the estimated sales per square foot of *GLA* yields the estimated sales of retail products and services in the market area by category—i.e., supermarket, drugstore, discount store, and speculative space. Adding these figures together yields a grand total of $235,780,000 in retail sales in the market area.

Residual Analysis

Once the appraiser has calculated the purchasing power within the market area that can be directed towards retail expenditures (demand analysis—Table 4.1) and estimated retail sales in the market area (supply analysis—Table 4.2), these two figures can be compared to evaluate residual purchasing power. The calculation is show below.

Retail purchasing power (*RPP*)	$252,250,000
Retail sales (*RS-OCC*)	235,780,000
Residual purchasing power for retail	$16,470,000

If *RPP* in the market area is greater than *RS-OCC*, demand is greater than supply. This implies that consumers who live in the market area are spending money in retail establishments outside the predetermined market area. This additional purchasing power could be redirected or attracted to retail establishments in the market area. Two situations could result. If the right tenants are obtained, vacancies could decrease and rent levels could increase in the near future. Also, these favorable purchasing power conditions could lead to the construction of new retail space.

In the preceding numerical example, residual analysis demonstrated that purchasing power exceeds the total sales of retailers in the market area by \$16 million. If retail space remains constant, vacancies should continue to drop and sales per square foot should increase.

Consider another market in which retail purchasing power (*RPP*) is equal to the estimated retail sales for occupied space (*RS-OCC*) in the market area. This market is in balance at the existing vacancy rate. In this situation, future growth in purchasing power will lead to reduced vacancies and increased sales volume per square foot for the existing retail establishments in the market area.

Now assume that *RPP* is less than *RS-OCC* in the market area, indicating that supply exceeds demand. Here two conclusions can be drawn. On the positive side, local retail establishments are selling goods and services to consumers that reside outside the market area. The appraiser will need to determine whether this trend is likely to continue in the future. On the negative side, there is excess retail space in the market area.

The presence of excess retail space in a market area indicates that there is little opportunity for rent increases or vacancy reductions until the level of *RPP* increases. If the *RPP* figure derived was based on estimated sales for total space (*RS-TOTAL*), occupied plus vacant, this conclusion would be strengthened. Where *RPP* is less than *RS-OCC*, there may be opportunities for the construction of retail space in adjacent geographic market areas because retail space in the subject property's trade area is attracting customers who reside in these adjacent market areas. If this new retail space is constructed, sales volume in the subject property's market area may decline, vacancies may rise, and rent levels may fall in the future.[4]

Residual analysis is a useful tool, but the results need to be checked for accuracy and interpreted carefully. Inaccuracies can enter the analysis through population and household estimates, income estimates, square footage estimates, vacancy estimates, freestanding space estimates, and estimates of sales per square foot of *GLA*. Errors can also result from improper delineation of the subject property's market area. All of these items must be addressed and validated by the appraiser.

---

4. Caution is warranted when *RPP* is less than *RS-OCC*. Using a high sales-per-square-foot figure to estimate *RS-OCC* can result in a low *RPP*. If sales per square foot are high, economic profits are being made, which will attract new competition and increase the demand for new retail space. On the surface, it is difficult to interpret the significance of an *RPP* that is less than *RS-OCC*.

After residual analysis has been performed for the current period, it should be extended into the future to see if market conditions are expected to change. Extending the analysis is especially important if the appraiser discovers that new shopping center construction is underway or will begin in the near future.

For example, assume that a 100,000-sq.-ft. shopping center is currently under construction in the subject market and due to open next year. In addition, a 200,000-sq.-ft. shopping center is in the planning phase and will probably open in four years. These factors can be considered by extending the residual analysis shown in Tables 4.1 and 4.2 five or more years into the future. Then the future retail purchasing power (*RPP*) can be compared to the retail sales in occupied space (*RS-OCC*).

The residual is analyzed in another manner in Table 4.3, which employs growth rates for population, income, and retail sales per square foot. Assume that the appraiser discovers that population is forecast to grow by 4% for two years and then by 3.5% for one year. After that the growth rate will decline by 0.25% per year until it reaches a stable growth rate of 2% nine years from now. Per capita income is expected to grow by 2%, 2.5%, and 2.75% in the next three years, and then by 3% per year for the remaining years in the forecast period. Retail sales per square foot are forecast to grow at 4% for four years and then by 3% per year for the remaining years.

These data are shown in Table 4.3. On the demand side, the growth rates for population and per capita income are combined into a single growth rate using simple multiplication. Between Year 0 and Year 1, the combined growth rate is 1.04×1.02, or 1.0608. This combined growth rate is used to calculate retail purchasing power (*RPP*) in Year 1 and subsequent years.

On the supply side, newly constructed space is added into the analysis at the time when the space opens. It is assumed that the space is fully leased during the year it is opened. This assumption can be changed, however, by prorating the total space over two years and using only the portion that is expected to be occupied. Retail sales per square foot are increased by the anticipated growth rate.

When both demand and the supply factors are addressed, the residual value can calculated. Based on the growth factors and new construc-

Table 4.3 Residual Analysis

	Year 0	Year 1	Year 2	Year 3	Year 4	Year 5	Year 6	Year 7	Year 8	Year 9
Demand										
Purchasing power	$252.25									
Population growth	—	4.00%	4.00%	3.50%	3.25%	3.00%	2.75%	2.50%	2.25%	2.00%
Income growth	—	2.00%	2.50%	2.75%	3.00%	3.00%	3.00%	3.00%	3.00%	3.00%
Combined growth	—	6.08%	6.60%	6.35%	6.35%	6.09%	5.83%	5.58%	5.32%	5.06%
Purchasing power	$252.25	$267.59	$285.25	$303.36	$322.62	$342.27	$362.23	$382.44	$402.78	$425.34
Supply										
Existing sales	$235.78									
Existing space	1179.8									
Additional space	—	100	0	0	200	—	—	—	50	100
Total space	1179.8	1279.8	1279.8	1279.8	1479.8	1479.8	1479.8	1479.8	1529.8	1629.8
Average sales per sq.ft.	$199.85									
Sales growth	—	4.00%	4.00%	4.00%	4.00%	3.00%	3.00%	3.00%	3.00%	3.00%
Average sales per sq. ft.	$199.85	$207.84	$216.16	$224.80	$233.80	$240.81	$248.03	$255.48	$263.14	$271.03
Sales	$235.78	$265.99	$276.64	$287.70	$345.98	$356.35	$367.03	$378.06	$402.55	$441.72
Net	+ $16.47	+ $1.60	+ $8.61	+ $15.66	–$23.36	–$14.08	–$4.80	+ $4.38	+ $0.23	–$16.38

Note: Dollars are in hundreds of thousands; square feet are in thousands.

tion specified, the residual analysis shows cyclical market activity. Initially there is an undersupply of retail space in the market. Construction of the first 100,000 square feet of additional retail space brings the market closer to a balanced position, with a residual value in Year 1 of –$540,000. Then, with the addition of 200,000 square feet of space in Year 4, the market becomes oversupplied and a residual value of –$30,540,000 is shown. Over the next three years the market moves back toward balance with a residual value of –$3,450,000 in Year 7. The additional space constructed in Years 8 and 9 will cause the market to experience larger amounts of oversupply.

In conclusion residual analysis is a very useful technique applied to show the present and anticipated state of the market in which the subject property exists. It allows the analyst to see the impact of future changes in the variables that are important in retail analysis.

Market Saturation Benchmarks

Some investors and developers use a retail space saturation index to identify retail opportunities or signs of an oversupply of retail space. This index is a ratio of the *GLA* in the market area to its total population. The definition of *GLA* is determined by the data sources available in the market. For example, the gross leasable area considered may or may not include freestanding retail space or it may only include space in centers of more than 20,000 square feet. Because no national data collection service with standard definitions is available, users of a saturation index must be exceedingly cautious.

The ratio of *GLA* to population may be useful for tracking changes in a particular market over time. Large developers and investors may want to establish their own data banks and standardize the definition of *GLA*. After studying a specific market, one investor decided that a ratio of approximately 13 square feet of *GLA* per capita indicates additional retail opportunities that probably should be explored; the presence of 25 or more square feet of retail space per capita suggests that retail space is probably adequate and extensive research would be needed before any additional retail space were considered. Obviously such market saturation indexes are crude indicators; differences in trade mix, demographics, and other characteristics can significantly affect their reliability.

Marketability Analysis for Shopping Centers

Marketability analysis starts with the delineation of the retail trade area for the subject property and proceeds to a survey of the competition (supply analysis) and retail trade area analysis (demand analysis). The survey of the competition in a marketability analysis is more detailed than the supply analysis portion of a market analysis. In market analysis the appraiser only examines the competition's gross leasable area and sales per square foot of *GLA* by principal retail categories. A retail trade area analysis provides a more detailed estimate of retail purchasing power.

Delineation of the Retail Trade Area

In delineating the retail trade area for the subject property, the appraiser applies recognized distance and travel time relationships for various classes of shopping centers. These relationships were presented in Table 1.2 in Chapter 1 and are repeated in Table 4.4.

Table 4.4 **Distance and Travel Times for Retail Trade Area Delineation**		
Type of Shopping Center	**Distance**	**Travel Time**
Neighborhood	1.5 miles	5-10 minutes
Community	3-5 miles	10-20 minutes
Regional	8 miles	20 minutes
Superregional	12 miles	30 minutes

Source: Urban Land Institute, *Shopping Center Development Handbook*, p. 22.

The use of distance and travel times to delineate the trade area can be shown in reference to Figure 4.1. Let each square of the grid represent one square mile. Starting with the subject property, N_S, and using the 1.5-mile distance criterion for a neighborhood center established by the Urban Land Institute, neighborhood shopping centers N_1 and N_5 fall in the subject property's retail trade area.

After studying travel times in the vicinity of the subject property, the appraiser discovers that in nonrush hour periods it takes approximately 2.5 minutes to travel one mile. This rate takes into account the 30-mile-per-hour speed limit and the frequency and timing of stoplights. Applying the travel time criterion of 7.5 minutes, the retail trade area delineated by travel time would include neighborhood shopping centers N_1, N_4, N_5, N_7, and community centers C_1, C_2 and C_4.

Distance and travel time mapping is the first stage in delineating a trade area, but it does not produce definitive results. To establish the subject property's retail trade area, the appraiser also needs to understand the concepts of intervening opportunities and market area sharing.

Intervening Opportunities and Market Area Sharing

The second step in the delineation of a retail trade area is consideration of intervening opportunities and market sharing. To apply these two concepts, the appraiser must have a detailed survey of the competition. However, since a full discussion of the survey of the competition is provided later in this chapter, let it suffice to say that the appraiser inspects each of the neighborhood and community shopping centers identified in the retail trade area delineated by travel time to uncover the following facts:

- The gross leasable area of each center
- The nature of the anchor tenants
- The tenant mix in speculative space
- The access characteristics of each site
- The age and condition of the centers

Guided by this information, the appraiser can identify intervening opportunities.

Simply stated, an *intervening opportunity*, or *intercept location*, is a shopping center that potential customers will not drive past to get to the subject property. A relative analysis of the subject property and neighborhood shopping center N_5 can reveal the significance of intervening opportunities. For example, if center N_5 is an exact replica of the subject property, then a consumer who lives south of center N_5 would have no reason to drive past it to get to the subject property. Thus N_5 curtails the subject property's trade area in that direction. At best the subject property's trade area would extend to the south only to the location of neighborhood shopping center N_5.

If, on the other hand, the consumer considers shopping center N_5 markedly inferior to the subject property with regard to its anchor tenant, age and condition, accessibility from the street, and tenant mix, then he or she would probably drive past N_5 to reach the subject property. In this case center N_5 is not an intervening opportunity and the subject property's trade area would extend south past the location of N_5. The same analysis can be applied to shopping centers N_1 and N_4, both of which are included in the trade area because they are within 7.5 minutes of travel time.

The concept of market sharing comes into play after intervening opportunities have been identified. For example, assume the appraiser discovers that neighborhood shopping centers N_1, N_4, and N_7 are sufficiently comparable to the subject property to be considered intervening opportunities. Community shopping centers C_1, C_2, C_4, C_5, and C_6 are also considered intervening opportunities. Only center N_5 is not because it is markedly inferior to the subject property.

The appraiser's task then is to use this information about intervening opportunities to identify the specific retail trade area from which the subject property will draw its customers. The simplest method is to divide the space between the subject property and each of its intervening opportunities into equal parts. Consequently, the primary trade area of the subject property will extend halfway between the subject and shopping centers C_1, C_4, C_5, C_6, N_1, N_4, and N_7. These boundaries extend the trade area somewhat beyond shopping center N_5. This simple analysis indicates that the subject property shares the geographic market area with its competition. The geographic "breaking point," or halfway point, has been used to allocate the geographic market area among the competitors and establish the subject property's share of that market area.

Trade Area Delineation

Using distance and travel time mapping in conjunction with the concepts of intervening opportunities and market sharing, the appraiser can identify the subject property's primary trade area. Note that defining the primary retail trade area requires appraisal judgment and knowledge of the subject property's market area and competition. The retail trade area for the subject, neighborhood center N_S, is depicted in Figure 4.2. Matching this defined trade area to the census tracts will be discussed later in this chapter. For now, note that the retail trade area includes most, but not all, of Census Tracts *A* and *B* as well as small portions of Census Tracts E, G, H, and I.

Retail trade areas are not simply one-, three-, and five-mile rings around the subject property. The precise boundaries of a retail trade area depend on many factors. To review the delineation process and dispel the simplistic notion of trade area rings, consider the following list, which identifies important factors that the appraiser must consider:

- Distance as the crow flies is not the same as distance along the street system. These concepts would be identical only in a community where the street pattern is laid out as a hub with spokes radiating from the subject property. This is not the case in the example.

- To measure travel time the analyst must select the appropriate time to do the measurement and consider the influence of traffic volume at that time, the existence of traffic lights and stop signs, and the duration of traffic lights.

- Knowledge of the competition is needed to determine whether a competitor is an intervening opportunity.

- An examination of the competition helps determine how the geographic market area is shared among the subject property and its individual competitors.

Economic and demographic data supplied by vendors of secondary data can be useful to the appraiser. But these data in and of themselves, especially when they relate to distance rings around the subject property, do not determine the subject property's retail trade area. In most instances such distance rings do not even approximate the trade area.

In addition to the factors already discussed, the appraiser may need to consider the following items:

- Land use patterns near the subject property. An uninhabited area such as a park, nature center, golf course, or rock quarry may exist within the 7.5-minute travel time radius and thus be considered within the geographic trade area, but it will not generate either customers or sales.

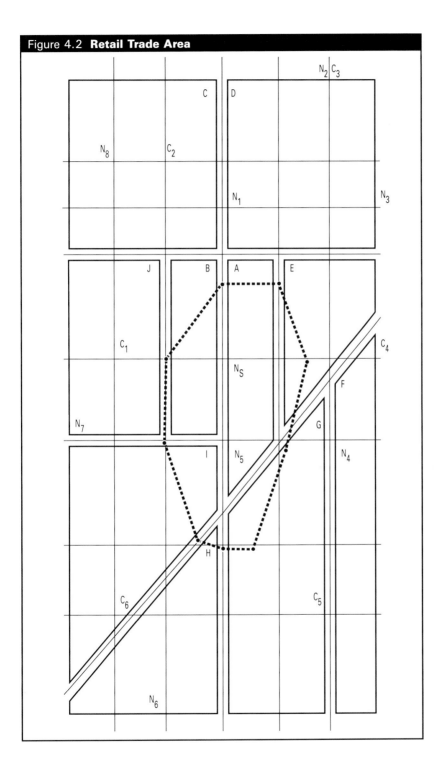

Figure 4.2 **Retail Trade Area**

- Natural barriers such as rivers, ridges, cliffs, and lakes as well as man-made barriers such as railroad tracks and elevated and limited-access expressways. Such barriers can curtail or truncate a retail trade area.

- Psychological factors associated with the travel route. Consumers may be unwilling to drive through areas with high accident or crime rates, poor road surfaces, excessive congestion, unappealing scenery (e.g., areas with heavy industry), or highway blockages such as railroad crossings.

These additional factors may need to be considered in defining the shape and extent of the retail trade area.

Matching the Trade Area to Data Sources

In our example the appraiser judged the subject property's trade area to be the breaking point between itself and shopping centers N_1, N_4, N_7, C_1, C_4, C_5, and C_6. The appraiser concluded that the trade area could extend south to the intersection where shopping center N_5 is located, but not much beyond that point because of the influence of center C_5 to the southeast and centers N_6 and C_6 to the southwest. Based on these judgments, the retail trade area for the subject property can now be matched to census tracts.

Geographically, the subject property's retail trade area includes almost all of Census Tracts A and B, minor portions of Census Tracts E, G, and I, and virtually none of Census Tract H. However, based on the spatial relationships between the subject property and its intervening opportunities, the appraiser must realize that the subject will not capture all of Census Tracts A and B.

Note that the breaking point between the subject property and shopping center N_1 occurs midway between these two competitors. This means that potential consumers living in the northern portion of Census Tracts A and B will be closer to shopping center N_1 than to the subject property. Moreover, consumers living in the southwest corner of Census Tract B are closer to neighborhood shopping center N_7 than they are to the subject property. Finally, consumers living in the southeast corner of Census Tract

A are closer to neighborhood shopping center N_4 than they are to the subject property given the street system.

The appraiser will need to judge how much of the purchasing power directed towards shopping center-type retail expenditures in Census Tracts A and B will be captured by the subject property. To do this he or she must factor out the potential customers lost in the northern portion of the Census Tract A due to the influence of neighborhood shopping center N_1; in the southeast corner of the census tract due to the influence of the intervening opportunity, center N_4; and in the southwest corner due to the existence of the inferior shopping center, N_5. In examining Census Tract B, the appraiser must recognize that potential customers will be lost from the northern portion of the census tract to center N_1, from the southwest portion of the census tract to shopping center N_7, and from the southeast portion to shopping center N_5.

In assessing the subject property's ability to capture the purchasing power in Census Tracts A and B, the relative location of competitors is one important variable and the population distribution in the census tract is another. If the population distribution is uniform throughout the census tract, then a simple geographic examination is sufficient. If the population distribution or the distribution of purchasing power is not uniform, however, these facts must be considered to estimate the subject's capture rate. Finally, issues concerning street systems, land use patterns, and physical and psychological barriers must be addressed.

Analysis of the subject property's impact on Census Tracts G, H, and I could lead the appraiser to conclude that so few potential customers will be attracted from these census tracts that they need not be considered in the analysis. Or, their minimal effect can be included by increasing the values obtained from Census Tracts A and B by a small percentage.

Additional Trade Area Delineation Techniques

In addition to distance and travel time mapping, the analyst can use gravity models and the customer spotting technique to assist in trade area delineation. Two recognized gravity models are Reilly's Law of Retail Gravitation and Huff's Probability Model. Space considerations prohibit a full discussion of these alternative techniques here. Among market analysts these alternative techniques occupy a subordinate position. They are sometimes used to verify the appraiser's conclusions, but they are seldom, if ever, used as the principal means of delineating a retail trade area.[5]

Supply Analysis—Survey of the Competition

For the most part, the phrase *survey of the competition,* as used by real estate market analysts, is analogous to the analysis of the elements of comparison undertaken to identify comparable properties. Whichever phrase is preferred, the analysis focuses on the following items:

- Physical characteristics of the site
- Physical characteristics of the structure
- Financial characteristics of the asset (the shopping center)
- Locational/neighborhood characteristics
- Legal and regulatory factors affecting the shopping center
- Economic characteristics at the time of the sale (the time adjustment)
- Financing conditions underlying the sale
- Condition of sale (arm's-length transaction)
- Real property rights involved in the transaction (e.g., fee simple, leasehold)
- Personal property included in the transaction

The survey of the competition does not require market sales; the process is similar to the selection of market rent comparables in the gross rent multiplier technique. The level and extent of the analysis depends on the appraiser's judgment. For example, a study of the subject property's market area requires data on the gross leasable area of each comparable property (a physical characteristic of the structure) as well as each comparable's occupancy level and square foot sales value (financial char-

---

5. For a more complete discussion of these alternative techniques, see Neil G. Carn, Joseph Rabianski, Ronald Racster, and Maury Seldin, *Real Estate Market Analysis: Techniques and Applications* (Englewood Cliffs, N. J.: Prentice-Hall, Inc., 1988.); David Huff, "A Probabilistic Analysis for Shopping Center Trade Areas," *Land Economics* (February 1963); and William Applebaum, "Method for Determining Store Trade Areas, Market Penetration, and Potential Sales," *Journal of Marketing Research* (May 1966).

acteristics). A retail trade area analysis may require additional information such as data on the proximity of intervening opportunities (a locational characteristic) and parking requirements and buffer zones (regulatory characteristics).

To analyze intervening opportunities or intercept locations, the following variables are identified:

- Gross leasable area and occupied space (physical characteristics of the structure)
- Access from the street to the site (physical characteristic of the site)
- Age and condition of the structure (physical characteristic of the structure)
- Nature of the anchor tenant and the tenant mix in speculative space (financial characteristics of the property)
- Visibility of the storefronts and signage from major arterials (locational characteristic)

Analysis of these variables can help the appraiser decide whether or not a competitive property is an intervening opportunity. Consumer attitudes and preferences are also important to this determination.

The following discussion describes the most thorough survey of the competition that can be undertaken. The actual extent of the survey of competition depends on the appraiser's judgment. The appraiser determines which characteristics need to be addressed in the analysis or, from a more pragmatic perspective, what set of characteristics can be studied given the time and monetary constraints of the assignment.

Our discussion focuses on four types of characteristics: financial, site, building, and locational.

Financial Characteristics

The financial characteristics to be identified in the survey of the competition are

- Rent per square foot of gross leasable area. The appraiser may choose to obtain information about the asking rental rate, the extent of rent rate concessions or abatements, the nature of the rental agreement (e.g., net lease, percentage lease), and any indexing or escalation of the base rent.

- Common area charges
- The term of the lease
- Vacancy rates by type of space

With this information the appraiser can calculate current effective gross income and predict future levels of effective gross income.

Site Characteristics

A complete discussion of site characteristics is presented in the next chapter. The most significant items are

- The amount of parking available
- The physical condition of the parking surface
- The design characteristics of the parking area
- Visibility of the shopping center from the street
- Ease of entry and exit
- The cleanliness and attractiveness of the site
- The nature and extent of accrued depreciation in the site improvements
- The quantity and quality of lighting fixtures in the parking area

These site characteristics are important to potential consumers and can determine whether or not a competitive shopping center is an intervening opportunity. The appraiser needs to understand the desires and motivations of potential customers in the market area to identify a specific competitor as an intervening opportunity.

Building Characteristics

A full discussion of building characteristics also appears in the next chapter. The main considerations are

- Square footage of gross leasable area

- Age and condition (effective age) of the gross leasable area
- The cleanliness and attractiveness of common areas and shopping areas
- The exterior appearance of the structure
- Exterior and interior signage
- The nature and extent of accumulated depreciation

Locational Characteristics

The locational characteristics of a shopping center fall into three major categories:

- Location relative to the street system and traffic patterns
- Location relative to points of origin of potential customers
- Location relative to competing or competitive retail establishments

Analysis of a shopping center's location relative to the street pattern and flow of potential customers principally focuses on traffic counts past the site. The smaller the retail establishment, the more significant traffic counts become. For example, a superregional shopping center and its anchor tenants generate traffic flow to the site. For a superregional shopping center, traffic flow along the main arterial road is less significant than the number of potential consumers in the trade area. For a small strip center or a freestanding retail establishment, however, traffic counts are an important determinant of gross sales.

The location of a shopping center relative to the points of origin of potential customers is another important consideration. Potential customers can come from various points, most importantly their residences. Additional customers may come from surrounding employment sites—i.e., office buildings, industrial plants, and other retail establishments. When dealing with multiple customer sources, the appraiser must avoid double counting. Individuals who work in the office building adjacent to the shopping center may also live within the boundaries of the primary trade area. Double counting occurs when the analyst adds the number of potential customers coming from residential points of origin to the number of customers coming from employment sites. An individual who lives and works nearby will be counted twice, once as a resident of the trade area and again as an employee in the office building.

The analyst needs to determine what proportion of the office employees do not live in the trade area. This is an important piece of information, but will be difficult to obtain. Typically the appraiser will use his or her judgment to allocate office employees between trade area residents and non-trade area residents, and then add only the nontrade area office employees to the potential customers who reside in the trade area.

To assess the shopping center's location relative to competing retail establishments, the appraiser constructs a map showing the location of the subject property and its competition and then decides which competitors represent intervening opportunities.

Competitive Properties To Be Surveyed

When a competitive survey is undertaken, all existing competitive properties need to be included in the analysis. Shopping centers currently under construction or in the final stages of planning should also be considered. Most surveys of the competition focus on existing and planned properties. These are the properties that affect the subject property now and will have an effect in the near future. The construction and planning of a shopping center development takes approximately two years.

A third type of property may also be surveyed, especially if the appraiser's analysis extends beyond two years. Vacant sites that have a high probability of future development may be important to the analysis, particularly in rapidly developing market areas in the path of urban growth. They are not a concern in well-established market areas where there are no vacant sites suitable for development.

Vacant sites can be considered in the analysis on a site-by-site basis. To judge a specific site's relevance, the appraiser needs some knowledge or insight into the prospects for future development by major shopping center developers. This issue can be handled in a more general way by estimating the amount of gross leasable area that will be developed in the urban growth path at specific points over the next three to 10 years.

An Analytical Framework

Table 4.5 offers a framework for displaying the data obtained from the survey of the competition. Along the left-hand margin, properties are identified as existing, under construction (pipeline), or vacant sites that could support competitive units in the future. Under one of these three categories the appraiser lists each competitive retail establishment in the market area. The columns to the right represent the four major elements of comparison: financial, structural, site, and neighborhood/locational characteristics. Information on the characteristics of competitors can be recorded here. Each broad category can be expanded to include as many specific points of comparison as the appraiser deems necessary.

Table 4.5 **Suggested Framework for Survey of the Competition**				
	Financial Characteristics	Structural Characteristics	Site Characteristics	Neighborhood/ Locational Characteristics
Subject Property				
Existing Competitive Properties	1. 2. 3. 4. 5.			
Competitive Properties Under Construction	1. 2. 3.			
Vacant Sites That Could Support Competitive Units in the Future	1. 2. 3. 4.			
The Market Standard				
Competitive Differential				

Information reported in the competitive survey is gleaned from field inspection of existing competitive properties and inspection of documents relating to facilities that are under construction or near the end of the planning process. This field inspection is tempered by judgment because the appraiser selects the specific elements of comparison to be included in the study. Interviews with retail leasing agents (as distinguished from shopping center managers) will help reveal the market standard and the competitive differential. Leasing agents usually know what size and type of space is renting quickly and what type of space is not in demand.

As mentioned previously, a major purpose of the survey of the competition is to decide to what extent a competitive property represents an intervening opportunity and determine its effect on the delineation of the retail trade area. However, the survey of the competition can also be used as a planning document for the shopping center developer, which is discussed in the next section.

The Market Standard and Competitive Differential

Once information on competitive properties is gathered, the analyst must find a means of summarizing or synthesizing the data from the various properties on a characteristic-by-characteristic basis. For example, the appraiser may have discovered that speculative space in all existing properties is renting at $10 per square foot while the rent projected for the speculative space in two new shopping centers being developed is $14 per square foot. This information can be synthesized in several different ways. A range of $10 to $14 per square foot can be derived, or the two pieces of information can be recorded as separate items—i.e., existing space at $10 per square foot and new space at $14 per square foot. In either case, the appraiser has identified the market standard with regard to rental rates.

This market standard can be compared to the current rent charged for the subject property. If the subject property is an existing shopping center that charges $15 per square foot, the appraiser will quickly realize that the rent structure of the existing shopping center is out of line with the market. If current vacancies are high, the asking rental rate is obviously too high and needs to be reduced to approximately $10 per square foot, which is what the competition is charging for existing, but not new, space. However, if vacancies are low at the property charging $15 per square foot, then the appraiser knows that there must be some other financial, structural, site, or locational characteristics affecting the property.

Establishing a market standard for competitive properties and comparing that standard to the subject property on a characteristic-by-characteristic basis leads to an analysis of the subject property's competitive differential. The subject property will have a positive competitive differential with regard to a characteristic when the subject property is better or more in tune with market needs than the competition. The subject property will have a negative competitive differential if it is worse than the competition or does not meet the needs of the market with regard to that characteristic. Establishing a competitive differential allows the appraiser to identify things that the property is doing well as well as things that need to be changed to improve the subject property's competitive position in the market area.

The information entered in the market standard and competitive differential sections of the survey of competition table can be facts or the appraiser's subjective judgment about how each competing property compares with the subject property. The appraiser can enter a number, a percentage, or a comment. Explanatory notes can be used to expand on the information contained in the table.

For example, under the financial characteristics of Property 2, the appraiser may note a competitive advantage in that the landlords are willing to offer 12 months of free rent; all else being equal, this may make that property 10% more attractive. At the end of the row the appraiser can summarize the net effect of all the relevant characteristics of Property 2. This measure can be used later to make adjustments in the rental rates, sale price, or functional or external obsolescence of the property.

Finding Gaps in the Market

The survey of the competition can also help the appraiser discover gaps in the market. There are two dimensions to this discovery. First, analyzing the spatial distribution of shopping centers and freestanding retail establishments in the trade area can lead to the discovery of a geographic area that is not adequately served by a particular type of retail establishment.

For example, there may be a vacant corner site halfway between two neighborhood shopping centers that could be developed with 15,000 to 20,000 square feet of gross leasable area. If the closest convenience goods retailers (e.g., gas stations, dry cleaners, convenience stores, video rental stores) are two miles away in any direction, this vacant site at the intersection of two reasonably busy streets could fill a need in the market.

Using the survey of the competition to find gaps in the market requires much more than a cursory field inspection of existing shopping centers. The survey of the competition framework shown in Table 4.5 would have to be expanded to include more columns in which the analyst could identify the types of tenants in both the subject and the comparable shopping centers. More rows might be needed to provide a subsection under existing properties for freestanding retail establishments in addition to shopping centers.

The second benefit of uncovering gaps in the market comes from analyzing the tenant mix within shopping centers. Market researchers have discovered that consumers like to complete multistop shopping trips within a single shopping center. The ability of a shopping center to satisfy this preference depends on the tenant mix in that shopping center. By surveying the competition, an appraiser may be able to discern the difference between the tenant mix in a successful shopping center and the tenant mix in a less successful shopping center. Such a comparison could be a form of paired data analysis. This analysis could facilitate the developer's search for tenants for a proposed shopping center and direct the leasing strategy of the owner or manager of an existing shopping center. In addition, analyzing the tenant mix of shopping centers and the nature and extent of freestanding retail establishments may lead to a final benefit—i.e., the identification of a type of retail establishment that does not currently exist in the market area.

Survey of the Competition and the Three Approaches to Value

For several reasons a survey of the competition is an integral part of shopping center analysis. The survey provides an estimate of the gross leasable area in the market, which the analyst needs to undertake residual analysis. It provides the information used to determine the extent to which a competitor is an intervening opportunity, and thereby affects the size and shape of the trade area. It allows the appraiser to establish a qualitative market standard and explore competitive differentials and gaps in the market. These conclusions can provide a basis for judgments and adjustments in the sales comparison approach, estimates of both functional and external obsolescence in the cost approach, and estimates of market rent levels and absorption periods in the income approach.

Information on financial factors obtained in the survey of the competition can be used to form judgments concerning the generation of effective gross income in a stabilized income forecast or cash flow statement. The survey can provide the appraiser with information about rental rates in the market and the effective rental rates after abatements and concessions. Market vacancy rates by type of shopping center (e.g., neighborhood, community, regional) and by location can be gathered as well as information about escalation clauses, percentage rental rates, and kickout clauses by type and location. A survey of the competition can also identify the lease terms and lease renewal dates of key tenants in competitive facilities. All of these factors can be important in applying the three approaches to value.

Demand Analysis—Retail Trade Area Analysis

The estimation of demand within a marketability analysis generally makes use of the same procedure and data sources employed in analyzing the aggregate market. In marketability analysis, however, the geographic market area is restricted to the retail trade area. Demand analysis has four steps:

1. Estimate the purchasing power in the retail trade area as the product of population times per capita retail expenditures or total households times mean household income.
2. Estimate the total purchasing power allocated to the subject site using data on the percentage of total income spent on various retail categories such as food eaten at home and apparel.
3. Estimate sales by retail category for the shopping center.
4. Estimate the square footage of construction warranted or justified based on the estimates of retail sales.

The final step, estimation of the warranted or justifiable square footage for the subject property, is primarily applicable to a proposed center, but it can also be useful in assessing the need to expand an existing center.

Estimating the sales of an existing property allows the appraiser to compare actual sales performance to expected sales performance. If actual sales exceed expected sales, the property has good future prospects; if actual sales fall below expected sales, the property could be experiencing problems, which could indicate functional obsolescence.

Estimating the potential sales of a proposed property though residual analysis can help the appraiser judge the market and the financial feasibility of the center as well as its anchor(s) and the tenants that occupy its speculative space. Such analysis can be integral to the estimation of highest and best use. If the existing retail space can absorb all of the trade areas potential retail expenditures, a retail use may not be the highest and best use. If further examination indicates a redistribution of present market shares, however, the project may be warranted.

Sample Demand Analyses

Demand analysis can be performed for an existing shopping center or a proposed shopping center. The structure of the analysis undertaken in each case is similar, but different techniques are employed. The first example relates to a proposed shopping center to be built on the site that has been analyzed throughout this chapter. Demand analysis for an existing shopping center is discussed later.

Demand Analysis for a Proposed Shopping Center

Demand analysis for a proposed shopping center starts with delineation of the trade area (see Figure 4.2). Based on an analysis of time and distance relationships and intervening opportunities, the retail trade area for the proposed property was identified as the area enclosed by the thick line of dashes. As noted earlier it contains most, but not all, of Census Tracts A and B; a very small portion of Census Tracts E, G, and I; and virtually none of Census Tract H.

Once the delineated trade area is matched with an appropriate data source, numerical analysis can begin. The following points relate to data sources:

- Census tracts can be used as sources of purchasing power data. In this case the appraiser must allocate the total purchasing power of the census tract to the subject property.

- A customized ring can be constructed as a proxy for the trade area. An appraiser using this technique will have to make adjustments for areas where the ring and the trade area do not match. This will involve both additions and deletions. (A customized ring refers to any radius other than the one-, three- and five-mile rings for which private vendors typically provide data.)

- A polygon that traces the shape of the trade area can be constructed. With this method, like the preceding technique, the appraiser has to make additions and deletions where the polygon and the trade area do not match.

Thus when either the customized ring or the polygon shape is used, the appraiser has to rely on the internal manipulations made by the private vendor of the data. The mechanical process that the vendor employs to convert census tract-based data to reflect the customized ring or polygon may not make sense in the market area or the retail trade area being studied.

The numerical example that follows makes use of census tract-based data after appropriate allocations have been made by the analyst, not the data vendor. Table 4.6 shows the estimation of the total purchasing power in the trade area. First, each census tract in the trade area is listed in Column 1. Then population and per capita income statistics for each census tract are listed in Columns 2 and 3 respectively. Purchasing power, shown in Column 4, is the product of Columns 2 and 3. The appraiser's estimate of how much of each census tract's purchasing power is allocated to the subject trade area is presented in Column 5. Finally, the purchasing power directed toward the subject property's trade area is presented in Column 6.

Table 4.6 **Purchasing Power Allocation**					
Census Tract	Population	Per Capita Income	Purchasing Power (in millions)	Allocation Percentage	Purchasing Power in Trade Area (in millions)
A	14,200	$15,250	$216.55	70%	$151.585
B	13,800	$14,700	$202.86	55%	$111.573
E	12,900	$16,400	$211.56	15%	$ 31.734
G	14,000	$14,800	$207.20	5%	$ 10.360
H	13,500	$14,000	$189.20	1%	$ 1.890
I	15,250	$16,250	$247.81	8%	$ 19.825
Total purchasing power in trade area					$326.967
Percent spent on retail goods					× 0.41
Purchasing power for retail goods and services in trade area					$134.056

The development of allocation percentages can be illustrated in relation to Census Tracts A and B. The allocation factor for Census Tract A is less than 100% for two reasons. First, the northernmost 10% to 15% of the tract is in the trade area for shopping center N_1. Second, the southern portion of the tract includes shopping center N_5, which reduces the subject property's penetration into this area. The appraiser judges that the presence of N_5 reduces the subject property's share, or capture, in Census Tract A by an additional 15%. Thus the appraiser estimates a total reduction of 30%, leaving a capture or penetration rate of 70% in Census Tract A.

This analysis is highly dependent on the population distribution. If the population density is uniform throughout Census Tract A, analysis based on geographic allocation is appropriate. However, if the population were dense in the southern portion of the tract and very sparse in the northern portion, then the 10% to 15% of the tract that lies in the trade area for shopping center N_1 would represent a smaller percentage of lost purchasing power—i.e., 5% to 8%. In allocating purchasing power, the population distribution must be considered.

A similar analysis of Census Tract B reveals that approximately 30% to 35% of its northern portion lies in the trade area of either shopping center C_2 or N_1. Furthermore, consumers in the southern portion of the census tract are doing some of their purchasing at shopping center N_5.

This lost purchasing power is estimated to be 10% to 15%. Thus the total loss is 45%, leaving a penetration rate of 55% for the subject property.

Multiplying the purchasing power in Column 4 by the allocation percentage in Column 5 yields the purchasing power directed toward the trade area shown in Column 6. Summing this column yields a total purchasing power figure of $326.967 million.

Now this $326.967 million must be allocated among retail expenditures, housing, insurance, transportation, utilities, and other expenses. The discussion of demand analysis presented earlier in this chapter revealed that approximately 41% of consumer income is spent on retail goods and services (see Table 4.1.) Applying this percentage indicates that $134.056 million of the purchasing power in the trade area can be spent in retail establishments.

In Table 4.7 sales and justifiable square footage are estimated for selected retail establishments. To construct such a table for an existing shopping center, the appraiser starts with information about the shopping center's tenants. A tenant list is obtained during site inspection. For a proposed shopping center, tenant information can be obtained from an inspection of competitive properties, from the survey of the competition, or from the Urban Land Institute's *Dollars & Cents of Shopping Centers*, which publishes the typical tenant mix for shopping centers. The retail establishments in Column 1 of Table 4.7 are typical.

In Column 2 the appraiser estimates the percentage of purchasing power that the trade area's population will spend at retail establishments in the subject property. For the most part, a neighborhood shopping center provides a high percentage of convenience goods and services such as groceries and personal care items. The subject property should be able to capture a large portion of the purchasing power directed toward these items. This is evidenced by the 90% capture rates for the supermarket, drugstore, and dry cleaners, and the 70% capture rate for the liquor store. These percentages are less than 100% because there are freestanding convenience stores in the trade area that lower the potential capture of the shopping center.

The capture percentages for the retail establishments selling shopping goods and services are much lower because consumers want a wide selection. To fulfill this desire they may go to a regional mall or other

Table 4.7 Estimated Sales and Square Footage by Selected Retail Establishment

Retail Category	Capture Rate (%)	Budget Allocation (%)	Estimated Sales	Sales Per Sq. Ft.	Estimated Justifiable Sq. Ft.
Supermarket	90	12.12	$14,622,828	$300	48,743
Drugstore	90	1.50	$ 1,809,756	$170	10,646
Restaurants	40	4.10	$ 2,198,518	$145	15,162
Men's & boys' clothing	40	1.50	$ 804,336	$154	5,223
Women's & girls' clothing	30	1.85	$ 744,010	$140	5,314
Shoes (family)	40	0.70	$ 375,356	$120	3,128
Dry cleaners	90	0.45	$ 542,927	$100	5,429
Liquor/wine	70	0.85	$ 797,633	$200	3,988
Subtotal		23.07			97,633
Miscellaneous retail					
Included	45	5.00	$ 3,016,260	$120	25,135
Excluded		12.93			
		17.93			
Total retail		41.00%			122,768

neighborhood and community shopping centers in the market area. In this instance much of the purchasing power of consumers who live in the subject property's trade area is spent outside the trade area. Capture percentages in the 30% to 40% range indicate that consumers living in the trade area will buy most of their shopping goods outside the trade area. Most food consumed away from home is not captured by the trade area because lunches are bought near job sites and dinners for special occasions are often consumed at fancy restaurants in another part of town. Clothing also has a low capture rate because most clothing is purchased at the regional shopping center and some is purchased at the community center, but very little is purchased at the neighborhood shopping center.

The capture rates used in a table such as Table 4.7 can be based solely on judgment, if the appraiser has significant experience in the market area being analyzed. However, capture rates are usually based on facts extracted from the market. The simplest way to estimate capture is to establish the appropriate fair share for each retail category based on the total square footage in the market area.

Supermarket Example

Consider the supermarket to be built within the proposed shopping center. Assume that it will be the only supermarket in the trade area and will contain 42,000 square feet. The trade area now contains two convenience stores of 1,000 square feet each and a bakery of 1,200 square feet. Using this information, the capture percentage for the supermarket in Table 4.7 will be 93% (42,000/45,200).

Now assume that an existing supermarket of 32,000 square feet also shares the subject property's retail trade area. Because this supermarket is in a shopping center across the street, or just down the street, from the subject property, the capture percentage of the proposed supermarket changes. In this case the fair share calculation indicates a capture rate of 54.4% (42,000/77,200). This fair share calculation is appropriate if the two supermarkets and the two shopping centers in which they are located are judged to be comparable. If the smaller supermarket is considered inferior to the subject property, the fair share ratio understates the subject property's capture rate. In this case the market share ratio is more appropriate.

To calculate a market share ratio, the appraiser must first make a judgment about the relative positions of the two supermarkets in the trade area. Since explicit, historical financial data are not available for the subject property, the market share ratio has to be developed by comparing the characteristics of the proposed center to those of the existing center. A rating chart such as the one shown in Table 4.8 can be used.

Based on observation and an analysis of the data displayed in the survey of the competition, the appraiser identifies the significant characteristics to be analyzed and evaluates each characteristic to derive input values for the proposed subject property and the existing competitor. Hypothetical values are shown in Table 4.8.

The market share capture rates generated for the subject and the competitive property are 61% and 39% respectively. Note that the convenience stores and the bakery have not been specifically incorporated into the analysis, but they are not to be ignored either. Two techniques can be applied. First, their 4.1% share of the market (3,200/77,200) can be retained and the remaining 95.9% can be allocated between the two shopping centers. This technique will be used in this analysis. Alternatively, the convenience stores and the bakery can be combined and included in the analysis as a second competitor. This method is demonstrated in the example that follows.

Assuming that the two supermarkets comprise 95.85% (74,000/ 77,200) of the market for food consumed at home, necessary adjustments are made to yield the following market share capture ratios: 58.5% (95.85% × 61%) for the subject supermarket, 37.4% (95.85% × 39%) for the competing supermarket, and 4.1% for the convenience stores and the bakery.

Table 4.8 can be expanded to include any number of direct competitors located in the subject property's trade area. The weighting or rating scheme used reflects the appraiser's judgment and preference. (Some analysts prefer to use a 10-point system, rather than the five-point system used here.)

The rating method used should also provide for the weighting of individual characteristics. In Table 4.8, each characteristic is equally

Table 4.8 Rating of Property Characteristics To Derive a Market Share Ratio: Supermarket Example

Characteristic	Subject	Competitor
Price/quality/selection of the store	5	3
Parking for the store		
Availability (no. of spaces/*GLA*)	5	4
Convenience to entrances	5	3
Quality of surface/cleanliness	5	3
Appeal/image of the store	5	2
Visibility and signage	5	4
Tenant mix/diversity of supporting shops	5	3
Access to the site	5	4
Attractiveness/cleanliness of center	5	2
Convenience to trade area customers	4	3
Other		
Total	49	31
Market share	61%	39%

5 = superior; 4 = above average; 3 = average; 2 = below average; 1 = poor

weighted; availability of parking is considered as important as visibility. At the discretion of the analyst, however, each characteristic can be weighted differently. (An example of this procedure is shown in the appendix to this chapter.)

Women's Clothing Store Example

Assume that the developer-owner of the subject property wants to include 2,000 square feet of space to be leased to a women's clothing store. In the market area there are 1,200 square feet of such space in the competing shopping center and 11,000 square feet of space devoted to women's clothing at the regional mall that serves the customers who reside in the subject center's trade area. The 11,000-sq.-ft. area at the mall includes the space allocated to women's apparel in department stores as well as in-line store space in the mall.

On a fair share basis, the subject property will capture 14% of the women's clothing market while the regional mall will capture 77.5%. Note that the 14% capture rate for a specific category of goods and the capture rates for other shopping goods can vary greatly depending on the type of shopping center that is being analyzed. The capture rate for shopping goods can be zero for a strip or small neighborhood center; 15% for a community center that competes with both another community center and a regional mall; 25% to 30% for a community center that competes only with a regional mall; and 70% to 90% for a regional mall depending on the competition posed by community centers in its trade area.

To estimate capture on a market share basis, consider the analyst's ratings shown in Table 4.9. The ratings established by the analyst are used to derive percentage distributions. These percentages are then used to weight the number of square feet of space allocated to women's clothing in the market. The calculations are shown below:

Subject:	2,000 sq.ft.	× 0.355	= 710	(13.1%)
Comparable 1:	1,200 sq.ft.	× 0.242	= 290	(5.3%)
Comparable 2:	11,000 sq. ft.	× 0.403	= 4,433	(81.6%)
		Total	= 5,433	(100%)

The market share calculation for the subject property dropped its capture rate from 14% to 13.1%, while the capture rate for the regional mall increased from 77.5% to 81.6%. The analysis discussed in the preceding examples can be applied to each retail category shown in Table 4.7. The capture figures shown in the table were generated in this way.

The difference between the terms *allocation percentage* in Table 4.6 and *capture rate* in Table 4.7 may need clarification. The allocation percentage in Table 4.6 is used to separate the consumers residing in the trade area from those residing outside the trade area. The capture rate in Table 4.7 is also an allocation percentage which describes how consumers living in the subject property's trade area allocate their purchasing power between the subject property and other retail alternatives. For convenience goods the allocation rate is high; for shopping goods the rate is low.

Column 3 of Table 4.7, budget allocation, contains information that the appraiser can use to estimate these percentages; these data come from three primary sources. The first is a Department of Commerce publication titled *The Relative Importance of Components in the Consumer Price Index*. This publication provides annual information for selected metropolitan areas and for the nation as a whole. A second data source is the *Census of*

Table 4.9 **Rating of Property Characteristics To Derive a Market Share Ratio: Women's Clothing Store Example**				
Characteristic	**Subject Center**	**Competing Center**	**Regional Mall**	
Price/quality/selection of the store	4	3	5	
Parking for the store				
Availability (no. of spaces/*GLA*)	5	4	5	
Convenience to entrances	5	3	5	
Quality of surface/cleanliness	5	3	5	
Appeal/image of the store	4	2	5	
Visibility and signage	5	4	5	
Tenant mix/diversity of supporting shops	2	2	5	
Access to the site	5	4	5	
Attractiveness/cleanliness of center	5	2	5	
Convenience to trade area customers	4	3	5	
Other				
Total	44	30	50	124
Market share	35.48%	24.20%	40.32%	100%

5 = superior; 4 = above average; 3 = average; 2 = below average; 1 = poor

Retail Trade. This publication provides information on a countywide basis, but only every five years. The most recent data at the time of this writing are from 1987. By the time this book is published, however, the 1992 census of retail trade will be underway.

Information is also available from private vendors that publish reports on consumer spending patterns and retail sales volume. Such a report may be called a *consumer expenditure survey* or a *consumer buying power survey* and provide information on annual retail spending in selected retail establishments in the census tract or trade area.

For example, the appraiser may obtain the information that the per capita expenditure in grocery stores in the census tract was $2,000 and per capita income was $16,500. This yields a budget percentage of 12.12% ($2,000/$16,500). This percentage is highly dependent on the level of per capita income in the trade area; high-income consumers spend 5% to 7% of their income for food consumed at home, while low-income consumers spend 14% to 20% of their income on grocery store items.

The budget allocation derived should be as area-specific as possible. For this reason, using data provided by private vendors is recommended.

In all cases, checking the accuracy of the data used is the appraiser's responsibility.

Returning to Table 4.7, all the percentages shown in Column 3 are derived from data provided by the three sources identified above. Once the capture rate and budget allocation are estimated, they are multiplied by the total purchasing power for retail goods and services in the trade area, the $134,056,000 figure calculated in Table 4.6. The resulting estimated sales figures for each of the retail establishments listed in Table 4.7 are shown in Column 4 of the table.

Column 5 shows sales-per-square-foot figures, which can be obtained from local sources such as the property managers of shopping centers in the market area. *Dollars & Cents of Shopping Centers* publishes sales figures that represent the median sales per square foot reported to the Urban Land Institute by members who develop and/or operate shopping centers.[6] The sales-per-square-foot figures in Column 5 are divided into the estimated sales figures in Column 4 to obtain the justifiable or warranted square footage by selected retail establishment shown in Column 6.

In the lower portion of Table 4.7, miscellaneous retail establishments are considered. When the budget allocation percentages for the stores identified in the top portion of the table are summed, the figure 23.07% is obtained. Since the initial assumption is that 41% of consumers' total purchasing power is directed toward retail products, 17.93% is not accounted for. The appraiser must allocate a portion of this 17.93% to the subject property.

To make the allocation, the appraiser compares the other retail establishments that are in the shopping center with those that are not in the shopping center. For example, part of the 17.93% of purchasing power is spent in barber/beauty shops, photography shops, video rental stores, record/tape/CD shops, jewelry stores, sporting goods stores, hobby shops,

---

6. These sales-per-square-foot figures developed from comparable properties can be applied directly in the analysis of a proposed center, or they can be used as a point of reference to compare the actual sales per square foot of an existing center. In the latter case, if the sales per square foot for comparable supermarkets in the subject property's market area equal $280 while the actual sales per square foot for the subject property equal $220, the subject property is not competitive in the market due to its age or condition, location, merchandise mix, price or quality of goods, or some other characteristic.

Of course the other properties in the subject property's market area and the properties represented in *Dollars & Cents of Shopping Centers* must be evaluated for their comparability.

pet shops, arts and crafts shops, and hardware stores. In this instance the appraiser analyzes the trade area and determines that the other retail establishments in the subject property — a barber shop, a photography shop, a video rental store, and a record store — account for an additional 5% of the consumers' budget; the subject property should capture 45% of the purchases and these stores have approximately $120 in sales per square foot.[7]

The conclusions of the analysis are the estimated sales and sales-per-square-foot figures, which are based on market demand information for the specific retail establishments identified in the top portion of Table 4.7. The justifiable square footage for additional retail establishments seems plausible.

The appraiser can use the data in Table 4.7 to assess the economic viability of the subject property. Assume that the subject property has a 45,000-sq.-ft. supermarket with annual sales of $10,000,000; a 9,000-sq.-ft. drugstore with annual sales of $850,000; a 3,000-sq.-ft. restaurant with annual sales of $200,000; and other retail establishments. Using the information in the table, the appraiser can estimate the rent and vacancy prospects for the shopping center and derive three conclusions.

1. The supermarket has sales of $222 per square foot, which is below the market norm of $280 to $320. The grocery store may be inefficiently managed or it may not meet consumers' preferences for products, service, and attractiveness. The problem may derive from demand factors, supply factors, or both. In any event future rent increases at lease renewal are unlikely and, if things get worse, the anchor lease may not be renewed.

2. The drugstore has sales of $94 per square foot, which is substantially below the market norm of $170. It is likely that the store will

---

7. These miscellaneous retail establishments are handled in general terms because one or both types of required data are not readily available. For example, the 1990 edition of *Dollars & Cents of Shopping Centers* reports sales per square foot for video stores ($90), film processing shops ($140), record and tape stores ($142), sporting goods stores ($163), arts and crafts stores ($64), import shops ($114), pet shops ($85), barber shops ($98), and beauty shops ($85), but data on the percentage of income spent on these items is not specifically stated.

A second problem involves the identification of comparable properties. Since the example is concerned with a neighborhood shopping center, retail establishments such as furniture and appliance dealers are not considered because they are typically freestanding establishments or are located in community shopping centers.

go out of business. If this happens, the vacancy rate will go up and rent receipts will decline.

3. The restaurant has sales of $68 per square foot, significantly below the market norm of $130 to $150 per square foot. If it continues to stay in business, it probably cannot support a rent increase. A vacancy rate increase is likely.

The examples presented in this section have focused on a proposed neighborhood shopping center. The analysis can easily be adapted to a proposed regional center. The principal differences will concern the nature of the tenants in the shopping center, the geographic size of the retail trade area, and the magnitudes of the two allocation percentages used in Tables 4.6 and 4.7.

Demand Analysis for an Existing Shopping Center

Demand analysis for an existing shopping center can take two forms, which are discussed in the following sections.

Form 1: Estimated and Actual Sales Volume and Justifiable Square Footage Compared

Demand analysis for an existing center is much like the analysis for a proposed center. The major difference is that the subject property is tangible, not conceptual. This fact implicitly affects the entire analysis, but it is most specifically addressed in the calculation of the allocation percentage (Table 4.6) and the capture rate (Tables 4.7, 4.8, and 4.9). When the estimated sales and estimated square footage by retail category are calculated, they can be compared to actual sales and occupancy figures. This comparison will show whether the subject property is meeting market expectations.

If actual sales exceed estimated sales, the subject property is in an excellent position to obtain rents at or above market rents and to generate rent increases in the future. If, on the other hand, actual sales are less than estimated sales, the subject property will probably not obtain market rents and may experience above-market vacancy rates.

Form 2: Comparison of Rent, Vacancy, and Operating Expense Characteristics

For a number of reasons, an appraiser may choose not to apply the procedure presented in the previous section. Actual sales data may not be available from the tenants in the shopping center if the rent is not charged on a percentage-of-sales basis. Alternatively, the appraiser may decide that the level of analysis required is too extensive for the assignment.

In these instances the marketability aspect of demand analysis can be accomplished by comparing the effective rents and vacancy rate of the subject to those of its immediate competition and the general market. In this case the analysis depicted in Tables 4.1, 4.2, and 4.3 can be conducted to determine if the market area is overbuilt or undersupplied with retail space presently and in the near future. Then the recent rent and vacancy rates of the subject property can be compared to the rates of its direct competitors. As discussed in relation to the survey of the competition, Table 4.5, existing competitors, competitive space under construction, and potential new competition can be incorporated into the analysis.

Four possible scenarios can arise and each can lead to different conclusions on the part of the appraiser.

- Scenario 1—The market is undersupplied and the subject property's performance is better than the performance of the competition.
- Scenario 2—The market is undersupplied and the subject property's performance is worse than the performance of the competition.
- Scenario 3—The market is oversupplied and the subject property's performance is better than the performance of the competition.
- Scenario 4—The market is oversupplied and the subject property's performance is worse than the performance of the competition.

A brief discussion of these scenarios is presented along with the probable conclusions that may be reached. The appraiser's actual conclusions will depend on the extent of the oversupply or undersupply, how long the condition is expected to last, and the actual difference in performance between the subject and its direct competitors as measured by their effective rents and actual vacancies.

Scenario 1. If the market is currently undersupplied and the situation will continue in the near future because population, households, and income are expected to grow and new retail space is not forthcoming, the subject property is in a very favorable economic position. It should continue to receive market rents, which will increase over time. Given that its present performance is better than its competitors' performance, this trend should continue but the gap will narrow as the competition decreases vacancies and increases rent levels.

Scenario 2. If the market is currently undersupplied and will continue to be in the near future because population, households, and income are expected to grow and new retail space is not forthcoming, the subject property is again in a very favorable economic position. It should continue to receive market rents and experience increases over time. Because its present performance is worse than its competitors' performance, this advantage should diminish over time as the subject property is able to reduce the gap in vacancies and increase rent levels.

Scenario 3. If the market is currently oversupplied and the subject property's performance is better than its competition, it should be able to retain its existing rent revenue and occupancy. It will be the first to benefit if the oversupply is eliminated by increased retail purchasing power in the market.

Scenario 4. If the market is currently oversupplied and the subject property's performance is worse than its competition, it may not be able to retain its existing rent revenue and occupancy. It will be the last to benefit if the oversupply is eliminated by increased retail purchasing power in the market. If the oversupply is not reduced and subsequently eliminated in the near future, the subject property will experience stagnant or even declining rent levels and possibly higher vacancy rates.

Summary

Market and marketability analysis for shopping centers is basically an analysis of the demand for and supply of retail products and, therefore, retail space. In a market analysis, the appraiser estimates the relationship between the demand for and supply of retail space to see if there is excess space or excess demand. Residual analysis is performed by subtracting an estimate of the retail expenditures allotted to all present competitors (using industry estimates of average sales) from the total retail purchasing power.

In marketability analysis, an estimate is made of the expected sales volume and justifiable square footage of the subject property. This is accomplished by estimating the total purchasing power in a trade area and allocating it among the various retail products and places or locations where they can be purchased. This estimate, although simple in form, can support a highest and best use analysis.

Finally, competitive analysis can provide benefits: it will help estimate the market sharing within the estimated retail trade area; it will indicate the market rental rate; it will refine the character of the highest and best analysis; and it may contribute a basis for adjustments in all three approaches to value.

Appendix to Chapter 4

The material that follows expands on the rating of property characteristics presented in Table 4.9 by including a second weighting scheme in the analysis. In Table 4.9 each of the characteristics of the three properties is implicitly assumed to have the same relative importance. The weighting scheme presented here turns this implied assumption into an explicit statement by attaching a level of importance ranging from 5 to 1 to each characteristic. Each characteristic is rated as follows: 5 = very important; 4 = important; 3 = average importance; 2 = relatively unimportant; 1 = no bearing in the analysis.

A copy of Table 4.9 appears on the next page. The following table, Table 4.10, uses the weighting scheme to show how market share can change when the various characteristics are judged to have different levels of importance.

Table 4.9 Rating of Property Characteristics To Derive a Market Share Ratio: Women's Clothing Store Example

Characteristic	Subject Center	Competing Center	Regional Mall	
Price/quality/selection of the store	4	3	5	
Parking for the store				
Availability (no. of spaces/*GLA*)	5	4	5	
Convenience to entrances	5	3	5	
Quality of surface/cleanliness	5	3	5	
Appeal/image of the store	4	2	5	
Visibility and signage	5	4	5	
Tenant mix/diversity of supporting shops	2	2	5	
Access to the site	5	4	5	
Attractiveness/cleanliness of center	5	2	5	
Convenience to trade area customers	4	3	5	
Other				
Total	44	30	50	124
Market share	35.48%	24.20%	40.32%	100%

Table 4.10 Rating of Property Characteristics To Derive a Market Share Ratio: Women's Clothing Store Example

Characteristic	Weighting Factor	Subject	Competing Center	Regional Mall	
Price/quality/selection of the store	5	20	15	25	
Parking for the store					
Availability (no. of spaces/*GLA*)	4	20	16	20	
Convenience to entrances	3	15	9	15	
Quality of surface/cleanliness	4	20	12	20	
Appeal/image of the store	5	20	10	25	
Visibility and signage	5	25	20	25	
Tenant mix/diversity of supporting shops	5	10	10	25	
Access to the site	4	20	16	25	
Attractiveness/cleanliness of center	4	20	10	20	
Convenience to trade area customers	5	20	15	25	
Other					
Total		190	133	225	548
Market share		34.67%	24.27%	41.06%	100%

Note: Weighting factors that indicate the importance of the various characteristics are shown above. The weighting factors are multiplied by the ratings shown in Table 4.9 to produce new, more precise ratings that reveal the importance of the characteristics.

Oakbrook Center, Illinois　　　　　　　　　*R. Krubner / H. Armstrong Roberts*

Chapter Five

SITE AND BUILDING CHARACTERISTICS OF SHOPPING CENTERS

Introduction

For a shopping center to be financially successful, it must possess appropriate site and building characteristics. However, desirable site and building features, in and of themselves, do not guarantee an adequate flow of revenue to make the shopping center profitable. The economic circumstances of the trade area must work in concert with the site characteristics. If we assume that the economic environment in which the shopping center is located is adequate, then possession of particular site and building characteristics will greatly affect the profitability of the shopping center.

Site Characteristics

Ten important site characteristics will be discussed in this chapter:

1. Size of the site, including

- The footprint of the building
- Customer parking
- Parking lot circulation
- Parking lot lighting and security
- Parking in relation to building entrances
- Employee parking
- Other site requirements

2. Shape of the site

3. Access to the trade area

4. The site's relationship to the street pattern

5. Ease of access

6. Visibility

7. Signage

8. Landscaping

9. Topography and drainage

10. Utilities, zoning, subdivision regulations, and construction codes

Size of the Site

The shopping center site should be large enough to accommodate the footprint of the building and the required parking. Other considerations that affect the site size are: buffer areas and setback requirements, merchandise delivery areas, outparcels or commercial pads, and space for possible future expansion.

Footprint of the Building

The shopping center site must have enough square footage or acreage to contain the shopping center structure as well as all attendant ancillary facilities. Although this seems obvious, several important considerations must be noted. Neighborhood and community shopping centers are typically single-story structures. However, in some market areas such shopping centers may have a second floor.

Two-floor centers usually follow one of two models. In an area with level terrain and thus a completely flat site, a second story is normally constructed above first-floor retail space. In some market areas, office space is put on this upper floor; in other areas, retail space may be found on the second floor if customers find this arrangement acceptable. In this case the size of the footprint is not equal to the gross building area of the shopping center. The percentage of the gross building area represented by the footprint depends on the relationship of upper-floor space to lower-floor space. The appraiser simply needs to recognize the existence of second-floor space and measure it appropriately.

A two-floor neighborhood shopping center can be built on a site that drops off at one end so that ground level entrances can be created for both floors. The footprint of such a building is typically one-half of the gross building area.

Regional and superregional shopping centers exhibit greater variety. Older regional shopping centers constructed before the 1970s tend to be single-story structures. The footprint of the center contains not only the gross leasable area but also common areas, which may be walkways connecting individual structures or an enclosed mall area, which is more typical. Most newer regional shopping centers have two levels. Variety and design enhancement are provided by the anchor tenants, whose buildings may be two or three stories high. In these instances the footprint of the structure may represent 35% to 50% of the gross building area.

For regional shopping centers in densely populated areas, specifically downtown malls, the footprint may be only 15% of the gross building area. A prominent example is Water Tower Place on North Michigan Avenue in Chicago. This seven-story shopping center has a footprint that is approximately one-seventh of its gross building area.

In summary, a neighborhood shopping center with 80,000 square feet of gross leasable area may have a footprint of 80,000 square feet, while a superregional shopping center containing 1,000,000 square feet of gross leasable area may require a site footprint of only 450,000 square feet.

Customer Parking

Much of the material that follows has been derived from *Parking Requirements for Shopping Centers* and *Shopping Center Development Handbook* published by the Urban Land Institute.

The need for adequate parking is a major site requirement for a shopping center. The issue of parking can be approached from two perspectives. The first perspective focuses on parking standards, also known as the *parking index*, which is defined as the number of parking spaces per 1,000 square feet of gross leasable area of the shopping center. A second perspective analyzes the peak hour demand for parking space. Here the analyst studies the ability of the parking facility to meet the peak demand for parking at various times of day or on certain days of the week or days of special shopping activity—i.e., the day after Thanksgiving, the day before Christmas, and the day after Christmas.

In the vast majority of assignments, the appraiser only considers the first perspective—the parking standards. When a more extensive market study is required, the parking issue may be analyzed from both perspectives.

The following parking standards have been recommended by the Urban Land Institute:

- Four parking spaces per 1,000 square feet of gross leasable area for centers having a gross leasable area between 25,000 and 400,000 square feet

- Four to five parking spaces per 1,000 square feet of gross leasable area for shopping centers having a gross leasable area between 400,000 and 600,000 square feet

- Five parking spaces per 1,000 square feet of gross leasable area for those shopping centers with more than 600,000 square feet of gross leasable area.[1]

These guidelines can serve as a benchmark but they may be, and often are, superseded by specific zoning ordinances.

The amount of square footage allocated to each parking spot is governed by the zoning ordinance and by the design created by the architect. As a general rule of thumb, 325 square feet per parking space is considered adequate in markets where compact cars are prevalent, and 425 square feet per parking space is needed in markets where large cars are more common. With good parking surface design, less space is needed; inefficient design creates a need for more square footage.

For discussion purposes, assume that 375 square feet per parking space is typical. Of course, 375 square feet is an area much larger than

---

1. Urban Land Institute, *Dollars & Cents of Shopping Centers* (Washington, D.C.: Urban Land Institute, 1990.)

the dimensions of a typical automobile. The 375-square-foot figure includes not only the parking stalls but also the lanes in the parking lot, the entry areas into the parking lot, and the circulation area. Using this figure, the analyst can convert the parking standards mentioned above into square footage. Table 5.1 illustrates the relationships.

Table 5.1 **Recommended Parking Parameters**				
GLA	Parking Spaces Per 1,000 *GLA*	Square Feet Per Space	Square Feet of Parking	Per *GLA*
25,000	4.0	375	37,500	1.50
100,000	4.0	375	150,000	1.50
400,000	4.0	375	600,000	1.50
500,000	4.5	375	843,000	1.690
600,000	5.0	375	1,125,000	1.875

Source: Urban Land Institute, *Parking Requirements for Shopping Centers* (Washington, D.C: Urban Land Institute, 1982.)

The second aspect of parking requirements is the peak hour phenomenon. The parking standards identified earlier are based on a specific assumption about the peak hour problem, which is stated below:

> The provision of parking based on these standards . . . . will serve patron and employee needs at the 20th busiest hour of the year and allow a surplus during all but 19 hours of the remainder of the more than 3,000 hours during which a typical center is open annually. During 19 hours of each year which are distributed over 10 peak shopping days, some patrons will not be able to find vacant spaces when they first enter the center.[2]

Parking Lot Circulation

In addition to the quantity of space provided to accommodate parking, the layout or design of the parking lot is very important. "Ease of parking should be the guiding criterion for parking layout at any center. Parking at a shopping center must be simple, trouble-free, and safe."[3] There are six

2. Urban Land Institute, *Parking Requirements for Shopping Centers* (Washington, D.C.: Urban Land Institute, 1982), 2.

3. Urban Land Institute, *Shopping Center Development Handbook* (Washington, D.C: Urban Land Institute, 1985), 68

aspects important to parking lot layout. First, at the points of entry and exit (where the curbcuts are placed), the design should allow cars leaving the parking lot to line up and wait for a chance to leave the lot without interfering with the ability of other customers to park their cars. There should be separate entry and exit lanes that are physically removed from the area containing the parking spaces. This arrangement can minimize frustration for customers.

Second, the design of the lot and internal circulation features should discourage speeding and hazardous driving practices. This can be accomplished by minimizing the length of aisles (or straightaways) in the area containing parking spaces. Aisles can be interrupted by intersections with very visible markings and stop signs. If aisles are reasonably short, speeding will be discouraged or eliminated. Speed bumps can be installed to discourage speeding, but most drivers do not like these obstacles and they can be considered a disadvantage for the shopping center. A speed bump should be high enough to slow traffic, but not wreck the front-end alignment of the customers' cars.

Third, the design of parking stalls can affect both the space needed for the parking lot and customers' acceptance of the parking facilities. Angled stalls require narrower aisles for one-way traffic circulation, but there is a slight loss in the number of parking spaces in each aisle. In other words, with an angled design the parking lot will have more aisles with fewer spaces per aisle. No information concerning customer preferences for angled versus ninety-degree parking stalls is available, so it can be assumed that neither is more advantageous.

Fourth, the circulation of cars in the parking area should be continuous and preferably established as one-way traffic. The movement of traffic should be clearly indicated with directional arrows painted on the pavement and standing signs at the ends of the aisles. The management of the shopping center should repaint the arrows frequently to keep them visible.

Fifth, in regional and superregional shopping centers, adequate circulation of traffic typically requires circumferential roadways or beltways in the parking area. Most of these centers have an inner beltway along the perimeter of the parking lot. These major aisles allow for two-way traffic and should be marked with directional arrows. The inner beltway provides easy access to the structure for emergency vehicles (fire trucks, police, and ambulances) and drivers who are dropping people off or picking them up. The outer beltway allows customers to drive from one portion of the shopping center to another without having to travel through the parking area.

Finally, good parking lot circulation in smaller shopping centers requires that customers be able to drive from one part of the parking area to another without having to use the public street.

Parking Lot Lighting and Security

The parking lot should be well-lighted with no dark or unlighted areas. In the past good lighting was considered a convenience that allowed the shopper to watch his or her step while walking through the parking lot, finding the car, and opening the car door. Today lighting is a necessity for convenience and personal safety.

Parking bays should not be in obscure locations that are not visible or too far away from building entrances. Poor visibility and long walking distances represent potential dangers and can drive customers elsewhere.

Parking lots may require other forms of security in addition to lighting. Many superregional centers have security forces that patrol the parking lots. This visible presence reassures customers and deters burglary, robbery, and car theft. Security personnel may also carry a battery and cables to assist stranded shoppers. Some shopping centers provide space to local police departments for a precinct office or substation to have a police presence on site.

Parking in Relation to Building Entrances

In addition to an adequate number of spaces, the convenience of parking is important. In general, customers prefer to park as close to the entrance of the shopping center as possible. In regional and superregional shopping centers, the most distant parking spaces should be 300 to 350 feet from the entrance. As the size of the center decreases, so should the distance between the parking lot and the building.

The access aisles in the parking lot should make it easy to enter the shopping center. In a regional or superregional mall, the customer should be able to walk directly to an entrance of an anchor tenant or the entrance to the enclosed mall. The parking area should be designed so that the access aisles are perpendicular to the building. Aisles should lead directly to an entrance or the walkway in front of the building, so customers do not need to squeeze between cars. The same arrangement is recommended for community and neighborhood shopping centers.

Parking spaces for small strip centers are very often situated perpendicular to the storefronts. Access to the stores is easy because the customer can park in front of the establishment or a few feet away. This layout also facilitates quick visits and fast turnover of these prime spaces. When this design is used, measures should be taken to ensure that the cars do not protrude into the walkway in front of the stores. This can be accomplished with extended curb lines, bumper guards, or wheel stops.

Employee Parking

The existence and use of separate employee parking facilities should be noted.

> Between 15 and 20 percent of all center peak period parking is attributed to center employees. Analyses of center employment data during the busiest shift, on a peak Saturday before Christmas, indicate that during this period there are about 1.6 employees on site for each 1,000 square feet of GLA.[4]

If employees are allowed to park where they choose, they will park close to the store where they work in a neighborhood or community center and near the entrances to a regional shopping center. This practice affects customers in two ways. First, on ordinary days employee parking is a small inconvenience because the best parking spots are taken for the entire day. Second, on peak business days, employee parking reduces the effective number of parking spaces for customers and crowded conditions can drive customers away.

The Urban Land Institute offers the following recommendations:

---

4. Ibid., 185

1. At centers where employees must park on the site, provide parking behind or alongside the building. If the design will not allow this solution, employees should be required to park at the outer edge of the parking lot.

2. At centers where employee parking facilities are provided at a separate offsite location, the total amount of parking required at the center may be reduced by as much as 15 percent if all employees use the offsite parking area. A reduction of this magnitude requires prohibiting all employees from using the remaining available onsite spaces (reserved for patrons) and enforcing this regulation during peak periods.

Other Site Requirements

In addition to the footprint of the building and the parking requirements, the size of the site must be large enough to accommodate delivery and service space, outparcels or pads, expansion space, and buffer areas and setbacks.

Delivery and Service Space The shopping center site must be large enough to provide adequate space for delivery vehicles. Anchor tenants typically receive deliveries in large trucks. Local tenants tend to receive smaller loads and thus require less space for smaller trucks. The appraiser need not analyze the specific delivery and service requirements of each tenant; a reasonable rule of thumb can be applied to allocate a sufficient amount of space for these activities. In general the delivery space needed to receive merchandise for the various tenants in the shopping center plus service space for dumpsters and miscellaneous refuse should be approximately 10% to 15% of the gross building area. For aesthetic reasons, these service areas should be at the rear of a strip center and screened from customers' view at an enclosed mall.

Outparcels or Pads The shopping center's site should be large enough to provide space for outparcels—i.e., sites around the perimeter of a shopping center typically used for gas stations, fast-food restaurants, franchised restaurants, and banks. These outparcel tenants help generate customer traffic and are desirable additions. Each outparcel must provide adequate space for a structure and parking. The exact size of the outparcel depends upon the retail establishment to be built. Gas stations and branch banks have the smallest structural and parking requirements. Fast-food restaurants require more parking space and additional area for pick-up facilities. A sit-down restaurant typically has a larger building and a larger parking lot.

If the site is small, there may not be enough square footage or acreage to provide space for outparcel development. This usually occurs when the developer is unable to obtain rezoning approval for sites adjacent to or behind the shopping center site.

Expansion Space and Surplus Land If, at the time of development, the retail trade area has strong potential for growth, the developer may have additional acreage set aside for expansion of the shopping center. In this case both present and future site requirements for the footprint, parking, delivery, and service space must be investigated. As gross leasable area is added to the shopping center, more parking, delivery, and service area must be added. This area to be developed in the future will be considered surplus land in the original appraisal.

Buffer Area and Setback Requirements Shopping centers are affected by the local community's zoning ordinances and subdivision regulations. Police power allows the local community to establish buffer areas to insulate adjacent uses from the shopping center and to enforce setback requirements to position the parking areas in relation to the street system.

Typically a 30- to 50-ft. buffer area is established between a shopping center and residential land uses, especially single-family developments. Where possible, the buffer area is stipulated to be a wooded parcel so that the subdivision is separated visually and by distance. Often a larger buffer area is required between the rear of a shopping center and a residential neighborhood than between the side of the shopping center and the neighborhood.

In many communities setback requirements stipulate that green space must separate the street from the parking surface. Depending on community regulations and the developer's desire, the setback may be a grassy area or a landscaped parcel with ground cover and low-growing shrubs.

Site Size Rules of Thumb

Two rules of thumb for shopping center development are provided in the literature.

1. Each 40,000 square feet (about one acre) of the site will have roughly 10,000 square feet of building area and 30,000 square feet of surface parking area (including landscaping, circulation space, delivery area, etc.). . . A rough calculation of this sort is useful for gauging the adequacy of a shopping center site in an outlying suburban location, however, and would not be applicable for determining the adequacy of a downtown site.[5]
2. Physical improvements cover approximately one-third of the acreage.[6]

The second statement needs clarification because the phrase "physical improvements" is ambiguous. It can be interpreted to include the parking surface. The rule can be restated as: The total gross leasable area, including anchors and speculative space, covers approximately one-third of the site.

With these two rules of thumb, a reasonable relationship between *GLA* and site size can be established. If *GLA* is approximately 25% to 33% of the site size, a shopping center of 100,000 square feet of *GLA* will need a site of 400,000 to 300,000 square feet, or 9.18 to 6.89 acres. In short, a 10-acre site will accommodate 100,000 square feet of building area in a conventional shopping center development.

Rules of thumb can only be accepted as extremely rough approximations. Rules that are supposed to establish a relationship between *GLA* and the square footage of a site may not reflect the relationship between the building's footprint and the size of the site. This difference arises when the shopping center is an enclosed mall, because *GBA* is greater than

---

5. Ibid., 34

6. Glenn J. Rufrano, "Retail Acquisitions: Why?" *The Appraisal Journal* (July 1990), 292.

GLA, and when the shopping center is a multifloor structure, perhaps with two floors for speculative space and three floors for an anchor tenant.

Shape of the Site

Shopping center sites typically tend to be square or rectangular. However, due to the layout of streets, sites may not be perfectly rectangular; the corners along the perimeter of the site may not be perfect right angles.

Of principal significance is the relationship between the rectangular shape of the shopping center and the major street on which it has frontage. A shopping center site may have:

1. A normal frontage to depth relationship
2. Narrow frontage and great depth
3. Wide frontage and shallow depth
4. An irregular shape

A normal frontage to depth relationship generally reflects a one-to-one correspondence (i.e., a square site) or a configuration where the frontage on the main street is moderately longer than the depth (e.g., a 1.2 to 1.0 correspondence).

A site with a narrow frontage-to-depth ratio (i.e., approximately a one to three correspondence) lacks visibility from the major street. This situation will be discussed in a later section.

A site with wide frontage and shallow depth (i.e., a four-to-one correspondence) has less visibility from the intersecting street and a parking problem. The lack of depth on the intersecting street means that potential customers driving by the site will not have time to see the signs for the individual stores. Parking will have to be laid out along the front of the structure, which will probably force customers to drive from one side of the center to the other. This can be seen as a great inconvenience, especially at peak times when the parking lot is crowded. Irregularly shaped sites can be evaluated using the same principles applied to more regular sites, considering building to street depths, location, the visibility of buildings on the site, and the adequacy of internal circulation given odd boundary configurations or outparcels.

Access to the Trade Area

Each shopping center has a retail trade area. Delineation of the trade area was discussed in Chapter 4. Travel times along the street system serving the shopping center are used to identify the geographic extent of the retail trade area. As discussed previously, the relationship of the site to the street system and thus to its retail trade area is a very important site characteristic.

Relationship to the Street Pattern

The ideal shopping center location is almost always at the intersection of two major streets or highways. A neighborhood or community shopping center is typically placed at the intersection of two major streets that serve the community. Regional and superregional shopping centers are very often found at or near the intersection of a major surface street and an interstate highway. Sites at intersections benefit from their exposure to a large number of passersby and enhanced visibility.

If a location at the intersection of two major streets is not available, developers select sites with frontage on a major highway. In essence these are interior lots, not corner lots. It is difficult to determine whether a corner influence exists. Common wisdom suggests that corner lots should be more valuable as shopping center sites than interior lots, but this effect may be obscured in the market by the tenant composition of the shopping center or the reputation and prestige of the anchor tenant.

When a site at the intersection of two major streets is chosen, the shopping center typically faces the busier street. The developer will seek to acquire a site with more frontage on the major thoroughfare, but the depth of the site as measured from that thoroughfare is also an important consideration. The depth from the major thoroughfare is, in fact, the frontage on the other intersecting street. The frontage on the secondary street must be sufficient to give passersby adequate time to see the shopping center. Thus, while the ideal site at the intersection of two major roads tends to approximate a square, it is in reality a rectangle with the longer side along the major artery.

When a shopping center is developed on an interior lot, frontage is much more important than depth. The developer maximizes frontage to make the center more visible and provide several entry points into the facility. When the shopping center's frontage is adequate, potential customers driving by the site can see the front of the building as well as the tenant signs.

If the site has greater depth than frontage, customers driving by may not have enough time to see the signs, may be limited to only one entrance curb cut, and may only see the storefronts from a single direction. A structure constructed on an inordinately deep site must be positioned perpendicular to the street instead of parallel to the street.

Ease of Access

The design of the site must make it easy for potential customers to enter and leave the property. This is accomplished by providing adequate curb cuts and turn lanes. When the site is at the intersection of two major streets, at least one curb cut is needed on each of those streets and, if possible, two curb cuts should be provided on the principal street which ideally has more frontage.

Curb cuts are complemented by turn lanes. Right-hand turn lanes allow entering customers to slow down without affecting the traffic flow on the principal street and departing customers can merge into traffic easier. Left-hand turn lanes also make it easier for customers to enter and leave the site.

Access onto the site is also affected by the relationship between the parking surface and the street. If the parking surface is at grade, there is no problem. If the parking surface is below grade, however, the steepness of the ramp that leads from the parking lot to the street greatly affects the ease of access. Customers want a smooth transition. They dislike steep grades because they make leaving the shopping center site more difficult.

In addition to curb cuts and turn lanes, traffic congestion and street lights can affect access onto the site. Traffic congestion can minimize the benefit derived from left turn lanes entering and exiting the site. Customers may not want to wait and dodge through two or three lanes of oncoming traffic. A traffic light at the entrance to the shopping center or at the nearest intersection can eliminate this problem.

Visibility

Visibility is critical to the success of a shopping center. This truism is logical and well-documented in shopping center literature. A store must be visible to passing traffic. High visibility offers convenience to consumers and may lead to impulse purchases. "When many stores are visible, more customers are likely to be drawn to the center and will spill over to stores that were not the primary reason for their shopping visit."[7]

Evaluating visibility is a matter of judgment, but several factors can affect visibility, including street location, position on the site, obstructions, site elevation, and architecture.

Location Relative to Streets and Intersections

The location of a shopping center with regard to the street system greatly affects its visibility. Neighborhood shopping centers at the intersection of major streets have a great deal of visibility, especially if there are traffic lights at that intersection. Potential customers can see the stores from both streets as they are driving and when they are stopped at the light.

When neighborhood and community shopping centers are placed on sites away from the intersection of major roads, their visibility declines especially as the speed limit on the road increases. At speeds of 30, 40, 50, and 60 miles per hour, it is difficult for motorists to see the stores. Visibility is further reduced if the shopping center on an interior lot has a relatively small amount of frontage.

Placement of the Structure on the Site

The manner in which the shopping center structure is positioned on the site has a great effect on its visibility. A structure at an intersection should be placed so that the storefronts are visible from both streets. This is typically accomplished by using an L-shaped design with part of the center facing one street and part facing the other. If the site is not suited to an L-shaped structure, a rectangular configuration can be used and the build-

---

7. Nicholas A. Ordway, Alexander Bol, and Mark E. Eakin,   Centers," *The Appraisal Journal* (April 1988), 233
   "Developing a Visibility Index to Classify Shopping

ing can be placed parallel to the more heavily traveled street or at an angle so that stores can be seen from both streets.

On interior lots, visibility depends on the site's frontage along the street and the speed limit on the road. Visibility is enhanced by placing the structure parallel to the street. Visibility is minimized if the structure is at a right angle to the street or a U-shaped design is used.

Visual Obstructions

As mentioned earlier, the creation of outparcels is beneficial to a shopping center because it increases traffic volume and consequently the number of potential customers on or near the shopping center site. The creation of outparcels also gives the shopping center developer an additional source of revenue when the outparcel sites are sold to retail establishments such as gas stations, fast-food restaurants, banks, and convenience stores.

However, there is a trade-off. The construction of buildings on outparcel sites creates visual obstructions, so the relationship between outparcels and visibility needs to be analyzed. In general outparcels should be developed if the site size permits, but structures should be positioned so that the major portion of the shopping center and the anchor tenant(s) remain visible from the road and the intersection.

Site Elevation

The ideal shopping center site is level or almost level and at street grade. Such a site offers the greatest visibility. Visibility is diminished if the shopping center is above or below the level of the street.

Architectural Features and Building Elevations

Visual obstructions are sometime created by the architect. Many features that might make the shopping center attractive and convenient can reduce its visibility. Architectural features that reduce visibility include overhangs and canopies, which block the view of individual storefronts; recesses and indentations in the front of the building, which put some storefronts further back and limit their visibility from the roadway; and courtyards, which make the storefronts visible only when the customer enters the courtyard.

Other Major Obstructions

In addition to outparcel buildings and architectural features, other types of obstructions affect the visibility of a shopping center. The two most important factors to be considered are signs and landscaping. Each of these site characteristics will be discussed in greater detail.

Signage

The visibility of a shopping center can be enhanced by the proper use of signs. Signage has two components—the shopping center sign and tenant signs.

Shopping center signs are those monuments placed along the front of the site which give the shopping center name recognition. These signs are usually designed to be aesthetically pleasing and eye-catching. Such a sign is positioned for maximum visibility and enhances the visibility of the entire shopping center. For example, an attractive, visible shopping center sign can overcome the disadvantages of a below- or above-grade shopping center site. It can also overcome the disadvantages of an interior site with relatively little frontage.

Often the shopping center sign will identify both the shopping center and the principal tenants in that shopping center. Typically the sign will carry the names of the anchor tenant or tenants as well as the tenants in speculative space that could draw the most customers onto the site.

The second aspect of signage relates to individual tenant signs, which are typically placed on the front of the building above the space occupied by that tenant. These signs give each tenant greater exposure and visibility from both the street and the parking lot. Often these tenant signs attract more customers into the shopping center than the sign that identifies the shopping center itself. However, tenant signs can cause problems. The shopping center developer or manager must consider their attractiveness and try to prevent visual clutter. Following their own desires, each tenant would put up a sign that meets his or her needs and preferences. This could give the face of the shopping center a cluttered appearance because the signs would possess no uniformity. For this reason shopping center management typically controls the design and size of tenant signs to ensure that tenant visibility is enhanced, but the building's appearance remains uniform and attractive to potential customers.

Landscaping

Landscaping relates to both attractiveness and visibility. Because trees and tall shrubs can be obstacles that reduce the visibility of the shopping center from major roadways, the frontage areas of shopping center sites are cleared and leveled. If setbacks and greenspace are required, landscaping will consist of grassy areas and low-lying shrubbery. Such landscaping adds to the aesthetic appeal of the center, but does not obstruct visibility.

Landscaping on interior portions of the site is designed for attractiveness and has less impact on visibility. Neighborhood shopping centers may use flowers and ornamental shrubs along the face of the building and pedestrian walkways. Trees and shrubs may be planted on islands in the parking lot to serve as a visual break in the asphalt or concrete surface. Entryways into the parking lot may also be landscaped.

Attractive landscaping can enhance the desirability of the shopping center, but it imposes a burden on shopping center management. Landscaping must be maintained; dead trees and shrubs and weeds in grassy areas and flowerbeds are not attractive. The cost of operating the shopping center must increase if landscaped areas are to be maintained.

Topography and Drainage

Topography is a very important site characteristic because it can affect the physical design of the site as well as the design and construction of the building or buildings. The best shopping center sites are level or gently sloping. Sometimes a steeply sloped site can be used for a shopping center. In these cases customer access is provided at different levels of the structure and the parking area may have to be terraced.

Subsurface soil characteristics and drainage are also important. A shopping center needs underground utilities in order to operate. The site must be excavated to put in electric power lines, water mains, sewage disposal lines, and telephone lines to the building. A storm drainage system may have to be placed under the parking surface to eliminate standing water.

Utilities, Zoning, Subdivision Regulations, and Construction Codes

Obviously the availability of utilities is essential to the operation of a shopping center. If water, sewers, electricity, and gas are available to the site, are they off site, adjacent to the site, or in close proximity to the subject site? In other words, are they next to the property lines? If not, the cost of developing and operating the shopping center will be higher because additional expense may be required to obtain utilities.

Another issue concerning utilities is the level of service required by the different retail establishments within the shopping center. For example, a shopping center with a high percentage of eating establishments may need more water and sewer capacity than a shopping center that has no restaurants.

The principal zoning issues are whether the land is zoned to allow for construction of the shopping center and any zoning requirements that affect the provision of parking. In addition, the zoning ordinance may contain provisions that restrict certain tenants from the property. For example, fire safety requirements may prohibit a retail establishment selling paints, furniture refinisher, and other flammable products from locating in the center because the sprinkler system is not adequate.

Subdivision regulations and construction codes affect the development and construction of a shopping center and thus can have long-term effects on the center's revenue potential, maintenance and repair expenditures, and other line items in the income and expense statement. An inaccurate set of development regulations may have overstated the need for parking and consequently surplus parking area may have been built. This error can affect the property tax bill as well as the periodic expenditure to resurface the parking area. Inadequate subdivision regulations that understate the need for parking can be responsible for crowded parking lots, frustrated customers, and reduced sales during peak periods.

Exterior Building Characteristics

By inspecting the exterior of the structure, the appraiser can collect quantitative information about the building's size, shape, method of construction, and materials. In addition to quantitative factors, the appraiser studies exterior features such as entrances, signs, canopies, and lighting, which must be considered qualitatively.

Building Area

Usually the first quantitative measurement that the appraiser takes is gross building area. This figure should include the space for both anchor tenants and speculative tenants. For neighborhood and community shopping centers, gross building area is relatively easy to measure. The area measurements can be computed from the architect's plan for tenant leasing. If necessary, the appraiser can measure the exterior walls of the structure around the perimeter. Then the gross building area can be calculated from these perimeter measurements, which are usually illustrated in a hand-drawn representation of the building.

The second space measurement is gross leasable area. As defined in Chapter 1, *GLA* is the total floor area designed for the occupancy and exclusive use of tenants, including any basements, mezzanines, and upper floors. Gross leasable area is measured from the center line of joint partitions to the outside wall surfaces. For neighborhood and community shopping centers, gross leasable area should equal gross building area. The sum of the parts will equal the whole. The gross building area and gross leasable area of an enclosed mall differ. The difference is the common area inside the structure.

Gross leasable area is more difficult to measure with a tape measure than gross building area, but it can be done. However, the most practical procedure for an appraiser is to obtain measures of gross leasable area from the owner or manager of the enclosed shopping mall. This *GLA* information is provided in center leases if rent per square foot is used. The gross leasable area may also be specified in construction plans.

Building Configuration or Shape

Shopping center buildings can be constructed in various shapes, and shopping centers can reflect different configurations of buildings. The Urban Land Institute recognizes three general shapes and two configurations for shopping centers (see Figure 5.1). The building shapes are the linear building, the L-shaped building, and the U-shaped building. The two shopping center configurations are the mall, composed of two L-shaped buildings and two linear buildings, and the cluster, composed of five linear buildings and one truncated L-shaped building. Other options include one other building shape, the bent linear, and one additional configuration, the T-shaped mall (see Figure 5.2).

Building Elevation and Materials

A building's appearance, which developers call its *elevation*, and exterior materials are selected to create a visual image that is considered attractive according to community standards. "The image created should be one of harmony tempered by tasteful variation in selected details."[8] Achieving this goal may be difficult because many different entities with various elevations and materials must be brought together.

First the mall developer typically constructs all the structural space that will be leased by speculative, non-anchor tenants. If the center is a superregional mall constructed in an X-configuration, there will be four anchor tenants. Each of these anchors will want to construct a building with an elevation and exterior materials that are distinctive and express its corporate identity. One anchor tenant may select a traditional structure with a polished marble exterior. Directly opposite, a second anchor tenant selects an elevation constructed of glass and chrome. The speculative space between these two anchors may be clad with pink stucco. Each element could be tasteful, attractive, and aesthetically pleasing in and of itself, but in combination the image produced may be less than pleasing.

To achieve the goal of "harmony tempered by tasteful variation," the shopping center developer has to coordinate the anchor tenants' desire for distinctive designs and materials. This entails achieving harmony among the four anchors and smoothly incorporating the exterior materials, elevation, and design selected for the speculative space.

The appraiser's role with regard to building materials and elevation is mostly descriptive. However, there is a real possibility that an unattractive, aesthetically displeasing shopping center can suffer a loss of sales, which

---

8. Urban Land Institute, *Shopping Center Development Handbook,* 78.

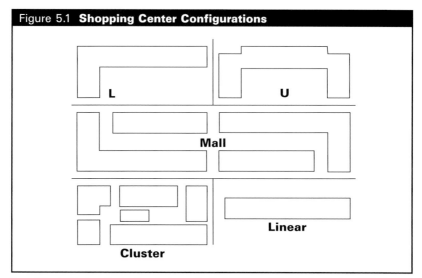

Figure 5.1 **Shopping Center Configurations**

Source: Urban Land Institute, *Shopping Center Development Handbook* (Washington, D.C.: Urban Land Institute, 1985), 61.

Linear. A line of stores tied together by a canopy over the sidewalk, which runs along the fronts of the stores. Economical for small stores, but must be kept to a reasonable length to avoid excessive walking distances and difficult merchandising.

The L. Basically a linear layout, but with one end turned. Good for corner locations.

The U. Basically a linear layout with both ends turned in the same direction.

The mall. Essentially a pedestrian way between two facing linear buildings. The mall may also take another shape—an L for example.

The cluster. A group of pedestrian buildings separated by small pedestrian malls or courts.

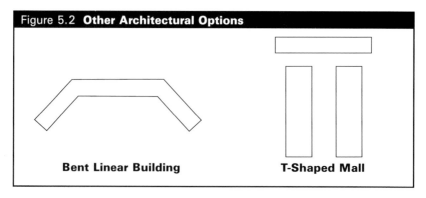

Figure 5.2 **Other Architectural Options**

Bent Linear Building   **T-Shaped Mall**

will decrease the rents collected through percentage leases and increase vacancy rates.

Building Entrances

The entrances to an enclosed mall should be prominent design features. This can be accomplished in one or more of the following ways:

- Creation of a distinctive facade
- Construction of a special canopy
- Increasing the roof height
- Constructing a wall extension or an indentation
- Using attractive and distinctive exterior lighting as a design feature as well as a means to highlight the entrance

Canopies

For neighborhood and community shopping centers, which are usually not enclosed, a walkway protected by a canopy is an important feature. However, a covered walkway has both advantages and disadvantages that the appraiser should recognize. First, the canopy provides weather protection. To serve this purpose, "experience has shown that 12 feet to 15 feet is a good width for the walkway.... Their widths and heights will be determined by the proportions appropriate to the architectural style."[9] If the developer chooses, the walkway can be enclosed with glass panels and either heated or cooled. This could make shopping along the storefronts more enjoyable at certain times of the year.

The disadvantage of canopies is that they can reduce the visibility of the storefronts. When canopies are used, individual storefronts are usually not visible from the street and, quite possibly, not visible from the more distant portions of the parking lot.

Signage

In a typical regional or superregional shopping center, exterior signage on the structure tends to be limited to the anchor tenants. Sometimes specu-

---

9. Ibid., 79.

lative tenants with exterior entrances may also have exterior signs. In this case there is less concern for the coordination and management of these exterior signs.

For neighborhood and community shopping centers with canopies, exterior signage takes two forms. Often, each retail shop wants to place its own distinctive sign either above the canopy or on the face of the canopy to improve the store's visibility from the street and the parking lot. This form of exterior signage requires the greatest amount of coordination and management by the shopping center developer. Without such controls, the elevation of the shopping center, which may be architecturally pleasing, can become a jumble of letters and colors as each tenant places its own sign on the building.

A second type of exterior signage on the structure is the placement of signs under the canopy at or near the entrance to each of the retail establishments. Once again, this form of signage must be coordinated and managed by the developer.

> It has been found that when all signs in a center are required to conform to the same guidelines of size and style, each tenant is more amenable to restrictions on his signage. The conclusion to be drawn is that when graphic controls are uniformly applied, shop keepers no longer feel the need of erecting signs that are larger or more dazzling than those of their neighbors and competitors.[10]

Sign control is usually accomplished through leases. The developer may include a clause in the lease that stipulates permitted and prohibited signage as well as an approval clause allowing the developer to investigate and approve each sign to be used. Typically these clauses prohibit signs that are constructed on the roof of the building, large projecting signs that hang over the top of the canopy, and signs that move or incorporate flashing lights.

---

10. Ibid., 81–82.

Lighting

Because a greater percentage of retail business is now being conducted during the evening, exterior night lighting has become an important safety as well as design feature. It helps to protect the public, and it can be used to create an image and character for the center.[11] Security lighting for the parking area was discussed under site characteristics. In another context, lights are used as a design element in signage. Distinctive lighting makes building entrances more attractive and decorative lighting adds to the aesthetic appeal of the elevation.

Interior Building Characteristics

Analysis of interior building characteristics focuses on the following topics:

- Storefronts
- Store size
- Building flexibility
- Multiple levels
- Food courts
- Interior signage

Each of these topics is discussed in the following sections.

Storefronts

In any type of shopping center, the attractiveness and appeal of the individual storefront may be the principal reason why a customer enters that particular store. The attractiveness and design of storefronts can affect the customer's overall impression of the shopping center and thereby enhance its image. To create an aesthetically pleasing array of storefronts, the developer must achieve a high degree of architectural integration.

In an enclosed mall, storefronts are usually open so the full width of the storefront becomes the entrance to the retail establishment. This arrangement allows customers to enter the sales floor at many different

---

11. Ibid., 82.

points along the storefront and gives the retailer many options for display-ing merchandise.

The principal disadvantage of an open storefront is shoplifting. Place-ment of the checkout area near the front of the store and the use of detec-tion devices can be deterrents. Some enclosed malls have storefronts that are partially open. This arrangement allows the retailer to have window displays.

A developer achieves architectural integration in an enclosed mall through the wall area above the storefronts and by imposing commonality or at least compatibility among the partially open storefront constructions.

As a general rule, the developer should try to create the greatest possi-ble number of storefronts along the pedestrian mall to provide exposure for the maximum number of merchants. This can be accomplished by de-signing the floor area in such a way that larger tenants occupy space be-hind adjoining retail establishments. In other words, the large retail establishments may have a floor area that is L-shaped or T-shaped.

Store Size

There is a saying in the shopping center industry: "Any store size is all right if it is not too big." Shopping center developers and managers are ad-vised that "each tenant should be held to the minimum space needed as it is better for a tenant to be a little tight on space than to be rattling around in too much room with insufficient sales to justify the rent. . . ."[12]

Store size is principally determined by width and depth, which to-gether indicate the gross leasable area, but ceiling height is also impor-tant. There is no standard or typical store width for any particular type of tenant. Major retailers generally have an idea of the store size and store width that they require. However, their desires often conflict with the de-veloper's desire to keep the mall to a reasonable length and to provide frontage on the mall to the largest possible number of tenants. An old rule of thumb limits store width to a maximum of 50 feet and many developers prefer a maximum width of 40 feet.

---

12. Ibid., 92.

Similar standards also apply to store depth. "The ability to provide stores of varying depths is an asset to any center. A range of depths from 40 to 120 feet is often both required and feasible. Where buildings must have uniform depths, small stores can be carved out of deeper space, leaving rear overlap areas for the neighboring larger stores."[13]

The store depth needed by a retail establishment depends on many factors. Each retail establishment must maintain a sales floor area, a storage area, a merchandise receiving area, and an administrative area (i.e., the store manager's office). If all of this gross leasable area must be provided on a single level, then the store depth must be greater. However, if basement facilities are available, especially for storage, then less depth is necessary for each retail establishment.

Ceiling heights enter the analysis in two ways. First, from a purely structural viewpoint, ceiling heights in shopping centers vary from 10 to 14 feet depending on the architectural design of the building and the tenants expected to occupy the space. For example, in a neighborhood shopping center, a grocery store anchor tenant requires more structural ceiling height than the speculative tenants (e.g., a dress shop, a shoe store). The top two to three feet of this height must be devoted to HVAC ducts, electrical wiring, recess lighting fixtures, plumbing lines, and other utilities. In addition to structural height, there is the issue of finished ceiling height. As a general rule, only the ceiling in the sales area is finished. In supermarkets finished ceiling heights range from 12 to 14 feet, which necessitates structural ceiling heights of 15 to 17 feet. Depending upon the nature of the tenants, speculative space may have finished ceiling heights between 9 and 11 feet. Thus, structural ceiling heights in this portion of the shopping center can be 12 to 14 feet. Usually the more gross leasable area rented by the tenant, the higher the finished ceiling height they desire. High ceilings bring a feeling of openness to a large retail space; smaller space users can be accommodated with lower ceiling heights.

---

13. Ibid., 93.

Building Flexibility

The design of the shopping center should allow as much flexibility as possible in creating tenant spaces of different size. To accomplish this, the use of load-bearing walls between tenant spaces should be minimized. Local fire codes may dictate the spacing between fire walls, but within the limitations imposed by these codes, the design of the building should provide the freedom to move interior partitions between tenants.

To achieve this flexibility as inexpensively as possible, mechanical systems such as plumbing, HVAC ducts, electrical wiring, and panel boxes should be placed on back walls or on the walls that are least likely to be removed in the process of enlarging a store. If utilities are on side walls, additional expense may be incurred to move them.

Multiple Levels

One aspect of multilevel shopping centers, their smaller footprints, was discussed under site characteristics. Two other aspects of multilevel shopping centers, tenant distribution and visibility, must also be analyzed.

Multilevel shopping centers can provide marketing benefits if the tenants are distributed to take advantage of the interplay between the floors. Tenant location is crucial. Several guidelines can be applied.

- The anchor tenant must have an entrance on each level.
- High-volume, popular retail establishments must be dispersed between the levels and at various places on each level.
- Access to the upper level must be easy. Escalators, elevators, and staircases must connect the common area on the first level with the common area on the second level. Anchor tenants will provide escalators and possibly elevators within their own structures that consumers can use to go from mall shops on the first level to mall shops on the second level.
- Customers on the second level should have ample opportunity to cross from one side of the second-floor common area to the other side. This is accomplished by placing bridges or walkways at several points along the length of the mall. The ability to cross from side to side on the second level will never approach the unlimited ability to do so on the first level, but free movement on the second

tier should be facilitated to the greatest extent possible given the structural integrity and desire for openness in the mall.[14]

Visibility is important in a multilevel shopping center design. As customers walk along the mall area on the first level, they should be able to see at least the upper portion of the storefronts (the signage) of the tenants across the mall on the level above. In addition, customers on the elevators, escalators, and stairwells should be able to see the shops on the second floor as they go up and down. This is accomplished with open escalators, glass-walled elevators, and open stairways.

There is an important connection between site design and a multilevel shopping center. If the terrain allows, entrances to the mall area should be placed on each level. This encourages customer traffic on the second floor.

Each of these points made about multilevel shopping centers generally apply to regional and superregional shopping centers as well.

It is seldom advisable for neighborhood centers to have two stories. Second floors do not necessarily increase earnings and extra costs are involved for construction, plumbing, heating, and maintenance. It is uneconomical to provide elevators or escalators to reach the second floor. . . . A small two-story center is likely to succeed only in an area of limited and high cost commercial land, high population density, and a high level of disposable income. Suitable second floor tenants are those that pull people to the center regularly and frequently, have visitors who will not park any longer than an hour during shopping hours, and require no display space on the ground floor. Some service tenants such as beauty shops, photographers, dance studios, and the like are appropriate for second floor locations.[15]

Generally, office tenants are not suited to second-level space in a neighborhood or a community shopping center. Office employees tie up parking spaces for nine or ten hours per day and most visitors to offices

14. Ibid., 88-89.   15. Ibid.

are working, not shopping. There is an old adage for neighborhood shopping centers with second floors: Ground floors are rented. Basements and second floors are given away.[16]

These statements apply to traditional neighborhood and community shopping centers, but they probably do not apply to theme centers established in downtown areas, historic areas, and renovated areas. Many older, historically significant buildings are converted into multilevel shopping malls. These centers are usually tourist-oriented and contain a high proportion of restaurants, taverns, nightclubs, and specialty retail shops.

Food Courts

Food courts are now a major component of regional and superregional malls as well as smaller specialty centers. A food court is simply a cluster of quick-service food vendors positioned around a common seating area. Three important considerations must be analyzed in evaluating a food court—location, design, and tenant mix.

The location of the food court must be considered in two ways. First, is the food court an anchor tenant or is it providing a convenience service? If the food court is a destination that attracts people from nearby offices and retail establishments around the regional mall, then it is viewed as an anchor. In this case, the food court should be located in an area of the shopping center where people are drawn past the retail shops. On the other hand, if the food court serves customers who are shopping at the mall, it should be placed where the volume of pedestrian traffic is highest. Generally this is at some point between the anchor tenants and near the geographic center of the shopping center.

Another aspect of location concerns whether the food court will remain open after the shopping center's regular business hours. If this is possible, then the food court can serve those patronizing late night establishments, typically cinemas, and provide a point of destination for people seeking a variety of quick-service foods.

A second important element of a food court is its design. "The design of the food court should provide a theme and a festive ambience. . . . amenities such as terraces, water features, and landscaping are

---

16. Ibid., 89, 91.

important, particularly to temper the visual impact of the seating area in a large scale food court.[17]

A third significant element is tenant mix. This aspect of a food court can be analyzed using the principles of cumulative attraction and compatibility, which we introduced in Chapter 1.

Interior Signage

Tenants in neighborhood and community centers may want to put various signs on their windows. The developer needs to control this practice through the lease. If tenants have unrestricted freedom with regard to signs, they may advertise all manner of fire sales, going-out-of-business sales, or two-for-one sales with signs of all colors and sizes. If this practice is allowed, the visual image of the shopping center can be greatly diminished due to the cluttered appearance of the windows. The same situation can result in an enclosed mall when tenants hang various signs across the front of the stores.

Plans and Specifications

Plans and specifications are obviously needed to appraise a proposed shopping center. The appraiser would be well advised not to accept such an assignment without them. When appraising existing centers, most appraisers prefer to rely on the measurements in these documents rather that risk making an error in their measurements. It is a good idea to reference the plans and specifications, identifying their date, page numbers, and the architect's name.

Summary

In conducting a physical inspection of a shopping center property and its comparables, the appraiser should be sensitive to a wide range of design elements that affect these properties' physical and functional adequacy. These elements comprise the site characteristics, including signage and landscaping, and building characteristics both inside and outside the shopping center.

---

17. Ibid.

Tabor Center, Denver   *R. Krubner / H. Armstrong Roberts*

Chapter Six

APPLYING THE THREE VALUATION APPROACHES TO SHOPPING CENTERS

Introduction

Traditionally, three approaches to estimating real estate value have been taught and practiced. Theoretically, each approach represents a way in which typical market participants make their purchase decisions. When substitute properties are available or have been sold, it is appropriate to investigate the motivations of the parties involved and the details of the transactions and make inferences to estimate the value of the subject property; this is, of course, the methodology of the sales comparison approach. When buyers would consider acquiring a site and constructing improvements to suit their purposes, reproduction or replacement cost minus depreciation tends to set an upper limit of value for the typical buyer. This is an application of the cost approach. If the subject property is most likely to be acquired for investment return, it is appropriate to view it in an income capitalization approach context, in light of the risks and returns available on comparable investments. If typical buyers would not consider the subject property in one of these three ways, then an appraiser would not either. As a forecaster of buyer and seller behavior, an appraiser seeks to simulate market behavior as closely as possible.

The following discussion does not review the theory and techniques of each of the three approaches to value; instead, it focuses on the special problems and considerations relevant in shopping center assignments.

Some of these considerations may not apply to smaller shopping centers, which do not have the synergism created by a centralized management and marketing strategy or an operating agreement.

Property Rights and Their Modification

Appraisers and assessors need to understand the property rights involved in the assets to be valued and how these rights are modified or transferred. Property rights, which are sometimes referred to as a "bundle of rights," are modified by leases, easements, cross-easements, and (in larger centers) the operating agreement and supplementary agreement. The following definitions can help the appraiser ask the right questions in defining and executing the assignment:

> *Fee simple estate*: Absolute ownership unencumbered by any other interest or estate, subject only to the four powers of government.
>
> *Leased fee estate*: An ownership interest held by a landlord with the right of use and occupancy conveyed by lease to others; the rights of lessor or the leased fee owner and leased fee are specified by contract terms contained within the lease.[1]

When appraising a fee simple estate, it is important to select as comparable sales other properties that have been sold with all of the bundle of rights intact. A property with leases, such as an operating shopping center with anchor tenants and mall tenants, is a leased fee estate or, as some practitioners identify it, a fee subject to leaseholds. The appraiser does not want to damage his or her credibility by defining the subject property as a fee simple estate and then analyzing leases.

In most states the assessed value for property tax purposes is to be based on the market value of the unencumbered fee simple estate, notwithstanding the existence of leases, easements, or other encumbrances.[2]

---

1. American Institute of Real Estate Appraisers, *The Dictionary of Real Estate Appraisal*, 2d ed., (Chicago: American Institute of Real Estate Appraisers, 1989.)

2. Gregory K. Lafakis, "Valuation Concepts and Issues and the Taxpayer's Responsibilities Concerning Regional Shopping Centers," a paper presented at the International Association of Assessing Officers Eighth Annual Legal Seminar, San Francisco, October 1988.

An example will illustrate the importance of properly identifying the property rights being appraised. Consider a shopping center appraisal assignment in which the land is leased under a long-term ground lease. The appraiser assumes that since the land is under long-term control, it is part of the shopping center. He therefore includes the land value in all three approaches and seriously overstates the value of the property. Because the land is ground leased, the rights being appraised include a leasehold estate. The appraiser should have estimated the present value of the differential payments that the estate would have received from the shopping center tenants minus those paid to maintain the estate.

It is also imperative that the appraiser determine which physical assets are included in a shopping center appraisal because some tenants own their own storefronts and interior improvements.

Value Definitions

In any valuation assignment the appraiser must first define very carefully *what* value is sought. Various types of value are defined below. Most of these definitions are quoted from the Appraisal Institute's *Dictionary of Real Estate Appraisal*, second edition.

> *Market value:*
> Market value is the major focus of most real property appraisal assignments. Both economic and legal definitions of market value have been developed and refined. A current economic definition agreed upon by agencies that regulate federal financial institutions in the United States of America is:
>
> The most probable price which a property should bring in a competitive and open market under all conditions requisite to a fair sale, the buyer and seller each acting prudently and knowledgeably, and assuming the price is not affected by undue stimulus. Implicit in this definition is the consummation of a sale as of a specified date and the passing of title from seller to buyer under conditions whereby:
>
> 1. Buyer and seller are typically motivated;
> 2. Both parties are well informed or well advised, and acting in what they consider their best interests;

3. A reasonable time is allowed for exposure in the open market;

4. Payment is made in terms of cash in United States dollars or in terms of financial arrangements comparable thereto; and

5. The price represents the normal consideration for the property sold unaffected by special or creative financing or sales concessions granted by anyone associated with the sale.[3]

The word *probable* in the definition implies a probability distribution of the possible sale outcomes for any property—from the very lowest price obtainable by a strong buyer to the highest price attainable by the strongest seller. The most likely price, which will fall in the middle of the distribution or bell-shaped curve, is called *market value*. In ad valorem property taxation, the usual focus is market value.

As William N. Kinnard has suggested, "In this framework, the purchaser-investor is 'typical,' the owner-operator-manager is 'typical,' and the developer-entrepreneur is 'typical.'"[4] Kinnard argues that when the purchaser is not a typical, passive investor who retains a normal good manager, but rather an unusually successful and credible business entity, then perhaps some value *other* than market value should be the focus of the appraisal. This value may more properly be termed *use value* or *investment* value, and may be an indicator of business enterprise value, which will be discussed later. It may be a value toward the high or low end of the probability distribution instead of the one in the middle. Several definitions of value follow.

Value:

1. The monetary worth of property, goods, services, etc.

2. The present worth of future benefits that accrue to real property ownership.

---

3. This definition appears in the Uniform Standards of Professional Appraisal Practice and conforms to Title XI of the Financial Institutions Reform, Recovery and Enforcement Act of 1989.

4. William N. Kinnard, Jr., "Valuing the Real Estate of Regional Shopping Centers Independently of Operating Business Value Components: A Review of Recent Research," prepared for the annual meeting of the American Institute of Real Estate Appraisers, Chicago, May 3, 1990.

Investment value:

The specific value of an investment to a particular investor or class of investors based on individual investment requirements; as distinguished from market value, which is impersonal and detached.

Business valuation:

An appraisal of a business, usually performed to determine the present and future monetary rewards of complete or partial ownership rights in the business.

Going-concern value:

Going-concern value is the value of a proven property operation; it is considered a separate entity to be valued with an established business. This value is distinct from the value of the real estate only. Going-concern value includes an intangible enhancement of the value of an operating business enterprise which is produced by the assemblage of the land, building, labor, equipment, and marketing operation. This process leads to an economically viable business that is expected to continue.[5]

Appraisal as a Behavioral Science

Real estate appraisal is applied urban land economics. It is micro forecasting, and good forecasters must understand market transactions. They ask: Who buys, why do they buy, and how? Who sells, and why? Who are the support people—brokers, lenders, property managers, etc.? What terms are typical in the market—time to sell, bargaining conventions, and financing terms?

Analysts can obtain this information by asking questions of buyers, sellers, lenders, property managers, present tenants, prospective tenants, and the retail tenants' customers—i.e., shoppers. Talking to as few as six to 10 people can reveal the major strengths and weaknesses of a center. Minor characteristics need not be studied in detail.

---

5. Appraisal Institute, *The Appraisal of Real Estate*, 10th
   ed. (Chicago: Appraisal Institute, 1992), 23-24.

For example, in interviewing the shopping center manager, the following questions should be asked. What feature seems to attract new mall tenants more than anything else? When a prospective retail tenant chooses another nearby location for his or her store, what reason is usually given? What maintenance complaint do you hear most often? What past mistakes—in leasing, construction, or management — would you most like to correct? By asking similar questions of mall shoppers, competing mall managers, and others, the appraiser can assess the competitive attributes of the subject property. These primary data will supplement the secondary data gathered from the courthouse, data services, comparable sales, and elsewhere.

Highest and Best Use Analysis

In highest and best use analysis, the appraiser integrates site-specific analyses undertaken in the three approaches to value with each other and with the general marketability analysis described in previous chapters. The appraiser needs to identify the highest and best use of the land as though vacant and the property as developed.

The analysis usually begins with four criteria. The highest and best use must be legally permissible, physically possible, economically viable, and maximally productive. In considering the uses that are legally possible, one constraint on land use is the operating agreement, when there is one. The operating agreement is a document that contains commitments from the anchors and the center operator to maintain the site in a specified type of use. Unless there is a genuine possibility that all parties could agree to cancel this agreement in favor of an alternative plan, the operating agreement has the same limiting effects as a zoning law.

The analyst can eliminate alternative uses that are obviously inappropriate and settle on two or three that merit closer scrutiny. The residual analysis described earlier will presumably indicate the center's capacity in terms of gross leasable area. Marketability analysis can indicate if the design of the subject space makes sense in light of recent transactions and demand and supply indicators.

Highest and best use analysis requires input from each of the three approaches to value—just as each approach probably requires some information from the others. This fact may be lost on the new appraiser because the highest and best use section of an appraisal report is usually presented before the discussions of the three approaches. This placement does not necessarily reflect the order of the appraiser's thought processes. Cost approach techniques will be especially helpful in identifying returns to the capital investment in the building and land, with the residual considered entrepreneurial profit for the developer. This is an important test of highest and best use. Then a limited land residual analysis can be performed for each of the alternative uses to determine which creates the highest land value.

A great many of the estimates required will be beyond the typical appraiser's expertise. For example, if an office building is being considered as a possible alternative to a shopping center, the analyst will need to make a decision about density without the advice of the architect or land planner. To make this decision, the analyst might investigate the density of typical, competitive office properties in the market.

The income approach may also be applied in highest and best use analysis to identify the residual income to the land from each alternative use. The sales comparison approach affirms that the market will reward the developer for construction and land assembly with an appropriate profit.

The Sales Comparison Approach

In the sales comparison approach, the appraiser studies and simulates the thinking of the buyers, sellers, and intermediaries who make up the market for the subject and comparable properties to forecast their behavior in future transactions. Conventional wisdom holds that market participants generally consider price and value on a common unit basis. In the shopping center submarket, this unit of comparison is typically dollars of sale price per square foot of gross leasable area. Of course, the appraiser must determine the appropriate measure and identify typical value ranges for the relevant property type.

The property rights appraised must be carefully defined. For example, some centers are sold without the anchor department store property included because these stores own their pads. In analyzing sales of these malls, the analyst should calculate the sale price per square foot of mall *GLA* only; that is, neither the sale price nor the *GLA* measurement should include values or areas attributable to the anchors when these properties are not owned and sold by the developer. It is also important to determine the precise areas and rights involved in comparable sales.

If market value is the value that falls in the middle of the probability distribution, not at either extreme, proper selection of comparable sites or properties is essential. The appraiser must avoid what Kinnard calls a *de facto classification*—i.e., only using sales of projects created by highly successful developer-operators. All available retail property data should be used. The sale price of a successful comparable shopping mall may need to be adjusted to remove the business enterprise value component before inferences are made for a subject property that is too new to have any such value.[6] When the comparables have substantial differences in the rights being transferred or the terms of the leases, other adjustments should be considered.

Appraisers have developed various techniques to collect, report, and analyze market data. One method for organizing important comparable sales data is shown in Figure 6.1.

Some appraisers apply a type of a gross income multiplier in evaluating regional malls, using the ratio between the price per square foot of mall space and the sales generated by that mall space. Glenn J. Rufrano, MAI, reported that his analysis of a number of market transactions indicated this ratio ranged between 1 and 1.35.[7]

It is standard appraisal procedure to make comparisons between similar properties that have been sold and to use this analysis as a guide in arriving at a value estimate, which is primarily an intuitive process. Some appraisers present these comparisons in a grid. Comparative judgments can be expected for all major differences revealed in the interviews with market participants, including financing, time of sale, property rights conveyed, lease clauses, demographics and trends in the trade area, traffic counts, property condition, access, visibility, and infrastructure. An issue that has not been addressed in the professional literature is how an ap-

6. Kinnard.

7. Glenn J. Rufrano, MAI, "Retail Acquisitions," *The Appraisal Journal* (July 1990), 291.

Figure 6.1 **Sample Comparable Sales Data**

Shopping Center Sale 4

Name:	Sand Hill Shopping Center
Location:	NW Corner U.S. Highway X and
	Sand Hill Road
	City, County, State
Grantor:	A. B. Cee
Grantor:	D. E. Eough
Date of sale:	October 12, 1989
Sale price:	$9,200,000
Sale price per sq. ft.:	$90.70
Financing:	Cash
Land area:	10.9 acres
Improvements:	Brick veneer, concrete block and steel frame
Age:	1987
Size:	101,425 sq. ft.
Anchors:	FoodMaster Store–40,000 sq. ft.
	Diamond Hardware–8,000 sq. ft.
	Chain Drug–9,450 sq. ft.

Estimated effective				
gross income:	$1,067,881	$10.54/sq. ft.	*EGIM:*	8.62
Net income:	$865,256	$8.54/sq. ft.	*OAR:*	9.40%

Comments: Local rents range from $10.50 to $13.90 per square foot with tenants paying prorated expenses over base year amounts. Leases typically include a stated annual increase of 5% to 6%. This center was 83% leased at the time of the sale and reached 92% occupancy approximately one year after the sale.

---

praiser might adjust unit price measures for differences in the demographic potential of the trade area or for the uncertainty of infrastructure improvements.

A grid used by one appraiser to make comparisons among sales is presented in Table 6.1. This appraiser finds it more practical to express the value derived in the sales comparison approach as a range rather than a point estimate. The sales summary grid helps identify which sales are most similar to the subject in terms of tenant composition and economic and physical characteristics. In this analysis Sales 2 and 4 appear to be most comparable, but they exhibit effective gross income multipliers of 7.2 and 5.7—a rather wide range. The appraiser judged Sale 4 to be the most comparable, considering all factors including the date of sale and the market condition changes that occurred after Sale 2. He concluded that an effective gross income multiplier of 5.75 to 6.0 was appropriate.

Table 6.1 Sales Summary Grid—Neighborhood Shopping Centers

	Subject	Sale 1	Sale 2	Sale 3	Sale 4
Real property rights conveyed	Leased fee	Leased fee	Leased fee	Leased fee	Leased fee
Construction	Class C	Class C	Class C	Class C	Class C
Age/condition	28 yrs./good	20 yrs./good	30 yrs./avg.	15 yrs./good	17 yrs./avg.
GLA	113,697	141,370	96,417	131,019	167,710
Percent anchored	83.1%	70.5%	81.9%	73.2%	85.5%
Percent occupied	92.1%	96.3%	94.8%	95.1%	91.9%
Consideration	N/A	$4,100,000	$3,700,000	$5,950,000	$4,100,000
Date of sale	01-Feb.92	15-Jan.89	30-Nov.90	12-Oct.91	18-Jan.92
EGI	$638,615	$619,201	$511,010	$767,742	$717,799
EGI per sq. ft.	$5.62	$4.38	$5.30	$5.86	$4.28
EGIM	N/A	6.6	7.2	7.8	5.7
Expenses	$229,840	$169,661	$133,885	$202,684	$283,094
Expenses per square foot	$2.02	$1.28	$1.39	$1.55	$1.69
Expense ratio	36.0%	27.4%	26.2%	26.4%	39.4%
Net income	$408,775	$449,540	$377,125	$565,058	$434,704
Net income per square foot	$3.60	$3.18	$3.91	$4.31	$2.59
Overall rate	N/A	11.0%	10.2%	9.5%	10.6%
Net income multiplier	N/A	9.1	9.8	10.5	9.4
Sale price per square foot	N/A	$29.00	$38.37	$45.41	$24.45
Average tenant credit rating (anchor/local)	A/C	A/C	A/C	A/B	A/C
Market conditions	Static	Static	Static	Static	Static
Upside potential	Limited	Slight	Limited	Moderate	Limited

Standard teaching materials often prescribe the application of percentage or dollar adjustments in sales comparison analysis. Adjustment grids are not popular with some practitioners because of the lack of paired data or other bases for the adjustments. Some appraisers believe they oversimplify the inherently intuitive judgment process and actually provide litigation adversaries with ammunition. Sometimes they are used as supporting documentation in the appraiser's file, but not included in the final appraisal report.

Significant information is conveyed in the sales comparison approach by analyzing the ratio of *NOI* per square foot of *GLA* for the comparable sales and inferring the results to the subject property. This technique is illustrated in Table 6.2. Here the sale price of the comparable sale is adjusted to reflect the relationship between the subject *NOI* per square foot and that of the comparable property. Critics of this method point out that this ratio is the reciprocal of the capitalization rate, and that its use compromises the independence of the sales comparison and income approaches. A mathematical demonstration shows this to be the case. Assume that M represents the adjustment and

$$SP = \text{sales price}$$
$$SF = \text{square foot}$$
$$NOI = \text{net operating income}$$

then $\quad M = (SP/SF)/(NOI/SF)$

Inverting fractions and multiplying

$$M = (SP/SF) \times (SF/NOI)$$

cancel *SF* and

$\quad M = SP/NOI$, which is the reciprocal of *NOI/SP*

A variant of this method is to compare the operating expense ratios of all the comparable properties and make adjustments to their sale prices based on how these ratios compare to the operating expense ratio of the subject property.

When selecting comparable sales of investment properties, the relevant market is not geographically limited to the local retail trade area. It is the entire region or nation throughout which investors are likely to operate. Similarly, operating expense ratios should be drawn from industry sources

Table 6.2 Sales Comparison Approach—*NOI* Adjustment Chart

Sale No.	(A) Sale SP/SF	(B) Sale NOI/SF	(C) Subject NOI/SF	(D) Difference NOI/SF	(E) Multiple (C ÷ B)	(F) Adjusted SP/SF (A × E)
1	$87.65	$7.89	$8.42	$0.53	1.07	$93.79
2	$105.58	$9.71	$8.42	($1.29)	.87	$91.85
3	$77.69	$6.82	$8.42	$1.60	1.23	$95.56
4	$90.80	$8.54	$8.42	($0.12)	.99	$89.89
5	$85.43	$7.70	$8.42	$0.72	1.09	$93.12
6	$74.35	$7.39	$8.42	$1.03	1.14	$84.76

that report norms for a range of properties, not just particularly successful or unsuccessful projects.

Kinnard argues that the economic life of a shopping center is probably only about 10 to 15 years because of the frequent modernizing they require—especially in competitive, overbuilt markets. Appraisers can attempt to make subjective adjustments for variations in economic lives in sales comparison. When adjustments have been made based on a total life of 40 or 50 years, they have been relatively small and sometimes erroneous.[8]

In the past sales of department stores only, separate from shopping centers, have been hard to find. Since 1983 they have become more common, perhaps due to leveraged buyouts and the restructuring of the retail industry. When these stores have sold the reported prices per square foot have been lower than the replacement cost of the buildings. It has been argued, however, that such transactions reflect a sale of only part of the bundle of rights in the property because part has been transferred through the operating agreement. (See the discussion of site valuation that follows.)

In comparing the sale prices of anchor stores, appraisers should be alert for any market evidence of price or performance differences between freestanding anchor buildings and in-line anchors. An in-line store is contiguous with its neighbors, so it might benefit from greater passing foot traffic. Alternatively, it could suffer from insufficient parking. Perhaps a

8. Kinnard.

comparison indicating that the stores have similar sales per square foot would convince a reader of the report that they are sufficiently comparable. In most cases making an adjustment for who the anchor is will present more of a challenge than an adjustment for the style of construction.

Financing

The value of an asset's cash flow stream to an investor is influenced by the financing structure of the asset. When appraising an existing shopping center, the appraiser should examine the mortgage documents to identify and analyze any participation or kicker clauses in the mortgages. The mortgage may call for annual payments to be made out of the minimum or percentage rents, in which case the owner might find it strategic to trade off those minimum rent payments in favor of greater tenant contributions to common area maintenance charges. A due-on-sale clause in a mortgage may limit property value in a sale that could otherwise be facilitated by a loan assumption. A closed period, during which the loan may not be prepaid, may deprive the owner of a source of cash flows from refinancing. Differences in financing can require adjustments in all three approaches to value.

Ground leases are not uncommon in the financial structure of shopping centers. When a center occupies leased land, it is important to determine whether the ground lease includes a purchase option and to analyze the price involved. In one market where typical ground lessors enjoyed a participation in net cash flow, the ground lessor was entitled to share the profits by collecting additional rent from operations set at 50% of the net operating income before depreciation and debt service. It is important to analyze how investors receive their payments from the mall enterprise.

Understanding the role of financing in the sales comparison approach is complicated by the private nature of improved property sales. Sometimes it is unclear whether a purchase was an arm's-length sale or merely a transaction such as a sale-leaseback used to accomplish a financing objective. Complicated questions may arise. Has the seller retained any contingent interest in the operating income of the center? What relationship might have been structured? Is there a guarantee by the seller? If the sale is of a partial interest, did the purchaser get the depreciation deductions?

Was any other property exchanged in the transaction? Was the transaction a forced sale to pay off acquisition debt or to accomplish some business retailing objective other than investment?

The Cost Approach

The cost approach may establish an effective upper limit for the market value of a shopping center property. To apply the approach the appraiser estimates the reproduction (or replacement) cost of the improvements minus accumulated depreciation plus the market value of the land as a site for that type of center.

If the appraiser chooses to estimate reproduction cost, the precise materials, workmanship, and design of the structure must be considered to estimate the cost of constructing an exact replica. All items of functional obsolescence built into the model are treated as depreciation. If replacement cost is sought, a cost service manual is used to estimate construction costs for a replacement structure, which may employ newer materials or design elements.

The cost approach, based on reproduction or replacement cost, is often the primary basis for the assessed values estimated by tax assessors. Assessors find the income approach too dependent on the capitalization rate selected and they usually do not have the resources to search for comparable sales outside the local jurisdiction.[9]

Some courts have determined that shopping centers are unique, specialized properties and that in some cases the cost approach is preferred because no comparable sales are available in the tax jurisdiction.[10] The Appraisal Institute prescribes the cost approach for a limited market property, . . . a property that has relatively few potential buyers at a particular time."[11] (Some of the conditions of this definition may not seem to fit shopping center anchor department stores, but the courts have accepted the argument. The Beebe article cited includes extensive legal references.) Application of the cost approach would result in more uniform property

---

9. Robert L. Beebe, "The Assessor and the Shopping Center: Valuation Issues and Problems," a paper presented at the International Association of Assessing Officers Eighth Annual Legal Seminar, San Francisco, October 1988.

10. Ibid.

11. Appraisal Institute, *The Appraisal of Real Estate*, 10th ed. (Chicago: Appraisal Institute, 1992), 21.

value estimates among different retailers, which has concerned some judges. It also removes going-concern or business value, but poses special problems in estimating functional obsolescence for the store building and, perhaps, the retailer's entrepreneurial profit.

Not all professional appraisers use the cost approach in appraising shopping centers. Many appraisers reach an understanding with the client that the approach is not warranted and so it is omitted. Other appraisers include it routinely. Two reasons for estimating site value are to allocate a depreciation basis to the improvements and to establish replacement costs for insurance purposes.

According to Kinnard, reproduction and replacement costs must include all agents of production, including the developer's overhead and profit, but not the overhead and profit that the manager or entrepreneur receives for creating the retailing enterprise. (Business enterprise value, or going-concern value, as separate from real estate value is discussed later.) The cost estimate includes both hard and soft costs. It must also include the time-related costs of completing the construction process—e.g, construction interest (or a reserve), property taxes, and insurance.

Some developers think that in smaller commercial developments their only profit is in the land and that a purpose for the project, once they have recovered the costs of constructing the improvements, is to support and retain their labor force. Appraisers have estimated entrepreneurial profit in various ways—i.e., as a function of the land value, the improvements cost, or the whole package. Few studies reveal profit margins on development projects of any kind. An appraiser might gain insight into this cost component by conducting interviews in the submarket of the subject property. Local builders and developers should be contacted to verify the cost estimates available from popular cost estimating services.

Most appraisers place little reliance on the cost approach because they believe that investors and lenders do not employ it. Land values are often difficult to estimate because few, if any, sales of comparable tracts can be found, especially within the small jurisdiction of a property tax assessor. When comparable transactions are found, extensive adjustments must be made for the date of sale, topography, shape, demography, traffic counts, developability, legal interest, terms, and timing of the sale. An economic feasibility study of all the comparables may be indicated to ensure similar highest and best uses. Further complications arise as the appraiser considers how to handle the sale of a nearby site sold for use as a service station based on the traffic to be generated by the subject shopping center. The utility of a site can be influenced by many factors besides differences in use, including size, topography, and other factors uncovered in standard site analysis.

Kinnard distinguishes between the cost of producing space, which is real estate, and the cost of producing income, which presumably is business income, not part of the real estate value.[12] Business income would include leasing expenses. He also warns against double charging — i.e., considering the costs for interior tenant improvements and then charging the property with a tenant improvement allowance. Kinnard questions the practice of including leasing expenses, selling expenses, and absorption expenses in the total reproduction or replacement costs, pointing out that a center that takes longer than average to lease up is not, as a result, more valuable. Some appraisers estimate increased expenditures of this type and then further adjust for them as external obsolescence in estimating depreciation in the cost approach.

Appraisers need to decide how to treat the special kinds of depreciation and obsolescence found in shopping centers. For example, if the anchor tenant departs or just stops operating while continuing to pay rent, what is likely to happen to the sales of other mall tenants? How will the percentage rents paid to the center be affected? Can leases be canceled? How many lease payment obligations will drop to percentage rentals only? Such a situation probably creates either curable or incurable functional obsolescence, but the current literature does not address these problems.

There are several methods for estimating accrued depreciation in the cost approach. The most detailed is the breakdown method in which deficiencies in the observed condition of the property are divided into three major categories: physical deterioration, functional obsolescence, and external obsolescence. The appraiser considers sources of value loss in each category. Some examples follow.

---

12. Kinnard.

- Physical deterioration is caused by deferred repairs and the normal aging of building components.

- Functional obsolescence may occur if some leases have escape clauses for tenants while comparable sales do not, or if the center has a poor tenant mix. If going-concern value is recognized, these items would be associated with this value, not with the value of the real estate. Some could argue that these items represent external obsolescence. Other examples of functional obsolescence include inappropriate space sizes or configurations, adverse tenant combinations, and failed sign control.

- External obsolescence can result from a loss of visibility due to off-site development or road changes or the development of more space than can be supported by the trade areas purchasing power or the number of potential retail tenants.

The treatment of these items may vary depending on how the appraiser chooses to handle going-concern or business value.

Economic Lives

Although the physical improvements of a shopping center may last for half a century, their economic lives are probably much shorter—perhaps only 15 years considering how often centers are modernized to keep them competitive. This short economic life is reflected in the three approaches to value as follows:

- In considering capital recovery rates in developing overall capitalization rates in the income approach

- In estimating replacement allowances in net operating income estimates

- In estimating age-life-based accumulated depreciation

- In adjusting the prices of comparable properties that exhibit different effective ages. When excessive economic lives are used in valuations, the indicated value of the real estate may be overstated.

Figure 6.2 shows how an appraiser might develop an estimate of reproduction cost and then adjust it for depreciation. If desired, further detail can be shown such as the square foot cost components of the anchor store and retail shops.

The appraiser must make clear which estate is being appraised in each of the approaches. For example, the estimate of functional obsolescence in Figure 6.2 may reflect the detrimental effect of below-market leases on the leased fee estate. Greater detail could be provided to support the estimate and help support any adjustments for this feature made in another approach.

Valuation of Land and Site

Neither the cost approach nor its associated land value estimate is popular with appraisers. Many of the estimates required in the approach are difficult to make and usually little emphasis is placed on the cost approach in deriving a final indication of value. The site value estimate, however, may have other uses—e.g., to support the highest and best use analysis, to verify the tax assessor's value allocation, or to establish a basis for allocating depreciation under federal income tax law. The land value estimate can also help an appraiser determine if it would be feasible for a competitor to develop a rival center or if the subject center contains business value (see Chapter 9). Analyzing land value estimates and construction costs can reveal the likely increase in competition. These considerations may be lost if no cost approach valuation is attempted.

Six techniques can be used to value sites: sales comparison, allocation, extraction, subdivision development, land residual, and ground rent capitalization.[13] The sales comparison approach seems to be the preferred method of estimating shopping center site value. A land sales adjustment grid is presented in Figure 6.3. A land residual approach is useful in feasibility and highest and best use analyses. Moreover, ground rents can sometimes be used to calculate the present value of an income stream.

Several problems arise in valuing a site through sales comparison. One problem is that the value of a large shopping center site increases

---

13. Appraisal Institute, *The Appraisal of Real Estate*, 10th
    ed. (Chicago: Appraisal Institute, 1992), 302.

Figure 6.2 **Sample Format for Reporting a Cost Approach Estimate**

The value of the shopping center estimated by the cost approach is set forth below.

Reproduction Cost

Direct costs
Building costs:

Anchor stores – 43,450 sq. ft.	@	$30.00/sq. ft.	$1,303,500
Retail shops – 46,316 sq. ft.	@	$28.00/sq. ft.	1,296,848
Restaurant – 3,130 sq. ft.	@	$50.00/sq. ft.	156,500
92,896 sq. ft.			

Total building costs $2,756,848

Site improvement costs:
 Includes grading, drainage, clearing, fill and compaction,
 paving, curbs and sidewalks, site lighting,
 irrigation, and landscaping

Total site improvement costs	900,000
Total direct costs	$3,656,848

Indirect costs

 Includes costs of architectural, engineering, and legal
 services; points, interest reserve, title, and permits; appraisal,
 leasing and marketing; and developer's overhead & supervision

Total indirect costs	$1,000,000
Reproduction cost–improvements	$4,656,848
Plus: entrepreneurial profit @ 35%	$1,629,897
Total reproduction cost	$6,286,745
Rounded	$6,300,000
	$67.82/sq. ft.

The estimated value after an allowance for accrued depreciation is deducted is shown below.

Total reproduction cost of the improvements		$6,300,000
Less accrued depreciation:		
Physical deterioration	$315,000	
Functional obsolescence	$400,000	
Total accrued depreciation		$ 715,000
Depreciated value of the improvements		$5,585,000
Plus site value		$2,200,000
Total indicated value		$7,785,000
Rounded		$7,800,000

Figure 6.3 **Comparable Land Sales Adjustment Grid**

	Subject	Sale 1	Sale 2
Location	115 W. Burgher Ave. State College Borough West County, PA	317 N. Wade St. Halseth Township West County, PA	Martin Street Halseth Township West County, PA
Grantor		Tunes	Taylor
Grantee		Hardcourt Associates	Tennis Associates
Consideration		$1,310,000	$497,400
Date	04/90	05/87	03/89
Land area	7.66 acres	15.07 acres	3.26 acres
Sale price/acre		$86,928	$152,577
Time adjustment		+ 6%	+ 2%
Time adjusted price/acre		$92,144	$155,629
Elements of Comparison			
Location	Good	Superior –5%	Inferior + 15%
Size	7.66 acres	Inferior + 20%	Superior –35%
Topography/utility	Level/good	Inferior + 20%	Similar
Utilities	All public	All public	All public
Zoning	Commercial	Commercial	Commercial
Access	Good	Similar	Inferior + 5%
Net adjustments		+ 35%	–15%
Value indications		$124,394	$132,285

during the development period. Therefore, in selecting comparable sales, the appraiser must pay attention to timing. When it becomes clear that the zoning changes required for development will be obtainable, the land appreciates; its value rises further when anchor tenant commitments are secured; still more value is added as the leasing program shows that the center is likely to be a success. If the sales of apparently comparable sites occurred at different points in their development cycles, their prices will reflect different values and some adjustment should be attempted. A time adjustment can sometimes be made based on the value growth of the site through the development process.

In the simplest applications, appraisers infer land value from sale comparables based on their sale prices per square foot of building area, adjusted for pad size. In selecting sales for analysis, an appraiser can follow two procedures: 1) consider *all* land sales within the vicinity regardless of their present use because the zoning can often be changed to accommodate a retail use after the sale, or 2) investigate sales of known shopping center sites in comparable neighborhoods.

Once sales are selected, their verified prices must be adjusted, especially if the sales were transacted at different stages in the development process. The data available are generally not sufficient for paired data analysis or discrete percentage adjustments made in the traditional way.

One seasoned professional employs personal judgment (Would I buy this?) and a simple data grid, which is filed with the working papers but not included in the report.[14] To develop a grid, comparable sales are listed down the side of a page and key attributes that distinguish the utility of alternative sites are listed across the top (see Figure 6.4). For land sales these attributes might include the time elapsed since the sale, utilities, location, traffic count, the commitment of an anchor, some demographic considerations, topography, and other factors considered important by the market participants interviewed. Then an arrow is drawn in each cell of the grid to indicate whether that transaction price should be adjusted up or down to better resemble the subject. At the right end of each line of data a final up or down arrow is drawn to indicate the net effect on that sale. No effort is made to specify quantitative adjustments. The results of the grid are posted on a scatter diagram of the unadjusted unit prices of the comparable sales, which are arrayed from left to right in descending order of comparability so that the pattern flares out. After half a dozen sales are plotted, a level emerges on the chart and the appraiser can discern the level or range of adjusted price indications for the subject.

Excess land is identified and segregated so that an appropriate economic unit of land is appraised. Depending on the client's needs, the excess land may be appraised too. To be considered excess land, a parcel must be unnecessary to the present use and usable or salable in light of its

---

14. The adjustment system works for land sales, improved sales, rent comparables, and expense comparables.

Figure 6.4 **Sample Sales Adjustment Grid**							
	Time	Utilities	Access	Traffic Count	Anchor Commitments	Demographics	Subjective Net Effect
Sale 1	↑	—	↓	↑	↑	↓	↑
Sale 2	↑	↓	—	↑	↑	↓	↑
Sale 3	↑	—	↑	↑	—	↓	↑

Note: Up arrows mean subject is better; down arrows mean the comparable sale is better. Length of arrows indicates relative size of adjustments.

shape, topography, and other dimensions. If it cannot be used or sold, it is not excess. The highest and best use and unit land value selected for the subject property are presumed to be equally applicable to the excess land, but some discussion may be warranted. One interesting question that arises in connection with excess land is whether the associated carrying costs (for taxes and maintenance) should be treated as nonoperating expenses.

When pads are involved, some appraisers interview pad buyers to determine their purchasing criteria. Other appraisers may be familiar with this market and have sufficient data in their files. Often pad buyers' criteria are openly known; they have certain demographic target profiles and make purchases in a pre-set price range.

The Dynamics of Outparcels

Outparcels are generally those parts of the shopping center site that lie at its periphery and along major traffic thoroughfares.[15] Outparcels are popular locations for banks, fast-food restaurants, and auto service stores. Their uses and economic structuring are quite different from those of the in-line

15. This section is based on William P. Crawford, "Out-Parcel Leasing Strategies: Part of Total Financing Picture" from *ANDREWSREPORT*, 1991, vol. 5, no. 3, pages 1 & 3. Crawford is manager of peripheral development for Melvin Simon & Associates, Indianapolis, the fifth largest firm in open center development, according to *Monitor's* 1991 ranking.

space within the mall. Sometimes they produce the only profit realized by the developer of the mall. Usually they have a great impact on the image, visibility, and drawing power of the shopping center.

Outparcels become feasible when mall development is completed and its operations commence; thus they benefit from its agglomeration economics. Because they are used by a different class of tenant and are the subject of transactions made after the mall site is acquired, they make poor comparables for the land within the mall or the anchor pads.

When appraising outparcels it is important to understand the nature of their probable uses and the complex ways in which these deals are structured. Popular techniques for structuring outparcel deals include unsubordinated ground leases, outright sales, and build-to-suit options. Each of these alternatives is examined below.

Some developers use an unsubordinated ground lease to put an outparcel into production. This method is preferred because, when the outparcel site is part of the original larger mall site acquisition, the developers' investment in the site is less. With a ground lease the developer retains ownership of the site while its value is enhanced by the tenant who improves it and constructs a building. At the end of the lease term all the improvements can revert to the owner. Until then, the manner in which the site is used can be substantially controlled by lease covenants.

This arrangement makes it difficult to finance the improvements. The lease is unsubordinated, so the lender who makes the tenant's improvement loan must rely on the value of the building alone. Because it is so difficult to finance the construction of improvements under these conditions, these deals are only made by very strong national restaurant chains, financial institutions, and a few retailers who are able to fund their improvements on their own. In the words of one developer,

> . . . an unsubordinated ground lease usually offers the developer the best of all worlds: minimal investment by the developer; enhanced value to the property; the ability to borrow against the financial strength of the tenant; and the ultimate recapture of an improved property.[16]

---

16. Ibid.

Structuring a ground lease that is subordinated to the user's construction lender is possible, but unlikely. Normally these outparcels are used as additional security for the lien on the shopping center and the shopping center lender probably will not be willing to subordinate its lien.

Selling the outparcels may appeal to a developer because it is simpler than ground leasing and can quickly raise equity capital. Shopping center development generates substantial appreciation in outparcels over their acquisition costs as part of the larger parcel. Purchasing an outparcel is usually more attractive to the user than ground leasing because future occupancy costs can be controlled and financing the improvements is simplified. The sales contract can contain agreements and operating restrictions that control the appearance and use of the outparcel after the sale. In analyzing sales of comparable outparcels for appraisal purposes, the analyst should procure sales contracts and examine any restrictions they contain.

When a build-to-suit lease is used, the developer builds or finances the construction of improvements on the outparcel to suit the tenant's needs and then leases the combined land and improvements back to the user. This type of construction is difficult for the developer to finance, and if a loan is secured, the developer will probably have to contribute additional equity capital to complete construction. If the tenant should later default, the developer will be left with a property that may be too specialized to appeal to other users and has no rental income to cover the debt service obligations.

Outparcels were once considered "the icing on the cake" for a shopping center development, but they are now an integral part of the mall and require careful planning by the developer and careful analysis by the appraiser.

The Income Approach

Many appraisers think that the income approach is the most applicable approach to shopping center appraisal. According to one writer,

> The regional shopping center is almost always viewed by owners and potential owners as an investment from which a certain minimum return ought to be realized. Hence the income approach is the one with which the appraiser should be most concerned. Re-

placement and original costs appear to have little or no effect on the marketability of such a project if it has had several years of successful operation; and comparables are usually difficult to identify due to differences in demographic areas, shopping themes, tenant mixes, etc., found in the different centers.[17]

The complexities of the income approach can be intimidating. Each component of a complex income stream must be forecast judiciously and the capitalization rate for each of the income stream components must be selected carefully. Major income approach techniques are explored in detail in the following chapter.

Consistency in the Three Approaches

Items requiring adjustment in one of the approaches should be handled consistently in the other approaches. For example, an oversupplied market that necessitates rental rate concessions may be treated as an item of external obsolescence in the cost approach by capitalizing the loss in *NOI*. This market obsolescence can be addressed in the income capitalization approach by specifying the actual receipts or landlord outlays in a discounted cash flow (DCF) analysis or by capitalization of effective rentals in a stabilized income forecast. (A sample DCF analysis appears in Chapter 8.) If comparable sales transacted in the same market with the same concessions are available, no adjustment may be required. If the subject property is an investment-grade center and its comparables reflect a different market, however, an adjustment should be considered.

In all three approaches, differences between the subject property and the comparable sales should be treated consistently. These differences may relate to a wide array of characteristics including lease differences, physical condition, location, trade area demographics, shopping center design, and tenant mix.

---

17. Robert R. Trippi and Robert J. Spiegel, "Computer Assisted Appraisal of the Regional Shopping Mall," *The Real Estate Appraiser and Analyst* (September/October 1978), 24.

Preparing a Credible Report

An appraisal report may be divided into four main sections: the introduction, the premises of the appraisal, the presentation of data, and the analysis of data and conclusions. The introduction will contain a table of contents, the certification of value, and a letter of transmittal. The second section, the premises of the appraisal, states the assumptions and limiting conditions, definition of value, property rights appraised, and purpose of the analysis; it also specifies whether the value estimate is in terms of cash, terms equivalent to cash, or other precisely defined terms. The third section presents legal, economic, geographic, and demographic data and other descriptive information, which will form the basis for the appraiser's adjustments and conclusions. The appraiser must ensure that the circumstances described here are consistent with the analysis and conclusions that follow. The fourth and most important section is the valuation analysis, which presents the appraiser's reasoning and conclusions. This section must describe the appraiser's analysis clearly and allow the reader to trace the reasoning that leads to the conclusions. An addenda can be provided for supporting information including legal descriptions, statistical data, lease summaries, and background operating information.[18]

A number of general books and seminars are available to help appraisers improve their writing technique. Some of these publications are listed in the bibliography along with specific appraisal-oriented style guides.[19]

A good appraisal report should inform the reader about the property type and its special economic, investment, and operational characteristics. Given the complex nature of shopping centers and the sophistication of the investors and lenders attracted to this property type, many appraisers may be at a disadvantage. Appraisers affiliated with large, well-connected firms are better equipped to obtain and apply the data required for reliable shopping center valuations. They are often parts of teams that include other experts such as:

---

18. Appraisal Institute, *The Appraisal of Real Estate*, 10th ed. (Chicago: Appraisal Institute, 1992), 569-581.

19. See John R. White, "Some Thoughts on Lexicon and Syntax," *The Appraisal Journal* (July 1989), 419-421

and William P. Pardue, Jr., "Writing Effective Appraisal Reports," *The Appraisal Journal* (January 1990), 16-22.

- Engineers who can recognize the difference between high cost-to-build systems and high-maintenance systems (e.g., ammonia cooling systems vs. Freon)
- Construction experts who have built additions to owned centers (e.g., decked parking) and have reliable, in-house cost records
- Affiliated commercial brokers who sell and lease space and have client data and proposal packages with property histories and other hard-to-get information.

The Uniform Standards of Professional Appraisal Practice require that appraisers divulge their level of expertise and experience in accepting an assignment. If they find themselves to be underqualified, they must acquire the necessary skills or seek assistance from a qualified expert.

Ethical considerations are involved in the use of data. Within a large real estate firm, clients' confidences must be preserved. For example, a client's lease terms and expiration date might be useful to the commercial leasing division of a firm, but the appraiser must not share it. Even within the appraiser's own professional network, the plans, motivations, and problems of clients cannot be discussed.

Summary

The income approach to value is generally preferred in appraising large properties with complicated income streams and reversion benefits. Nevertheless, the sales comparison and cost approaches should not be dismissed. Since the objective of the appraiser is to simulate the thinking of potential investors, these two approaches should be used if they reflect market behavior. For example, the difficulty of estimating adjustments to comparable sales should not be used as a basis for dismissing these comparables if market investigation reveals some common rules of thumb in shopping center purchases. Such rules of thumb might focus on sale prices expressed in dollars per square foot or as a multiple of a retailer's average sales per square foot. Furthermore, if investors consider the acquisition cost of land in relation to the construction cost of a rival center, this is a legitimate avenue of investigation for the appraiser of the subject property.

The Gallery, Philadelphia   *J. Nettis / H. Armstrong Roberts*

Chapter Seven

PREPARING INCOME FORECASTS FOR SHOPPING CENTERS

Introduction

Estimating market value for a shopping center with the income capitalization approach is a two-part process. The appraiser first prepares an estimate of the returns from the asset and then selects a method for capitalizing these benefits into a value estimate. This chapter will discuss how benefits are forecast and the next chapter will review alternative capitalization techniques.

The extent of detail required in the benefits forecast depends on the capitalization method to be employed; similarly, the method of capitalization selected may depend on the benefits forecast. Appraisers can choose from a variety of direct and yield capitalization techniques, but the most popular are

- Direct capitalization of a stabilized net operating income (or balance) with an overall capitalization rate
- Discounted cash flow (DCF) analysis with specified yearly cash flows (usually before taxes) and a reversion estimate, both converted to present value with a discount or target yield rate.

Direct capitalization of stabilized income is employed in most assignments to appraise smaller centers. Often DCF analysis is used as a check of reasonableness. Investors and lenders focusing on larger centers will expect a DCF analysis, and some specify the software to be used.

Since a shopping center has income streams derived from contractual leases with a number of retailer tenants, the preferred approach is to analyze the leases of the anchors and other mall tenants and forecast the likely components of the income stream over a projected holding period. The holding period used should reflect the expected holding periods of actual investors in that specific property type in that submarket. An appraiser valuing a smaller center will probably read all the leases; in larger assignments all the anchor leases will be read, a representative sample of the mall store or shop leases will be reviewed, and abstracts of the rest will likely be studied. The extent of the appraisers review of the leases should be agreed upon with the client and specifically stated in the appraisal report.

The various components of a shopping center's income stream include base rents, extra rents accruing from percentage of sales clauses, expense recoveries, revenue from other services provided by the center operator, and miscellaneous income. The terms of typical lease contracts will be discussed and methods of treatment will be suggested.

Because the components of the income stream will vary in their reliability and hence their perceived risk, some experts suggest they be capitalized at appropriate, risk-adjusted discount rates. Selecting these rates and processing income forecasts will be discussed in a subsequent section, which focuses on the use of computer simulation models.

To review the descriptive and strategic elements of lease agreements, many appraisers use a form, which guides them through the abstracting and analysis of the lease. (Samples of two lease abstracting forms are provided in the appendix.) Some appraisers find that leases vary so much that use of a form is not feasible; in older centers with substantial retenanting and possibly several owners or managers, considerable time may be required to do a proper analysis.

Important Lease Clauses[1]

The information and clauses appraisers will encounter in shopping center leases include

1. Dates and parties to the lease
2. Identification of premises
3. Term of lease
4. Location
5. Rental payment
6. Repairs clause
7. Alterations clause
8. Insurance clause
9. Eminent domain clause
10. Tenant's right to assign or sublet
11. Fixtures clause
12. Destruction clause
13. Estoppel clause
14. Default clause
15. Use and exclusive use clauses

Date and parties

The date of the lease, the parties to it, and their addresses will be listed. The landlord is the lessor and the tenant is the lessee.

Identification of premises

The premises will be identified to include all land, buildings, fixtures, equipment, and personalty to be used by the tenant.

Term of lease

The time period or term covered by the lease will be specified, including both the initial term and any renewal options. In a typical shopping center,

---

1. Much of the following discussion is derived from Jack P. Friedman, Waldo Born, and Arthur L. Wright, *Develop-ing and Managing a Freestanding Store* (College Station: Real Estate Center, Texas A&M University).

the initial term may be four or five years or as long as 50 years or more for an anchor. Some leases provide for multiple renewal terms. Sometimes the beginning of the lease is not known because construction has not been completed; the lease may take effect when the occupancy permit is given, when the retailer opens for business, or at the time of some other contingent event.

An important development in retailing is the use of kick-out clauses in leases. Appraisers must understand the impact of such clauses. A kick-out clause allows a retailer to cancel a long-term lease of five or 10 years after one, two, or three years if sales have not reached a specified level. What might appear to be a long-term lease to an appraiser forecasting incomes may really be a short-term lease with an option to renew.[2] In a competitive market a clever tenant may bargain for an unrealistically low threshold, which gives him the option to leave at any time. The developer may agree to this in desperation, hoping to achieve a specified occupancy level so the lender will disburse funds or an institution will purchase the center. The lender or buyer may accept the arrangement through carelessness or be under pressure to employ funds.

A variant of a kick-out clause allows the tenant to cancel its lease if the landlord is unable to replace a departing anchor tenant within a specified period of time.

Location

When the store property to be leased has not yet been constructed, the tenant provides the center owner with its specifications and dimensions. Site improvements such as parking facilities, walkways, driveways, and sidewalks may be described. The lease usually specifies that the construction will comply with zoning regulations, building codes, and insurance requirements, and will be free of encumbrances and liens (unless the parties have agreed otherwise). An "act of God" clause allows extra time for construction when extraordinary difficulties arise that the landlord cannot control; it may serve as an escape clause for the tenant if construction is not begun or completed by a specified date.

2. Howard C. Gelbtuch, "Shopping Centers Are A Business Too," *The Appraisal Journal* (January 1989), 57.

Rental payment

The payment of rents is described in substantial detail, beginning with the base rent which is normally payable at the beginning of each month. The lease may call for additional rental payments based on increases in the Consumer Price Index (CPI), a percentage of tenant sales above a breakpoint, and a share of operating expenses. The terms *gross lease* and *net lease* describe who pays operating expenses. Net leases generally mean the tenant pays some or all of the operating expenses; the phrase *net-net* (or *net-net-net*) indicates that the tenant pays property taxes and insurance (or property taxes, insurance, and maintenance). *Gross lease* describes a contract in which the landlord pays the operating expenses. A stop clause sets an upper limit on the expenses to be paid by the landlord, with the tenant paying amounts above that ceiling.

Many expenses are incurred by a shopping center operator. The lease should address each expense individually, specifying how it is paid, by whom, and what form of evidence will be required to prove that payment was made.

A cost-of-living clause entitles the landlord to additional rent based on increases in a particular cost-of-living index. The lease should clearly identify the index to be used, its source, and the frequency of adjustments. Sometimes a lease will provide for a partial increase, such as 50% of the change in the CPI. A cost-of-living index adjustment is commonly used to protect the purchasing power of the owner's rental income from being eroded by inflation. Such a clause may be used in conjunction with other clauses that increase the rent.

A percentage rent clause in a lease obligates the tenant to pay additional rent to the landlord calculated as a percentage of its gross sales, perhaps in excess of a breakpoint or specified threshold level. This clause allows the landlord to share in the increasing economic productivity of his underlying fee estate. A lease may provide that the landlord is entitled to rent equal to the base amount or a percentage of sales, whichever is greater. In a variable scale lease, the percentage rate changes with the amount of sales—e.g., the percentage rate might decline as higher levels of sales are reached. When the lease is renewed, a new breakpoint is calculated.

Percentage rates often differ among retailers, depending on their profit margins on sales and their inventory turnover ratios as well as the type of shopping center. Reference tables are available from retailing information sources such as the International Council of Shopping Centers and the Urban Land Institute.[3] Of course, percentage of sales clauses give the operator an incentive to maintain the competitive status of the shopping center. The reporting obligations of the tenant are likely to be discussed in the lease contract.

Ad valorem property tax stop clauses pass real estate tax increases above a certain level on to the tenant. The landlord normally pays the base year amount and the tenant pays amounts in excess of the stop amount. The base amount is adjusted at the time of renewal, typically to include the amounts recently paid in excess of the stop amount.

A landlord burden clause allows an anchor tenant a lower stop for common area maintenance (CAM) expenses, with a greater burden shifted to either other mall tenants, which is typical, or to the owner. Frequently sought-after anchor tenants dictate the ceiling. The remaining CAM may be allocated among the non-anchor tenants. This greater burden may be expressed so subtly in the mall tenants leases that they do not realize the impact. This clause is not well known in some markets and its impact varies according to how astute the mall tenants and their agents are.

Repairs clause

The repairs clause sets responsibility for maintenance, repairs, alterations, replacements, and improvements. The assignment of responsibilities may be a matter of custom in the submarket. The landlord is typically obligated to correct problems in the original construction; heating, ventilation, and air-conditioning systems; and major mechanical systems as well as in the common areas. The lease should establish whether the tenant has rights of offset—i.e., the right to reduce regular rental obligations for payments made for repairs that the landlord has failed to provide.

---

3. See Section 8B of *Dollars & Cents of Shopping Centers, 1990*, published by the Urban Land Institute and the International Council of Shopping Centers.

Alterations clause

The alterations clause sets forth the tenant's obligation to get the land-lord's permission before making any alterations. Usually the landlord must approve the plans and the tenant must obtain insurance and accept responsibility for any claims or liens that may arise.

Insurance clause

The insurance clause requires the tenant to protect the landlord from claims during the lease term. Both liability and hazard insurance must be obtained. Such a clause sets the minimum amount of coverage to be main-tained by the tenant and normally specifies how the tenant can prove com-pliance. Rental insurance may be required, made payable to the landlord, the tenant, or the mortgagee, to ensure a continuous rent stream. Rental insurance can cover both the rental and real estate taxes so that both the tenant and the landlord are protected. The tenant will be able to meet his obligations even if the space is not usable. The landlord will need to main-tain his income source since most leases contain a clause excusing the ten-ant from occupancy and rent obligations if damage to the space exceeds a specified limit.

Eminent domain clause

The eminent domain clause holds that if a substantial portion of the build-ing or parking is taken in eminent domain proceedings, the lease may be terminated.

Tenant's right to assign or sublet

A clause requiring the landlord's approval for assignment or subletting protects the operator's tenant mix and credit risks. Under such a clause, the original tenant is likely to be liable for any obligations.

Tenants in many types of business have begun to realize that they are also in the real estate business. They have found that they can profit by surrendering an advantageous lease after rental rates have risen. This op-tion was a factor in some of the consolidations and takeovers among retail-ers in the 1980s. In their lease negotiations, shopping center operators should be prepared to indicate under what conditions they will consent to lease clauses permitting sublet and assignment. It is common for land-lords to grant liberal clauses in connection with traditional mergers, con-solidations, and reorganizations, but they are likely to be less generous in cases of takeover or leveraged buyouts. A shopping center operator who has a reputation for being especially uncooperative with regard to assign-ments and subleases can affect the center's ability to attract new tenants. This factor can only be evaluated by an analyst who understands the atti-tudes prevalent in the submarket.[4]

Landlords may be concerned about the financial ability of a takeover company, which may have assumed excessive debt in the acquisition. On the other hand, retailers need the ability to expand to new store locations or sell old ones as their retailing or marketing strategies evolve. A reason-able compromise might involve some type of test to ensure the financial strength of the new tenant. Landlords may have legitimate reservations about the proposed tenant's character and integrity, the impact of the new tenant on the tenant mix, or the new store's draw on the center's services or amenities. Many leases contain a clause obligating the landlord not to withhold consent for subletting or assignments on unreasonable grounds. This type of clause has increasingly been interpreted by courts in favor of the tenant's interest.

Fixtures clause

A fixtures clause establishes the tenant's right to install fixtures, but only after approval by the landlord to ensure that they are of sufficient quality and character.

Destruction clause

A destruction clause allows either the landlord or the tenant to terminate the lease upon the total or partial destruction of the premises. In the case of partial destruction, the landlord may be allowed to rebuild.

---

4. What tenants cannot get through negotiations they may gain through changing judicial attitudes. See Jeffrey H. Newman, "Rights of Assignments and Subletting; Keys That Unlock Future Value," *Real Estate Review* (Spring 1989), 27-31.

Estoppel clause

An estoppel clause in a lease obligates the tenant to sign a certificate testifying to certain conditions or stating that obligations are being performed. This is usually intended for the benefit of a potential purchaser or lender and is not generally of concern to the appraiser.

Default clause

Default clauses list various types of tenant defaults, such as late rent payment, bankruptcy, or failure to operate on the premises. Termination of the tenant's occupancy rights by the landlord may result from one of these defaults.

Use and exclusive use clauses

A landlord will attempt to control the shopping center's tenant mix through a use clause, which prevents the tenant from putting the leased premises to any use other than the permitted use. Tenants often attempt to craft exclusive use clauses which grant them some degree of monopoly. An exclusive use clause prohibits the landlord from leasing space in the shopping center to competitors. The appraiser should be sensitive to these lease clauses and attempt to identify potential causes of friction. A landlord may inadvertently make conflicting promises to different tenants.[5]

For example, a prospective tenant in the fast-food business may seek an exclusive use clause for a particular line of food. The landlord knows that if such a request is granted, exceptions must be established for other restaurants and fast-food tenants in the center. It is possible, however, for the landlord to overlook a non-restaurant tenant such as a supermarket which may have a very broad use clause entitling it to sell the same type of food.

In general, department stores and supermarkets may always be exceptions to the exclusive uses granted to specialty retailers. A desirable lease would preserve the landlord's flexibility by including a clause that grants a

5. Robert A. Silverman, ''Pitfalls in Shopping Center Use and Exclusive Use Clauses,'' *Real Estate Review* (Summer 1990), 60-62.

tenant exclusive use for a type of operation, not for the sale of a particular product.

Vague words and imprecise language can cause problems for a landlord. Leases with use clauses that permit the sale of specified items and "related" products may generate conflict. Product lines may be broader in the future than they are at the time the lease is negotiated. Consider a clause that states "No other supermarkets will be operated in the shopping center." Under this clause the landlord might be accused of default if another supermarket were to start operating—even if that supermarket tenant had no legal right to operate there and the landlord was attempting to terminate the use. A better clause might read: "The landlord will not enter into a lease that allows the tenant thereunder to operate a supermarket."[6]

A radius clause may complicate future borrowing against the shopping center. Such a clause promises a major tenant that no other property within a specified radius *now* or *hereafter acquired* by the shopping center owner will contain that same use. Prospective lenders may be concerned that, should they have to foreclose on this shopping center, they will be unable to comply with this exclusive use clause. Use of the phrase "hereafter acquired" weakens the lender's control over future uses.

Well-drawn lease clauses that preserve the landlord's flexibility in managing the center's tenant mix may contain generic exceptions to exclusive use clauses for pre-existing tenants, such as: "The landlord will not hereafter execute any lease that permits the tenant to operate as . . ." Desirable exceptions clauses will identify the premises occupied rather than name a particular tenant. In this way a vacated space may be preserved for a new tenant selling the same product or service.

Bankruptcy

Leases frequently state that the lessor will consider a tenant's bankruptcy a default. The bankruptcy code nullifies such a clause and precludes the termination of a lease even though it may contain just such a cancellation clause. Once a business is in bankruptcy and a trustee has been appointed, that trustee has the power to either assume or reject unexpired

---

6. Silverman, 61.

leases. When a tenant has filed for bankruptcy, the trustee of that bankrupted tenant has the power to assign the lease to obtain the benefits of favorable terms provided there are no defaults or that the defaults will be cured. In the case of a shopping center, the court requires that the trustee for the bankrupt tenant must assure the continuing payment of rent, including percentage rent; that any lease assignment will not violate the shopping center restrictions; and that there will be no disruption in the shopping center's tenant mix.[7] The bankruptcy laws also cancel any non-assignability clauses.

When the landlord has filed for bankruptcy, the tenant may choose to terminate the lease and vacate the premises or to remain in occupancy for the remainder of the lease term and offset against the contracted rent the expenses incurred because of the landlord's failure to perform his contractual obligations.

Summary of Lease Analysis

The appraiser should expect to read the lease for each anchor tenant and at least sample leases for mall tenants. Some appraisers read all lease abstracts when they are available. Often the client will instruct the appraiser not to spend time and resources studying each lease. If the appraiser does not read all the leases, this fact should be included in the statement of assumptions and limiting conditions, which is generally found at the end of the report.

Any deviations from normal market practice should be noted by the appraiser, who should also indicate how unusual lease terms might affect the level of risk associated with the income stream to the owner. To do this the appraiser must be familiar with typical leasing terms and practices in the submarket. Significant differences may necessitate adjustments in the sales comparison approach to value and estimates of functional obsolescence in the cost approach.

---

7. William B. Brueggeman, Jeffrey D. Fisher, and Leo D. Stone, *Real Estate Finance*, 8th ed. (Homewood, Ill.: Richard D. Irwin & Company, 1989), 61-62.

The Operating Agreement

The operating agreement describes the rights and responsibilities of the anchor tenants and the shopping center owner or operator. Each anchor usually negotiates its own set of agreements, so the operating agreement is often a bulky, redundant document. Most appraisers discuss this document with the manager and refer to it only if a problem becomes apparent. Generally these agreements have a finite life and some early agreements are now expiring. When such an agreement expires, there may be uncertainty about whether the anchor tenants will renew, especially when they are acquired by a development firm as part of a vertical integration. This uncertainty can remove a property from classification as an investment-grade property by large institutions.

The operating agreement is also called a *reciprocal easement agreement* and is recorded at the local courthouse. The *supplemental agreement*, which contains additional important agreements, is typically not recorded. The supplemental agreement states the price of the anchor's land parcel and any reimbursement to be made for site improvements. Normally security is the responsibility of each of the anchors because they own the land, but a supplemental agreement may stipulate that the developer contract the security services and be reimbursed for this cost plus possibly a management fee.

Income Forecasts

The appraiser reviews the leases in preparation for a forecast of the gross income of the shopping center. This review supplements the appraiser's evaluations of the surrounding trade area and the marketability of the subject center, which have been developed through analysis of comparable rentals in the marketability analysis.

Preparing an income estimate for a shopping center generally follows the traditional appraisal procedure. Potential gross income is estimated to include base rentals, percentage rentals, and tenant reimbursements for expenses. Estimated vacancy and collection losses are subtracted to produce effective gross income. Operating expenses are subtracted to indicate net operating income or, as the Urban Land Institute and International Council of Shopping Centers call it, the *net operating balance*.

The estimate of potential gross income includes all regularly recurring, anticipated income including fixed minimum rent, percentage rent, common area charges, and recoveries. Each income source needs to be examined to ensure it does not reflect a special, nonrecurring event. Non-real estate income such as interest income should be excluded. Rents based on the renewal of leases should be consistent with the plans and expectations of the management and correspond to forecasts of the growth or decline in market rental rates as revealed in comparable property analysis. Payments to the merchants' association are not normally included as part of the gross income to the shopping center.

An appraiser might request the owner's certified or audited financial statements to reconstruct income and expense items. Some analysts find such statements of limited use because they are often calculated on a cash basis and include items like depreciation and debt service that must be adjusted or removed.

Two Methods: Stabilized Income vs. DCF

As mentioned earlier, two popular income capitalization methods are applied to shopping centers — stabilized income analysis and discounted cash flow (DCF) analysis. To apply the first method, the appraiser estimates the economic productivity of the real estate for one representative year of the income forecast and projects increases in income and expenses. It is assumed that the net operating income can, in fact, be estimated in this way. The resulting net operating income, or balance, is capitalized using a rate derived from an analysis of the ratios between the net operating incomes and sale prices of comparable properties. Gaps in the gross income stream, such as those created by concessions, can be converted into effective rental rates and an estimate of allowances for replacements can be used to stabilize these outlays.

When a more elaborate DCF analysis is performed, the appraiser estimates each revenue and expense item for each year of the projection period. Capital replacement expenditures and rent concessions are estimated for the particular period in which they are most likely to occur. Then the cash flows for each year plus the proceeds of resale are discounted to present value with a market-based yield or discount rate. A stabilized income analysis is adequate for smaller shopping centers, but DCF analysis is mandatory for larger ones. Either might be used as a check of reasonableness on the other. The estimates required for the capitalization of stabilized income, which are discussed below, will also be required for DCF analysis.

Stabilized Income

To estimate potential gross income, the appraiser begins with a listing of contract rents based on a review of the leases. Many appraisers include a copy of the current rent roll as an addenda to their report. After contract rents are established, rental rates for the space available for rent or renewal must be estimated based on an analysis of comparable rentals. A format for summarizing the characteristics of each selected rent comparable is presented as Figure 7.1. Additional data and judgments made by the appraiser in the marketability analysis may be useful. This format for rental comparables can be used in both the stabilized income estimate and DCF analysis.

Information on several comparable rental properties can be summarized using the format shown in Table 7.1. This information is used to

---

Figure 7.1 Sample Format for Rental Comparable

Rental No.:	7
Reference:	The Mill Shopping Center
Location:	Northeast corner of J Road and K Road
Construction date:	1985
Gross leasable area:	79,000 square feet
Occupancy:	90% +
Rental rates:	$10.00 to $15.00 per square foot

Comments: This center is anchored by a National Bros. supermarket. Average absorption was approximately 10,000 square feet per month.

Lease conditions: Tenants pay a pro rata share of real estate taxes, insurance, and common area maintenance charges.

Comparison to subject: The subject's anchor draw and access are comparable. The subject's trade area, design, and aesthetic appeal are inferior. The subject would probably have a lower average rental rate.

make and support intuitive judgments about shopping centers that appear to be competitive. The appraiser must first estimate the adjustments for tenant lease arrangements so the sales are on a common level; then adjustments for physical and economic factors can be made.

A complete rent roll for the subject property might be presented in an appendix to the appraisal report. Table 7.2 shows excerpts from such a rent roll to suggest a format for presentation.

An estimate of the most likely market rent rate for the subject property can be inferred from comparable rental properties and from the marketability analysis. The appraiser can estimate market rent either intuitively or by means of a detailed adjustment grid.

Most appraisers would prefer to work with current, audited statements of tenant sales to verify a shopping center's percentage rent capability, but this kind of data is rarely available. Instead they generally trust the data provided by center management. In assignments for institutional lenders and owners, many appraisers are given the center's rent data on precoded computer disks to be used with standard cash flow analysis software.

In analyzing historical income and expense data, it is important to determine whether the center's accounts are recorded on an accrual or cash basis. With this information major outlays can be assigned to appropriate operating periods for statistical purposes.

After rental analysis the appraiser estimates a growth rate for income and expenses, which can serve several purposes. First, it allows the appraiser to check the comparability of comparable sales to be used in direct capitalization. It also provides an input for use in a property yield capitalization model such as $R = Y - \Delta a$. A growth rate is needed to select a K factor when this method is chosen for stabilizing incomes, and growth rates are required in DCF analysis.

The increases in revenue forecast should be consistent with any statements the appraiser has made earlier in the report about the growth or decline in trade area purchasing power. Trade area competition is not always bad. According to the principle of cumulative attraction, which was discussed in Chapter 1, the extra drawing power of competitive properties may increase sales potential at the subject property.

In oversupplied markets it is common practice to grant concessions to some or all of the lessees. The appraiser must investigate these conces-

Table 7.1   Comparable Rental Summary Grid

	Subject	Rental 1	Rental 2	Rental 3
Type of center	Community	Community	Community	Community
Construction	Class C	Class C	Class C	Class C
Age/condition	28 yrs./good	28 yrs./good	35 yrs./avg.	25 yrs./avg.
GLA in sq. ft.	113,697	141,370	160,000	120,000
Percent anchored	83.1%	70.5%	87.5%	75.0%
Anchors	Hills	K-Mart	Shop 'N Save	Value City
	Kroger	G Eagle	Hills	G Eagle
Percent occupied	92.1%	96.3%	94.8%	98.0%
Parking ratio	5.3/1,000	4.7/1,000	4.2/1,000	4.3/1,000
Condition	Good	Good	Average	Average
Avg. tenant credit rating				
(Anchor/local)	A/C	A/C	A/C	A/C
Market conditions	Static	Stable	Static	Static
Upside potential	Limited	Slight	Limited	Limited
Lease arrangements				
Typical lease terms	3-5 years	3-5 years	3-5 years	1-5 years
Annual increases	No	No	No	No
Percentage rents vs. break	Yes	Yes	Yes	Yes
Cost allowance	As Is	As Is	Negotiable	As Is
Real estate taxes	Prorated	Prorated	Base year	Prorated
Insurance	Prorated	Prorated	Base year	None
CAM	Prorated	Prorated	Fixed/.35	Prorated
Management	Landlord	Landlord	Landlord	Landlord
Utilities	Tenant	Tenant	Tenant	Tenant
HVAC	Tenant	Tenant	Tenant	Landlord
Other	None	None	None	None
Base asking rent	$8.75	$9.00	$9.25	$8.75
Lease adjustments				
Lease terms	3-5 years	Similar	Similar	Similar
Annual increases	No	Similar	Similar	Similar
Percentage rent	Yes	Yes	Yes	Yes
Cost allowance	As Is	Similar	Similar	Similar
Taxes	Prorated	Similar	($0.90)	Similar
Insurance	Prorated	Similar	($0.15)	($0.15)
CAM	Prorated	Similar	($0.10)	Similar
Management	Landlord	Similar	Similar	Similar
Utilities	Tenant	Similar	Similar	Similar
HVAC	Tenant	Similar	Similar	Similar
Other	None	Similar	Similar	Similar
Total adjustments for				
Lease terms		0	($1.15)	($0.35)
Rent adjusted for lease terms		$9.00	$8.10	$8.40
Physical adjustments				
Age/condition		Similar	$0.50	$0.25
Location		($0.50)	Similar	$0.25
Center strength		Similar	Similar	Similar
Physical adjustments		($0.50)	$0.50	$0.50
Indicated market rent of subject		$8.50	$8.60	$8.90

Table 7.2 Shoppers Crossing Rent Roll as of August 1991

Tenant/ Bay	Tenant Name	Square Feet	Base Rates	Lease Commencement/ Expiration	Original Term/ Options	Year	Base Annual Rent	Per Sq. Ft.	% Rent Breakpoint/Sq. Ft.	Taxes	Tenant Reimbursement Insur./CAM	Free Rent	Buildout Allowance Per Sq. Ft.
Anchor Tenants													
1	Discounter	114,760	$4.24	1/27/90 1/26/2010	20 years 6-5 yrs.	1-20	$486,582	$4.24	.5% 7th year gross sales	Tenant	Tenant	—	—
						Options	$486,582	$4.24			$0.15 yrs 1-10 $0.20 yrs 11-20 $0.25 option		
2	Grocer	63,070	$5.00	9/1/90 8/31/2010	20 years 5-5 yrs.	1-3	$315,350	$5.00	None	Pro Rata	Pro Rata	—	—
						4-10	$502,668	$7.97					
						11-15	$485,639	$7.70					
						16-20	$529,788	$8.40					
						Options	$529,788	$8.40					
3	Furniture	32,400	$7.25 $7.50 $7.75	5/90 5/2000	10 years 2-5 yrs.	1-10	$234,900	$7.25	None	Pro Rata	Pro Rata	—	$34.00
						Option 1	$243,000	$7.50					
						Option 2	$251,100	$7.75					
Retail Shop Tenants													
A-1 4	Books	1,993	$11.75	11/90 10/93	3 years 1-3 yrs.	1	$23,418	$11.75	None	Pro Rata	Pro Rata	3	$1.69
						2	$24,354	$12.22					
						3	$25,331	$12.71					
						Option 1	$26,347	$13.22					
						Option 2	$27,404	$13.75					
						Option 3	$28,500	$14.30					
A-2 5	Jewelers	1,960	$11.00	10/90 10/93	3 years 1-4 yrs.	1	$21,560	$14.30	None	Pro Rata	Pro Rata	3	$0.00
						2	$22,638	$11.55					
						3	$23,775	$12.13					
						Option 1	$24,970	$12.74					
						Option 2	$26,225	$13.38					
						Option 3	$27,538	$14.05					
						Option 4	$28,910	$14.75					

sions and make one of two adjustments for them. To stabilize rent, rental rates can be referred to as "effective" or "average" rates in periods of reduced rental.[8] Alternatively, when a year-by-year discounted cash flow analysis is developed, the analyst estimates the timing of reduced rental collections for lease renewals. Another marketing tool, the granting of lease options, was popular in the earlier days of shopping centers and has recently returned. Although lease options limit the operator's chance to increase minimum rents, aggressive tenants have been able to bargain for them in soft markets.

When the appraiser selects growth rates for both gross revenues and operating expenses, some thought should be given to their relationship. Although it may be common to forecast growth in revenue and expenses at the same rate, it is likely that operating expenses will grow faster than rents. This is true because as a shopping center ages, operating expenses usually increase with deterioration and an older center cannot compete as well for rents.[9]

Business Income and Expenses

All shopping center income may not represent returns to the real estate. Those that do not must be sorted out. Center operators frequently sell additional services to tenants such as trash collection and utilities. There may be an override on expenses and common area maintenance that results in additional revenue to the operator. Some operators resell electricity, when the state permits this practice. Although the current literature has not settled this issue, these revenues may be treated as business income creating business enterprise value. To illustrate the economic separability of such a profit center, consider a Texas mall owner who sold only his garbage collection business and retained the shopping center. These revenues should probably not be included in reporting real estate income, nor should the associated expenses be considered real estate operating expenses. The

8. New financial calculators such as the Hewlett Packard 19-BII have a function key labeled *Net Uniform Series*, which converts an irregular income stream into its level equivalent. On other financial calculators this can be done by converting a varying cash flow series into a present value and then computing the equivalent level payment (*PMT*) for that present value.

9. Vernon Martin has demonstrated the increase in operating expense ratios for several different kinds of properties, including retail properties, by analyzing selected operating ratios taken from *Dollars & Cents of Shopping Centers*. See Vernon Martin III, "Reviewing Discounted Cash Flow Analysis," *The Appraisal Journal* (January 1990).

revenues and expenses attributed to the real estate, tangible personal property, and intangibles should be carefully separated.

Through empirical research, Jeffrey Fisher and George Lentz discovered that when a shopping center is aggressively managed, base rentals can be increased at the time of lease renewal and previous overage rental payments can generally be incorporated into the new base. Furthermore, tenants who renew leases in a center frequently pay a renewal base rental rate that is more than 20% higher than the base rental rate paid by new tenants.[10] Some appraisers consider ancillary income as a return on the business enterprise value in the center, which will be discussed later.[11]

A special source of income that needs to be considered is the sales revenue derived from a catalog operation. Should this income be included in the sales revenue of a subject's anchor store? Again, this area is controversial. The income probably should be included, at least in part, especially if there are no other catalog outlets in that market area. But what if there are several other catalog outlets? How should this income be apportioned? Should leased department income be added to an anchor's gross sales revenue or treated in some other manner? More study and discussion will be needed before these questions can be answered.

Reimbursable Items and CAM

Leases establish the tenants' obligations to reimburse the landlord for certain expenditures. These items are variously know as *recoveries*, *billables*, and *pass-throughs* in different parts of the United States. Some of these items might normally be considered operating expenses and others, such as parking lot repaving, might be considered capital investment renewal. One of the most important reimbursements is for common area maintenance, or CAM. CAM expenses typically include the cost of common area utilities, security, cleaning, repairs and maintenance, equipment depreciation, paving, trash and snow removal, and landscaping upkeep. They are treated in the income statement as a separate revenue item, not as expenses.

10. Jeffrey D. Fisher and George H. Lentz, "Measuring Business Value in Shopping Malls," a report published by the School of Business of Indiana University, Bloomington, September 1989.

11. Kinnard, 22.

CAM charges vary greatly among tenants and require careful study. The recovery varies because tenants were put under different leases at varying times and they had different bargaining power. Tenant obligations to reimburse can cover landscaping, interior maintenance, capital expenditures, and management and administration, even with a surcharge. A sample tenant's reimbursement calculation appears in Table 7.3.

Table 7.3 **Sample Tenant Reimbursement Calculation (in Dollars per Square Foot of *GLA*)**			
	1993	**1994**	**1995**
Base rent	$7.00	$7.00	$7.00
Prorated expense share	$2.50	$3.20	$3.50
Stop	$3.00	$3.00	$3.00
Cap	$3.40	$3.40	$3.40
Tenant's reimbursement	0	$0.20	$0.40
Base plus reimbursement	$7.00	$7.20	$7.40

Food courts in malls are frequently treated as separate entities for purposes of expense recovery. Trash removal is a major expense. Although some tenants may pay a fixed amount toward expenses, most will reimburse the landlord for the costs of maintaining this area on a pro rata basis. Proration is usually based on the square foot area of the food court occupied by the tenant. Tenants may also be responsible for shares of other mall expenses. The appraiser will need to study leases to determine whether the proration is based on gross leasable area (*GLA*) or occupied mall area (*OMA*).[12]

Some appraisers use a special computer spreadsheet program to organize and total the figures for as many as 10 to 15 various items that are passed through to tenants in large malls. The information in this spreadsheet is then used as input in other popular cash flow programs. Such a spreadsheet is shown in Table 7.4. Common area maintenance charges are frequently loaded for an administrative fee—often approximately 15%. The appraiser should read the tenant leases carefully to determine how recovery of common area maintenance costs is allocated. Frequently the

12. F. Brian Johnson, MAI, "Operational Items to Consider When Valuing a Regional Mall," *The Appraisal Journal* (October 1991), 553-556.

Table 7.4 Smith Road Shopping Center—Stabilized Year Expense Recoveries

Total Taxes: $575,000   Insurance: $59,764   Total CAM: $307,679

		Taxes		Insurance			CAM			Total	
	Square Feet	Pro Rata %	Total	Pro Rata %	Admin.	Total	Pro Rata %	Admin.	Total	Recoveries	$/Sq. Ft.
Anchor tenants											
Discounter	107,806	22.3%	$128,244	Carries own policy			22.3%	0%	$68,623	$196,867	$1.83
Pharmacy	65,520	13.6%	$77,942	17.4%	0%	$10,427	13.6%	0%	$41,706	$130,074	$1.99
Clothier	35,600	7.4%	$26,700	9.5%	0%	$0*	7.4%	0%	$20,559*	$47,259	$1.33
Food mart	33,000	6.8%	$39,256	8.8%	0%	$0*	6.8%	0%	$9,900*	$49,156	$1.49
Budget dress	24,000	5.0%	$28,550	6.4%	0%	$3,819	5.0%	0%	$15,277	$47,646	$1.99
Builder's store	104,400	22.2%	$127,761	28.6%	0%	$17,091	22.2%	0%	$68,364	$213,217	$1.99
Cinema	32,000	6.6%	$38,067	8.5%	0%	$5,092	6.6%	0%	$20,369	$63,528	$1.99
Total	405,326	83.9%	$466,520	79.2%		$36,429		Total anchor recoveries	$244,799	$747,748	
Mini-anchor tenants											
Fashion spot	9,000	1.9%	$10,706	2.4%	0%	$1,432	1.9%	0%	$5,729	$17,867	$1.99
Fabrics	16,000	3.3%	$19,033	4.3%	0%	$2,546	3.3%	0%	$10,185	$31,764	$1.99
Video rental	6,000	1.2%	$7,138	1.6%	0%	$955	1.2%	0%	$3,819	$11,912	$1.99
Liquor	5,000	1.0%	$5,948	1.3%	0%	$796	1.0%	0%	$3,183	$9,926	$1.99
Total	36,000	7.4%	$42,825	9.6%		$5,729		Total mini-anchor recoveries	$22,915	$71,469	
Shop tenants											
Footwear	4,000	0.9%	$4,996	1.1%	0%	$668	0.9%	0%	$2,673	$8,338	$1.99
Accessory	2,800	0.6%	$3,331	0.7%	15%	$512	0.6%	15%	$2,050	$5,893	$2.10
Phase I shops	30,836	6.4%	$36,682	8.2%	15%	$5,643	6.4%	15%	$22,573	$64,898	$2.10
Phase III shops	4,200	0.9%	$4,996	1.1%	15%	$769	0.9%	15%	$3,074	$8,639	$2.10
Total	42,036	8.7%	$50,005	11.2%		$6,689		Total shop recoveries	$30,370	$87,968	$2.09
Total	483,362		$559,351			$48,843		Total recoveries		$907,186	

* This recovery is not a standard pro rata recovery. Refer to the rent roll for details.

leases will provide that the landlord spread the cost over the tenants who are presently occupying the space. When a center has substantial vacancies, a smaller number of tenants have to carry the same expense load. Leases provide that the landlord will bill tenants at the end of the year to make up any deficits caused by underestimating these payments.

An expense stop sets an upper limit on the amount of expenses that the owner pays. Expenses above this limit are the obligation of the tenant. The owner's purpose in using stops is to ensure that the center's net operating income will not be eroded by expense increases. The level of the stop will be negotiated based on the tenants prorated share, the expense categories to be included, and the expense amounts established when the lease was negotiated. Management costs are frequently excluded from the tenant's reimbursements. An expense cap can be used to set an upper limit on the amount of expenses to be reimbursed by the tenant to the landlord. In Table 7.3 both an expense stop and a cap are shown.

Percentage or Overage Rents

The appraiser reviews the lease clauses that require the retailer to pay a certain percentage of its sales to the landlord and analyzes the history of these payments to forecast future percentage rent payments. Obviously this will necessitate judgments about the individual tenants' marketing abilities and the probability of their renewing their leases. The appraisaer should talk to mall management about any plans to alter the merchandising mix. A computer-supported analysis can help the analyst prepare these figures and keep track of renewals and any changes in breakpoints.

The appraiser's analysis may include a table that shows three or four years of sales for the tenants with percentage clauses (Table 7.5). This group will probably include the center anchors and a few significant mall tenants. For each tenant and year, total sales and sales per square foot can be shown along with the year-to-year rates of change and perhaps the average annual change rates (Table 7.6). Average anchor tenant sales at the subject property and the percentage rent paid by each tenant can be compared to relevant industry norms (Table 7.7). The appraiser can use a different rate of change to forecast each tenant's sales. The rates selected should reflect the growth potential and competitiveness of each tenant as

Table 7.5 **Forecasting Percentage Sales**

Subject Property Anchor Tenant Historical Sales Data

Type of Store	1989 Sales	Sales/ Sq. Ft.	1990 Sales	Sales/ Sq. Ft.	1991 Sales	Sales/ Sq. Ft.	Average Sales/ Sq. Ft.
Grocery store	$19,086,163	$323	$22,468,105	$380	$21,427,710	$362	$335
Discount store	$7,418,599	$86	$8,190,594	$95	$8,665,935	$100	$94
Junior dept. store	$4,391,728	$107	$4,682,036	$114	$5,244,909	$128	$117

Table 7.6 **Percentage Change in Sales**

Type of Store	1988 Sales	1989 Sales	1990 Sales	1991 Sales
Grocery store	N/A	37.14%	17.72%	−4.63%
Discount store	N/A	−9.12%	10.41%	5.80%
Junior dept. store	N/A	N/A	6.61%	12.02%

well as its merchandising ability. These rates should also be consistent with the conclusions reached in the trade area analysis.

A spreadsheet can then be developed to show the dollar amount of sales for each tenant per square foot for each year of the forecast period (Table 7.8). A reference column can identify each tenant's breakpoint. Another section of the spreadsheet can present the basic rents identified in the tenant leases plus any applicable percentage rents above the breakpoint. The total rents for these tenants can then be incorporated into the aggregate discounted cash flow analysis.

Industry norms can be used to check the reasonableness of percentage rents and to estimate rents for unidentified occupants (Table 7.7). One source, the Urban Land Institute's *Dollars & Cents of Shopping Centers*, reports median sales per square foot, percentage rent rates, and total rent per square foot for selected tenant types. Publications from the Institute for Real Estate Management provide similar information.[13]

Leases must always be read carefully, but the appraiser should pay particular attention to whether the percentage of sales rent is paid on top of the base rent or a comparison is made between the base rent and the

13. See *Income/Expense Analysis, Shopping Centers*, 1991 ed. (Chicago: Institute of Real Estate Management, 1991.)

Table 7.7 Comparison to Benchmark

| National Sample Data | | | | Subject Property | | | | |
Type of Store	Average Size in Sq. Ft.	Average Sales/ Sq. Ft.	Average Rate of % Rent	Type of Store	Size in Sq. Ft.	Average Sales/ Sq. Ft.	Rate of % Rent	Breakpoint/ Sq. Ft.
Super store grocery	36,617	$330.49	2%	Grocery	59,134	$355	1%	$148
Discount store	60,842	$133.24	1%	Discount store	86,479	$94	1%	$181
Junior dept. store	39,000	$110.29	1.5%	Junior dept. store	40,951	$117	2%	$148

Source: Urban Land Institute, Community Shopping Center Summary (Open Centers).

Table 7.8 Estimated Sales Per Square Foot

Growth rate:	Yr.1(0.0%)	Yr.2(2.0%)	Yr.3(4.5%)	Yr.4(4.5%)	Yr.5(4.5%)	Yr.6(4.5%)	Yr.7(4.5%)	Yr.8(4.5%)	Yr.9(4.5%)	Yr.10(4.5%)	Breakpoint/ Sq. Ft.
Grocery store	$362	$369	$386	$403	$421	$440	$460	$481	$502	$525	$839
Discount store	$100	$102	$107	$111	$116	$122	$127	$133	$139	$145	$181
Junior dept. store	$128	$131	$136	$143	$149	$156	$163	$170	$178	$186	$148

percentage of sales with the landlord receiving the larger amount. Sometimes the base rent is offset against the amount due under the percentage clause because some time will elapse before the base sales amount is known and the percentage rent to the landlord can be determined. Similarly, the lease may allow the tenant to offset payments for his share of CAM expenses against the landlord's entitlements under a percentage clause.

Another way to handle modest percentage rents is essentially to disregard them. Some appraisers report that investors and lenders consider such rents an unexpected bonus and are reluctant to assign value to them unless they are substantial and can be reliably forecast.

Vacancy and Collection Loss Estimates

The vacancy and collection loss rates forecast should be consistent with the analysis of the competitiveness of the subject property in its submarket, conclusions derived from demographic data analysis, the probability of tenant turnover, and the amount of new competitive space entering the market. Typically some vacancy is forecast for most centers, even if none is currently being experienced, because it is anticipated that over a projected ownership period some vacancy and collection loss will occur. The rate forecast for this item may depend on the credit strength of tenants. High-grade national tenants on long-term leases may be assigned a 1% loss rate, for example, while local tenants in start-up operations would warrant substantially higher rates.

The use of industry norms has probably persisted longer in forecasting vacancy and collection loss than other types of accounts. In most markets there are widely held perceptions as to what constitutes a reasonable vacancy allowance and how much credit loss is to be expected. These market norms can be supplemented with a good marketability analysis.

When projecting vacancies, care must be taken to consider different types of space separately. Space occupied by thriving anchor tenants could merit a 0% vacancy forecast, while non-anchor tenant vacancies may be expected to be substantially higher. Of course, anchor status does not guarantee prosperity and many large retailing companies are in precarious financial and marketing positions. A single rate forecast of, say, 12% may actually represent a careful analysis of two or more categories of space. The percentage rate established should be based on the dollar volume of potential gross income, not the area in square feet. A 10% vacancy in anchor space rented at $3.00 per square foot is less damaging than a 10% vacancy in shop space rented at $12.00 per square foot.

It is wise to explain how the vacancy statistics for the comparable properties were calculated. Ideally the appraiser would get rent rolls for these properties and explain how the calculations were made. Such an explanation could help establish the credibility of any gross income multiplier applied. The analyst should be prepared to explain the credit loss component added to the vacancy allowance. Using recent operating periods as a relevant base, the appraiser's forecast should reflect the tenant mix, the lease expiration schedule, and the outlook for retailing in the market area.

Total potential rental income, plus tenant reimbursements for expenses, less vacancy and collection losses equal the total effective gross income. These calculations are shown in Figure 7.2.

Forecasting Expenses

Operating expenses for the stabilized operating year are estimated one account at a time. Growth rates for these expenses can be estimated individually, or in simpler assignments a single growth rate may be applied. The appraisal report should explain what is included in each expense account, comment on the history of that expense, and explain how the peculiarities of the subject property may affect that expense in the future. The best data source may be the history of the subject property, checked carefully against the operating data for the comparable properties. Appraisers who have developed contacts with other professionals may have access to expense histories, operating data, and cost information from proposal packages for financing or brokerage or from similar transactions.

Comparative Analysis of Operating Results

To analyze the economic productivity of a shopping center, the appraiser needs to locate and use performance benchmarks. Operating expense ratios should be drawn from, or at least checked against, industry sources that report norms for a range of properties. Many appraisers use *Dollars &*

Figure 7.2 **Total Effective Gross Income**		
Rental income		
Anchor tenants:		
Food King 35,000 sq. ft. @ $6.70/sq. ft.		$234,500
Drugmaster 8,450 sq. ft. @ $7.56/sq. ft.*		$ 63,903
Total anchor rental income:		$298,403
(Average anchor income/sq. ft. = $6.87)		
Local tenants:		
49,446 sq. ft. @ $13.26/sq. ft.* (average)		$655,818
Total potential rental income		$954,221
Tenant reimbursements for expenses are based on the terms set forth in the leases held by the anchor and local tenants and are estimated as follows:		
Tenant reimbursements		
Anchor tenants:	$63,000	
Local tenants:	$91,956	
Total tenant reimbursements		$154,956
Total potential gross income		$1,109,177
Less vacancy		
Forecast for anchor space: $298,403 × 0.0% = $0		
Forecast for mall tenants: $655,818 × 4% = $26,200*		
Less collection loss		
For mall tenants only: $655,818 × 2% = $13,100*		
Total deduction for vacancy and collection losses:		$39,300
Projected effective gross income:		$1,069,877
		say $1,070,000 per year

*Rounded

Cents of Shopping Centers as a secondary data source in forecasting expenses. This report is published every three years by the Urban Land Institute in cooperation with the International Council of Shopping Centers and provides data based on surveys of operators. This publication can shed light on the accounting system used by shopping center operators, trends in shopping center operating results, and the performance of the subject center compared to other, similar centers in its market. Because surveys are only conducted every three years, these data are frequently outdated and useful only for trend analysis and general verification. As the forecast period for the subject property goes beyond the benchmark data used, adjustments can be made to reflect incremental increases caused by time and inflation (Table 7.9.) Another good source of survey data on operating expenses is *Income/Expense Analysis, Shopping Centers,* 1991 ed., published by the Institute of Real Estate Management in Chicago.

Table 7.9 **Adjustments to Benchmark Data for Time and Inflation**		
Market Operating Expenses Per Square Foot*	**1989 Range**	**1990 Adjusted Range**[†]
Centers 20 years old & older	$0.05-$0.24	$0.06-$0.30
Centers 10-19 years old	$0.04-$0.25	$0.05-$0.32
Subject region	$0.08-$0.31	$0.10-$0.40
All U.S.	$0.04-$0.25	$0.05-$0.32
	1989 Median	**1990 Adjusted Median**
Centers 20 years old & older	$0.12	$0.15
Centers 10-19 years old	$0.11	$0.14
Subject region	$0.17	$0.22
All U.S.	$0.12	$0.15
1989 range $0.04-$0.31	Adjusted 1990 range: $0.05-$0.40	
1989 median $0.12	Adjusted 1990 median: $0.15	

*From *Dollars & Cents of Shopping Centers: 1990.*
[†]Figures have been adjusted at a rate of 5% per year.

The key operating income account is called *net operating balance,* which is defined as, "... that part of total income remaining after operating expenses are taken out but before deductions are made for depreciation, debt service, income taxes, and the return on equity."[14]

The 1990 report covers four kinds of shopping centers in five age groups and six geographic regions. All of the expense and revenue items that comprise the net operating balances are categorized using the system of accounts suggested in the *Standard Manual of Accounting for Shopping Center Operations.*[15] The Urban Land Institute disseminates additional information in its books, continuing education programs, information packets, project reference files, and videos. Comparative operating data on

14. *Standard Manual of Accounting for Shopping Center Operations* (Washington, D.C.: Urban Land Institute, 1971).   15. Ibid.

convenience centers, fashion malls, off-price shopping centers, super community centers, and superstore centers are also available.

Each edition of *Dollars & Cents of Shopping Centers* provides definitions of terms, an explanation of the data collection process, a discussion of the reliability of the survey sample data, and suggestions for applying the reported data to a subject property. Two sample presentations of the data are shown in Figures 7.3 and 7.4. Figure 7.3 concerns a superregional center and Figure 7.4 refers to a neighborhood center. (Note: The reader should not use the reference data, but rather procure and study current, local data.) The comparative unit used in these presentations is dollars per square foot of gross leasable area (*GLA*). Obviously the appraiser must study the definitions applied to make consistent comparisons between benchmark data and a subject property.

Dollars & Cents of Shopping Centers also includes a bibliography, an alphabetical listing of the tenant classifications in the SIC code system, and data on the number of parking spaces required for each thousand feet of *GLA*. (Tenant classifications and SIC codes are listed in the appendix.)

In preparing an expense forecast, some appraisers start with the owner's operating statement and rework it into the format shown in the *Dollars & Cents of Shopping Centers* report. They then reformat the comparable properties' statements to provide clear comparability and support for their estimates of the subject property's expenses. Professional standards require that historical data for the subject property be procured; data for several years may be used to support the appraiser's forecast. A historical expense analysis is shown in Table 7.10.

The operating expenses for a shopping center are the expenses of the asset, not the investor. Thus, operating expenses do not include investor outlays such as debt service, income taxes, or gains or losses on asset disposition. Collections from tenants for the operations of the merchants' association are not included in the center's gross income forecasts.

Other items to be considered in estimating shopping center expenses are discussed below.[16]

---

16. This discussion is drawn from interviews with appraisers and developers and from Robert L. Garrett, et al, *The Valuation of Shopping Centers* (Chicago: American Institute of Real Estate Appraisers. 1976).

Figure 7.3 **Sample Data for Superregional Shopping Centers in Southeastern U.S.: Base Data, Mall Tenant Data, and Operating Results**

Number of centers in sample: 24

	Medians
Base data	**Area in square feet**
Center size (total occupancy area)	961,457
Unowned occupancy area	554,270
Department stores (owned and unowned)	536,687
Mall tenant data	**Mall area in square feet**
GLA of mall shops	350,987
Mall tenant data	***Dollars per sq. ft. of mall GLA***
Mall tenant sales	$218.72
Operating results	***Dollars per sq. ft. of mall GLA***
Operating receipts	
Rental income—minimum	$13.58
Rental income—overages	1.53
Total rent	15.92
Common area charges	3.03
Property taxes and insurance	1.29
Other escalation charges	1.23
Income from sale of utilities	2.34
Total other charges	3.50
Miscellaneous income	0.24
Total operating receipts	23.79
Operating expenses	
Building maintenance	0.20
Parking lot, mall, and other common areas	2.15
Central utility systems	1.13
Office area services	
Total maintenance and housekeeping	3.72
Advertising and promotion	0.21
Real estate taxes	0.95
Insurance	0.24
General and administrative	1.38
Management agent fees	0.61
Leasing agent fees	0.03
Total operating expenses	6.36
Net operating balance	$16.06

Note: Because data are medians, detail amounts do not add to totals.

Source: *Dollars & Cents of Shopping Centers: 1990*, Table 3-4.

Figure 7.4 Sample Data for Neighborhood Shopping Centers in Northeastern U.S.: Base Data, Mall Tenant Data, and Operating Results

Number of centers in sample: 29

	Medians
Base data	**Area in square feet**
Center size (total occupancy area)	60,448
Mall tenant data	**Area in square feet**
Gross leasable area	60,083
Mall tenant data	***Dollars per sq. ft. of GLA***
Tenant sales	$220.11
Operating results	***Dollars per sq. ft. of GLA***
Operating receipts	
Rental income—minimum	$6.87
Rental income—overages	0.38
Total rent	7.02
Common area charges	0.70
Property taxes and insurance	0.87
Other escalation charges	
Income from sale of utilities	0.24
Total other charges	0.75
Miscellaneous income	0.04
Total operating receipts	8.43
Operating expenses	
Building maintenance	0.22
Parking lot, mall, and other common areas	0.37
Central utility systems	0.23
Office area services	0.13
Total maintenance and housekeeping	0.72
Advertising and promotion	0.13
Real estate taxes	0.76
Insurance	0.26
General and administrative	0.71
Management agent fees	0.43
Leasing agent fees	0.19
Total operating expenses	2.84
Net operating balance	$5.01

Note: Because data are medians, detail amounts do not add to totals.

Source: *Dollars & Cents of Shopping Centers: 1990*, Table 6-2.

Table 7.10 **Historical Expense Analysis**						
	1989		**1990**		**1991***	
	Total	**Per Sq. Ft.**	**Total**	**Per Sq. Ft.**	**Total**	**Per Sq. Ft.**
Real estate taxes	$38,743	$0.42	$38,722	$0.42	$42,563	$0.46
Insurance	44,240	$0.48	32,938	$0.41	14,745	$0.16
CAM	62,246	$0.67	59,837	$0.64	67,150	$0.72
Management	35,304	$0.38	44,413	$0.48	45,100	$0.49
Repairs & maintenance	14,695	$0.16	4,231	$0.01	28,400	$0.31
Totals	$195,228	$2.11	$180,141	$1.96	$197,958	$2.14

* Annualized, based on 11 months in 1991.

Building maintenance

To determine who is responsible for repairs and maintenance, the appraiser should read the leases. Tenants are usually responsible for interior maintenance and replacements, while the owner is responsible for structural, roof, and exterior repairs. If the owner is responsible for the eventual replacement of mechanical equipment, the tenants may not care for it well and the owner should have a maintenance contract.

A careful inspection by an experienced appraiser will reveal any repairs needed and whether work has been deferred to boost earnings and cash flow. If the center has a maintenance supervisor, this individual can be helpful in the inspection. A maintenance supervisor may be more candid about conditions than the manager.

Parking lot, mall, and other common areas

The expenses in this account include paving maintenance and repair; parking lot striping; cleaning; lighting; security service; heating, ventilation, and air-conditioning (HVAC) of any enclosed mall area; maintenance for the public restrooms; power for any signs that are the landlord's responsibility; landscaping; scavenger service; and snow removal.

Central utility systems

Reviewing the leases and talking to the manager will reveal how utility expenses are allocated. It is important to ensure consistency between the subject and the comparable properties analyzed or to make appropriate adjustments. Tenants usually pay for their own utilities plus a pro rata share of the expenses for mall common areas and, in some cases, parking. Some leases require tenants to maintain a positive flow of heated or cooled air for the benefit of the enclosed mall area. Utility costs may rise faster than all operating expenses combined, or faster than inflation, because fuel costs are volatile. According to *Dollars & Cents of Shopping Centers*,

> Central utility systems vary considerably among superregional and regional centers. Therefore, the procedures used to compute this expense item depend on the type of system used in a particular center. If the shopping center uses a central utility system that is charged out to all areas of the center, including unowned occupants such as department stores or banks, this expense item is divided by total occupancy area. If, however, the utility system is used only by the owned tenants, the cost for the central utility system is divided by the *GLA* of the center.[17]

Sometimes a landlord makes a profit on utility services by purchasing them at wholesale and reselling them at retail. The legality of this practice should be checked against state law.

Office area services

This account includes the cost of janitorial services and lighting for tenant's office areas. The total expenses are divided by the *GLA* of the center.

Total maintenance and housekeeping

This is a summary category for office area services, central utility systems, maintenance of parking lot/mall/and other common areas, and building maintenance. One reason malls and their comparable sales must be identified carefully is that housekeeping costs vary with different types of mall design. This fact should be kept in mind when comparing the expenses of dissimilar rentals or sales.

---

17. Urban Land Institute, *Dollars & Cents of Shopping Centers*, 15

Advertising and promotion

Larger centers achieve the desired synergism in part through a merchants' association. The appraiser should ascertain the strength of and support for such an association in the subject property and comparable centers. A clause in the lease will likely set forth the obligation to belong to the merchants' association, voting rights, assessment payment rate obligations, and any limits on assessment increases. Anchor stores may have fewer obligations because they are expected to contribute through their own advertising. In unusually competitive circumstances, it may be in the owner's best, long-term interest to make extra contributions to the association.

The manager is often the promotional force behind the association; some appraisers comment that tenants are seldom satisfied with the manager's efforts. Discreet discussions with tenants, when feasible, may reveal the association's special strengths or new opportunities for marketing the center.

Real estate taxes

The manner in which property taxes are allocated must be studied and compared to other centers. One author observes that real estate taxes now make up about one-third of shopping center expenses. Frequently the anchor tenants define their own tax parcels for separate taxation; the mall tenants and the anchor tenants share the common area taxes. Depending on the terms of the lease, the mall tenants may pay pro rata shares based on *GLA* or *OMA*.[18]

Some centers pay taxes on personalty, while comparable centers in neighboring jurisdictions may not. The analyst should determine when the subject property was last assessed for property tax purposes and when the next reassessment is expected. Special assessments may be outstanding or contemplated to pay for improvements benefiting the property. Comparable sales should be investigated too. Tax assessed values will be influenced by recent sales, which may have been transacted at historically

18. Gregory J. Lafakis, ''Valuation Concepts and Issues and the Taxpayer's Responsibilities Concerning Regional Shopping Centers,'' a paper presented at the International Association of Assessing Officers Eighth Annual Legal Seminar, San Francisco, October 1988.

high prices. The appraiser should be especially sensitive to the possible tax impact of any impending sale of the subject property.

The tenant's responsibility to provide reimbursement for property taxes may include the costs of any protests or assessment appeal. The appraiser should see how property taxes are defined in the lease. They may include special assessments and state or local taxes. The tenants will probably be required to pay their tax shares in advance on a monthly basis, adjusting for any differences at the end of the year. The anchor tenants will probably negotiate to pay their own property taxes and will not be included in the recoveries with other mall tenants.

Insurance

Shopping center owners and tenants must have insurance. Typically the tenant pays the premium or the increases in the premium above an initial threshold amount. The premiums paid on many kinds of insurance coverage have increased greatly recently, so special investigation may be warranted. A full discussion of insurance coverage is beyond the scope of this work, but the following coverages are usually included in a business owner's policy.[19]

- Worker's compensation
- Broad general liability (perhaps $1,000,000 of coverage and a special umbrella liability policy to increase coverage to $5,000,000)
- Automobile liability (nonowned and owned)
- Building—physical hazard insurance (e.g., fire, extended coverage, vandalism). Replacement coverage is preferred to actual cash value, and an all-risk coverage is preferable to named peril coverage. Coverage is usually indexed for inflation in building costs and may include tenants' leasehold improvements.
- Contents
- Boiler and machinery option
- Plate glass
- Earthquake or flood coverage, if needed

---

19. James L. Athearn and S. Travis Pritchett, *Risk and Insurance*, 5th ed. (St. Paul, Minn.: West Publishing Company, 1984), Chapter 18 and Appendix D.

The appraiser should determine whether the subject center or its comparables are carrying loss-of-rent insurance. This type of coverage smoothes the center's cash flow stream during periods of property damage, thus reducing the property's risk and possibly justifying a lower capitalization rate. It might be worth noting whether the insurer recently inspected the property and any observations made during this inspection.

General and administrative

The general and administrative category is a pooled account so comparison with other properties may be difficult. The analyst must simply look at how expenses are grouped to make sure that all necessary expenses are accounted for.

Management agent fees

Management duties may include leasing, collecting rents, and managing operations; the fees negotiated will depend on the responsibilities involved. Careful analysis and comparisons must be made. Even when an owner argues that no historical expense has been recorded for this item, the services are essential and must be forecast to separate income returns to the real estate from services.

Leasing agent fees

The cost of finding tenants and negotiating leases should be estimated to reflect local submarket practices. Historical expenditures may provide general guidelines, but the expenses forecast should be based on the amount and type of space to be filled during the forecast period.

In direct capitalization of either first-year or stabilized net operating income, leasing commissions are frequently not subtracted as part of operating expenses. This is appropriate as long as the comparable properties from which the direct capitalization rates are derived would reflect comparable leasing commissions. In a stabilized income estimate, however, the management expense could be adjusted to reflect leasing commissions.

At various points in the appraisal process, the analyst may need to evaluate the quality of center management. This subjective judgment will affect the appraiser's forecasts of trade area penetration, tenant negotiations and renewals, expense control, and other factors. Although it would probably be in poor taste to express an adverse opinion of management in the report, it may be appropriate to offer this opinion to the client at an opportune moment.

Appraisers should be aware that owners sometimes attempt to underreport various expenses to produce higher net income forecasts and valuations. When maintenance has been neglected, the physical inspection may reveal the results. A more indirect way to underreport expenses is to record expenditures not as operating expenses for the property, but as a capital infusion. Note that at a 10% capitalization rate, each dollar of expense concealed might produce an extra dollar of sale price.

Allowances for replacements

Appraisal literature advocates the use of allowances for replacements to define the economic productivity of real assets. These allowances are not always used by shopping center owners and operators. Sometimes waning assets are adequately treated without the use of reserves. For example, some repairs and replacements are shifted to tenants, while others are handled as cash outlays in the cash flow computer simulation programs employed by larger centers.

Under prescribed practice, replacement allowances are estimated as a prorated annual charge for the replacement of property components that are expected to require replacement during the term of ownership. Replacement allowances may be estimated for roofs, signage, parking, and remodeling. In practice, allowances for many of these items are omitted in the belief that the deduction will depress net operating income and reduce comparability with the comparable sales. This need not be the case if the *NOI* for the comparable sales can be reconstructed before extracting their capitalization rates. A simplified example is presented in Table 7.11.

Table 7.11 **Replacement Allowances and Capitalization Rate Adjustment**			
	Subject	**Comparable 1**	**Comparable 2**
Stabilized *NOI*	$50,000	$70,000	$80,000
Sale price			
(after all other adjustments)		$700,000	$800,000
Less annual reserves required			
Roof	$4,000	$5,000	$6,000
Paving	3,000	4,000	3,000
Signage	0	500	1,000
NOI after reserves	$43,000	$60,500	$70,000
Adjusted cap rate		0.0864	.0875

Thus, by reconstructing income estimates after reserves, it is possible to calculate adjusted capitalization rates for the comparable sales, which can be used to infer a capitalization rate for the subject property.

When no reserves are estimated the appraiser is making an implicit assumption that the need for replacements is the same for the comparable properties and the subject property. If there are differences in the condition of the comparable properties and the subject, they will need to be made explicit. Consistency is most important. If capitalization rates are derived from a reconstructed *NOI* after reserves, this approach should be applied to all properties in the comparable analysis. If both a DCF analysis and a single-year income forecast are prepared, they should be consistent. Finally, in a multiperiod income forecast, the appraiser should consider adjusting the income for the extra year beyond the holding period before capitalizing it to calculate the reversion.

When it is obvious that a major replacement expenditure will be needed soon after the purchase and the appraiser has chosen not to estimate replacement reserves for this item, the appraiser is likely to treat the item like an investor would—i.e., subtract it from the estimated value. This is expected in a DCF analysis, but it may also be done in direct capitalization of stabilized income.

Stabilized Income, Leasing Commissions, and Tenant Improvement Allowances

Most regional malls have leasing staffs and do not pay leasing commissions, but smaller centers must deal with brokers who bring in tenants.

The appraiser will inspect the schedule of lease expirations and develop an understanding of local market lease commission rates and payment practices to forecast leasing commission payments.

Leasing commissions and tenant improvement allowances are not typically treated as operating expenses in a direct capitalization, stabilized income forecast. Instead, they are treated as capital expenditures after net operating income — i.e., "handled below the line" because of their variability and the unwarranted impact they could have depending on when they are forecast. Interestingly, few practitioners average these expenditures and subtract them from stabilized income. Although it is not common practice, when stabilized net operating income is forecast it could be appropriate to average or stabilize tenant improvements and leasing commissions separately or as a component of management expense. Treatment of these items is not consistent, however. When commissions are paid out over a period of time, some appraisers choose to forecast a stabilized amount as an operating expense.

Considering Tenants' Capacity to Pay Occupancy Costs

When all of the revenue sources for each tenant have been estimated, including recoveries and percentage rent in addition to base rent, some thought should be given to the tenants' ability to carry the burden of these occupancy costs. Occupancy costs can be calculated in two ways: as the rate of total rent per square foot of *GLA* or total charges as a percentage of sales. Both types of occupancy rates can then be compared to published benchmarks for various types of retailers in different kinds of shopping centers.

Dollars & Cents of Shopping Centers shows median occupancy rates, calculated as the rate of rent per square foot of *GLA* as well as the upper 10% and the upper 2%. Total charges as a percentage of sales can be compared to medians and to the top and bottom deciles. General industry rules of thumb suggest that supermarkets normally have occupancy-costs-to-sales ratios of about 2%; ratios as high as 3% probably indicate some financial distress. Similarly, apparel retailers are comfortable with occupancy cost ratios at or below 10%, while some sources report that specialty retailers without strong competition can tolerate ratios up to 15%. Many mall shops would be in distress with ratios above 10%. However, these rough guidelines lack empirical documentation.

If any tenant has total occupancy costs that exceed both the benchmarks and the market rate, as revealed by comparable rentals, there may be a risk that the lease will not be renewed. If the costs are extremely high, the tenant may go out of business. If, on the other hand, the cost ratio is comparatively low, there may be an opportunity to increase rents in the future.

The Importance of Minimum Rents

In many centers, especially large ones, pass-through provisions and the administrative loads on them may cover all the landlord's expenses so that the center's net operating income consists mostly of minimum rents and overage rents. Tessier writes

> Having established that the pass through provisions plus the other income opportunities are usually sufficient to cover all operating expenses of the owner, we can examine the minimum and overage rents that will fall directly to the bottom line (*NOI*). The minimum rents will vary with the size of the leased premises, store location, anticipated sales achievement, and the gross profit margin potential for the type of business conducted. . . . Minimum rents are the key to mall valuation and must be secured from the landlord, the managing agent or the mall tenants. . . . The percentage rent clause of the tenant lease usually adds 10-20% to the minimum rents.[20]

Sample Stabilized Operating Income Statement

A sample operating statement for a shopping center is shown in Figure 7.5. The appraiser who prepared this statement was asked for a value estimate as of the time the shopping center was expected to achieve stabilized occupancy. The client agreed that this would be when all the space was absorbed or initially leased and normal operations and tenant turnover could be expected. Unusually high vacancy and collection losses are

20. Vern Tessier, CPA, "The Valuation of Regional and Super-Regional Malls," *Assessment Digest* (Sept/Oct. 1991), 2-13.

forecast to reflect the rent concessions required in this soft market. Therefore, nominal rents are reflected in the potential gross income and effective rents are captured in effective gross income.[21]

Figure 7.5 **Sample Shopping Center Operating Statement Stabilized Year 1993**		
Potential gross rental income		$336,082
Tenant reimbursements		54,788
Total gross potential income, including reimbursements		$390,870
Vacancy & collection loss (23% of total income)		89,900
Effective gross income		$300,970
	Expense Per Sq. Ft.	Total Expenses
Fixed and operating expenses		
Real estate taxes	$1.06	$22,809
Insurance	0.27	5,675
Common area maintenance	1.33	28,379
Management	0.84	18,058
Repairs & maintenance	0	0
Replacement allowance	0	0
Total expenses		$74,921 or $3.50/sq. ft.
Net operating income before nonoperating expenses		$226,049, or $10.56/sq. ft.

The operating statement does not show a separate amount for repairs
and maintenance because these items are included in the common area
maintenance account. Replacement allowances are not used because the
leases pass depreciation allowances through to the tenants and owners in
this market consider replacements as cash outlays in a year beyond the
investment holding period. Net operating income is forecast before nonoperating expenses, which include leasing commissions and tenant improvement expenditures. Generally direct capitalization is performed
using *NOI* after verifying that similar commissions and tenant improvements are experienced by comparable properties in the submarket. A

---

21. The mathematics of converting an irregular income stream from leases with concessions into its level equivalent is beyond the scope of this work, but several examples are available in the professional literature.

See James D. Vernor, "Discounted Cash Flow Approach to Comparative Lease Analysis in a Differentiated Market" *The Appraisal Journal* (October 1988), 391-398.

computer-supported discounted cash flow analysis can track cash commitments for these items.

Discounted Cash Flow Analysis

Discounted cash flow analysis is preferred by lenders and investors in larger centers for its advantages in analyzing complex properties. Modern computer technology has brought DCF analysis within the grasp of all analysts. (Comments about DCF software are offered in the next chapter.)

The main advantage of DCF analysis is that incomes and expenses in the form of cash flows can be forecasted or "modeled" at the time they are expected to occur. This allows the analyst to track the turnover of leases as they expire and to account for other significant cash-related events such as maintenance and remodeling expenditures. DCF allows the appraiser to think like buyers do, assuming an after-tax, leveraged, cash-flow, equity yield basis if that is how investors make their purchase decisions. Many assumptions implicit in working with stabilized income must be made explicit in DCF modeling. This is now generally seen as an advantage. Estimating replacement expenditures directly may alleviate the need for reserves. Sensitivity analysis is greatly simplified with computer-supported DCF analysis.

Two disadvantages are associated with DCF: 1) Some important input data such as equity yields are difficult to derive. 2) Start-up costs are incurred in acquiring and maintaining computer systems and skills. In the past unsophisticated readers may have been misled by computer analyses with unrealistic assumptions, but as experience and training increase, this is probably no longer true.

Once the analyst decides to use DCF analysis, it becomes easy to separate out various sources of income. More reliable income derived from minimum base rents, as opposed to percentage rents, may be separated out and discounted with a lower capitalization or discount rate to reflect its lower risk.

In developing computer-simulated income flows, the analyst should ensure that the periods between leases, known as down time, are realistic in light of current vacancy periods. It is also important to guard against forecasting unrealistic increases in percentage rentals based on sales overages. Remember that the percentage rate applies to sales above a sales breakpoint, which may be computed by dividing the decimal percentage rate into the base rent. When the lease is renewed, the base rent will be recomputed and a new breakpoint will be established, thereby lowering the percentage sales revenue for the landlord during the early years of the renewed lease. It is to be expected that the percentage rental income to the landlord will decrease in the years immediately after several important leases are renewed at higher rent levels. Similarly, the landlord's expense recoveries may decline when lease renewals establish new stops.

Leasing Commissions and Tenant Improvement Allowances

Leasing commissions and tenant improvement allowances are more easily handled in DCF analysis than in a stabilized income estimate. Tenant improvement allowances are cash payments to new tenants. A typical rate in some markets is approximately $10 per square foot of leased area, but this rate is a product of local market negotiation. Leasing commissions are frequently about 4% of the total rent during the lease term, but this rate may also vary. Commissions upon renewals are also common. In performing cash flow analyses, it is important to determine when the payments are actually made. They may be cashed-out when they are earned or paid in installments. Leasing commissions and tenant improvement allowances are typically recognized "below the line," after the net operating income or balance is computed. In this way they are subtracted from cash flow.

If leasing commissions and tenant improvement allowances are considered before computing net operating income, the resulting *NOI* will be lower, which will reduce the indicated rate of capitalization. This should not have any adverse impact on the valuation process as long as the same treatment is given to comparable sales in the inferential analysis. Nevertheless, the casual reader who does not take time to study the report may wonder if there is an error in the capitalization rates and the credibility of the report may suffer.

Summary

The income capitalization approach is the most popular method for estimating the value of most shopping centers. Before applying the approach, the appraiser must study the leases and estimate next year's revenue items and their expected growth. Operating expenses and their growth can be estimated based on the history of the subject property, checked against comparable property data and secondary survey data sources. Additional cash outflows, not traditionally considered as operating expenses, are estimated to support a DCF analysis.

Grand Avenue Mall, Milwaukee   *Fulker / Miller / H. Armstrong Roberts*

CAPITALIZATION PROCEDURES

Introduction

Capitalization is the process in which the value of a property is estimated based on its income and other financial benefits. The process employs an arithmetic equation, or *model*. The appraiser can choose from at least three models to capitalize an income estimate into a value estimate: direct capitalization, discounted cash flow spreadsheet analysis, and packaged simulation. Each method has advantages and disadvantages. Because appraisers attempt to mirror market thinking, the approach that best reflects buyers' thought processes would be the most desirable. If no market activity exists, the method that best simulates investor thinking should be selected.

Direct Capitalization of a Single Year's Income

In direct capitalization a one-year net operating income forecast is divided by an overall rate (*OAR*). All parameters of typical investor return expectations are represented (explicitly or implicitly) in either the income forecast or the capitalization rate. These expectations include current operating income and cash flow, the security of that income and the principal, income growth, an increased resale price (or reversion), protection against inflation, tax shelter, refinancing proceeds, and equity build-up through amortization. The direct capitalization rate, as the ratio of income to value, serves as a proxy for all these implicit investor return assumptions.

A sample direct capitalization model appears below. Assume that a subject property's net operating income for the first year of operations is forecast at $50,000, and the ratio of forecasted net operating income to sale price for similar properties is .095. The direct capitalization model indicates:

$$V = I/R$$
$$= 50,000/.095$$
$$= \$526,315$$

This is the answer before rounding. Note that the capitalization rate is prospective—i.e., the rate for both the subject property and the comparable sales is applied to a forecast of a prospective, one-year income stream.

The net operating income is forecast for a single year, usually the first full operating year after the date of the appraisal. If the analyst thinks this year will not be representative of the ownership period, a stabilized net operating income may be used to smooth out an irregular income stream. Either choice is acceptable. However, the analyst must be careful to select a model appropriate to the income stream and apply it consistently to the subject property and to comparable sales when extracting their capitalization rates.

A capitalization rate is extracted from comparable sales by rearranging the algebraic equation $V=I/R$, into $R=I/V$. The cash equivalent sale price of the comparable sale is divided into either the first-year income forecast or the stabilized income estimate for the comparable property. The same income estimate must be chosen for the subject property.

Direct capitalization is most appropriate when investors use a similar decision-making method. This may be indicated if comparable sales analysis reveals a stable pattern of capitalization rates. A few interviews can corroborate this indication.

Direct capitalization carries many hazards. When an overall capitalization rate is inferred from comparable properties, there is a danger that these comparables will vary in some significant way and that this variance will not be captured in any adjustments to the cap rate. Here the proxy rate does not serve well. For example, one of the comparable centers analyzed may have a trade area with a substantially stronger demographic profile, which would warrant a lower capitalization rate to reflect its higher potential for income growth, all other factors being equal. Other factors that might be overlooked when direct capitalization rates are used include:

- Substantial differences in shopping center infrastructure, design, tenant mix, and lease rollovers
- Different loan-to-property value ratios
- Below-market financing
- Different investor motivation
- Different land-to-building value ratios

Another significant factor in setting direct capitalization rates is the economic life of the subject center, which may be shorter than its physical life. This must be reflected in higher allowances for capital replacements, higher projected capital expenditures, or an overall capitalization rate increased for greater capital recovery.

The gross income multiplier is a tool used in direct capitalization, but it is seldom applied in shopping center analysis except to estimate some forms of depreciation.

Direct capitalization is especially difficult to apply in valuing a property such as a hotel or shopping center, which may experience an extended absorption period before achieving stabilized income. Moreover, because a shopping center's income from percentage leases and penetration into the retail trade area may fluctuate, it is likely that an irregular growth pattern must be projected. For these reasons appraisers may choose to use discounted cash flow analysis, not direct capitalization, unless market participants report the purchase and sale of existing centers based on direct capitalization rates.

Limited Discounted Cash Flow Analysis

A limited discounted cash flow analysis may be prepared and supported with a simple computer spreadsheet such as Lotus 1 2 3, Quattro Pro, or

Excel, among others.[1] To perform a computerized discounted cash flow analysis, individual estimates may be developed for gross income, reimbursed expenses, vacancies, operating expenses, and other major cash flows. A computer program to simulate these cash flows could be specifically designed within the appraiser's office using one of the spreadsheet routines now available. In this way the program could incorporate the level of detail appropriate to the subject property and the client's intended use of the appraisal report. The disadvantages of a customized program include the possibility of introducing programming errors and a lack of credibility in the eyes of the reader or client. Often spreadsheets are used to organize and study data before they are used in a packaged routine.

Reversion Estimates

Simple direct income capitalization approach techniques do not require specification of holding periods and resale prices (reversions), but reversion estimates are required for more detailed discounted cash flow forecasts. Care must be taken in estimating reversions. It is common practice for appraisers to estimate a reversionary sale price in a future year by capitalizing the subsequent year's net operating income. The rate used for capitalization is known as the *terminal capitalization rate*. Conventionally, this rate is 50 or 100 basis points ($\frac{1}{2}$% to 1%) higher than the going-in capitalization rates applied under direct capitalization. (Direct capitalization rates can be observed in an analysis of sales.) There are two reasons for setting the terminal cap rate slightly higher than the initial capitalization rate.

1. Many analysts argue that because the reversion is realized at the end of the forecast period, it is much less reliable and this greater risk is reflected with a higher capitalization rate.

2. Analysts assign a higher terminal capitalization rate to the reversion because at the end of the holding period the subject property will be older, less competitive, and have a greater risk of functional ob-

---

1. Users of the spreadsheet applications and computer programs described in this book should be aware that the Appraisal Institute has not developed, reviewed, or approved these materials. Therefore, the Appraisal Institute takes no responsibility and assumes no liability for any damage that might result from their use. Users of these programs must verify their accuracy and assume all responsibility for their proper use.

solescence. This greater risk is reflected in a higher terminal capitalization rate.

Actually a case could be made for selecting a terminal rate that is lower than the initial rate. If the property is operating at less than stabilized occupancy, is in a weak market, or is expected to become a stronger, more attractive investment in the future, a lower terminal rate might be warranted. Lower capitalization rates are associated with more desirable properties, so a lower rate might be applicable to the reversion if the subject property is expected to get healthier.

After the resale price is estimated, it is sometimes desirable to approximate the transaction costs likely to be incurred. These costs vary with the size of the transaction, but will include a brokerage fee (which might be negotiated as low as 1½%), legal fees, title insurance charges, prepayment penalties on mortgage notes, and the costs of repairs requested by the buyer.

When capitalizing a net operating income into a reversion price, the cash outlay for leasing commissions and tenant improvements may or may not be deducted from the cash flows to be capitalized. The prevailing practice is not to deduct them. One popular packaged computer program, Pro-Ject, allows the appraiser to make this choice. As mentioned previously, deducting these outlays will result in a smaller cash flow amount and produce a lower capitalization rate. Some explanation should be included in the report for readers who are familiar with traditionally derived rates.

Specifying DCF Assumptions

Many assumptions must be made to support a discounted cash flow model. As the late Professor James A. Graaskamp told his real estate investment students at the University of Wisconsin, what you are really buying in a real estate investment is the assumptions. Since the analyst has to make many decisions in developing input data for any DCF model, this information can easily be shared with the reader of the report. A sample list of cash flow assumptions is shown in Figure 8.1. With this information the reader can evaluate the persuasiveness of the analysis against the backdrop of the local area data presented earlier in the report.

```
┌─────────────────────────────────────────────────────────────────────────┐
│ Figure 8.1  List of Cash Flow Assumptions                                 │
└─────────────────────────────────────────────────────────────────────────┘
```

Subject Property: Smith Road Shopping Center

Analysis period:	16 years, starting 4/92
	Property sold in Year 10.
Market rents:	$13.00/sq. ft. for new retail shop leases, escalated at 3% per year for leases signed in Years 4 through 16.
Growth rate:	Overall expense growth 3%
	CPI 4%
Renewal/re-leasing:	60% renewals; 40% new leases
Commissions:	In-house only: New leases—first month's rent + 5%
	Renewals—5%
	Co-brokered: New leases—1.5 months' rent + 7.5%
	Renewals—7.5%
	20% of leases are co-brokered
	Commission is paid over the term of the lease.
Alterations:	New leases $0/sq. ft.
	Renewals $2.00/sq. ft.
	Speculative renewals $0.40/sq. ft.
Free rent:	New 3-year lease 3 months
	Renewal of 3-year lease 0 months
	Speculative renewal of 3-year lease 1.2 months
Expenses (in	Taxes $575,000
stabilized Year 3	Insurance $0.15/sq. ft.
—4/95)	Common area maintenance $0.60/sq. ft.
	Management 3% of *EGI*
	General & administrative $0.05/sq. ft.
	Allowance for replacement $0.05/sq. ft.
Recoveries:	Anchor tenants typically pay pro rata share of real estate taxes and CAM. (Refer to the rent roll in the addendum for details regarding anchor tenant recoveries.)
Credit loss:	2% for retail shop tenants only
Speculative renewal:	3 years with 2 months' down time between tenants, with speculative renewal free rent, alterations, and commissions.
Reversion:	Year 11 net operating income capitalized at 9.5% and sales costs of 2% are deducted to arrive at net sales proceeds
Discount rate:	10%

Packaged Computer Simulation

A sophisticated, packaged computer simulation analysis specifies income at least on a year-to-year basis, but more likely on a monthly or quarterly basis. This level of sophistication is probably appropriate for regional and superregional malls and will be required by lenders and investors in larger shopping centers. In many cases computer simulation analysis best captures the way lenders and equity investors analyze these assets. A number of popular programs are identified in a following section. One of these programs may even be specified by certain large institutional clients. These models can be used to value large-scale, existing centers with many complex leases. The income approach section of a narrative appraisal report will usually include both direct capitalization, if this method is used at all in the submarket, and a discounted cash flow analysis.

Appraisers must understand the difference between capitalization rates and discount rates. A cap rate is an income rate and represents the ratio of one year's income to the value of the property. It includes no explicit assumptions about investment benefits other than *NOI*, but these are reflected implicitly when the cap rate is compared to average rates at that time. A discount or yield rate is a more complete and explicit measure of all the benefits forecast for the years in a projected holding period. When a discount rate is applied, each of the cash flows is weighted to reflect its timing within the investment according to the compound interest theory.

The discount rate, which is also called the *target yield* or *desired internal rate of return*, is used in discounted cash flow analysis to capitalize investor benefits into a value estimate. The yield can be computed for all the cash flows from the investment, or just for the mortgage lender's cash flows or the equity investor's cash flows after the debt service is paid. In other words, total property yields, mortgage yields, or equity yields can be identified. When a DCF model is used, the appraiser should be consistent in discount rate selection and cash flow modeling. Moreover, in extracting yields from comparable sales and secondary data sources, the rate selected should correspond to its intended use. That is, a property yield which ignores borrowed money should not be used to discount the cash flows to an equity investor after the debt service on mortgage financing is paid.

Discount rates should reflect market rates of return on invested capital appropriate to the risk being assumed. When there are various sources of gross and net income with different levels of reliability and stability (risk), multiple discount rates can be applied in estimating the components of present value. Overage rental collections are considered less reliable than base rental collections and therefore a higher capitalization rate is justified. Rental income from anchor stores may be considered more reliable than income from mall tenants and may warrant a lower capitalization rate. When business income and business enterprise value are present, a higher discount rate may be applied to reflect the greater risk associated with these value components. If a single, blended discount rate is applied, it might be higher than the rate applicable to assets without recognized business enterprise value. Of course, few comparable transactions may be available to support these discount rates, so judgment and discretion will be required.

The discount rate for the DCF analysis should be based in part on local, primary empirical evidence and checked against secondary data sources. The narrative report should identify the secondary sources from which data were obtained and make clear whether the quoted discount rates or yields are for "free-and-clear" properties or those financed with leverage capital. Secondary data are periodically released by real estate consulting companies, accounting firms, and other real estate service companies.[2] For example, one newsletter recently reported that in one major urban market the typical going-in cap rate for community malls was 9.0, the typical reversion cap rate was 9.5, and the typical discount rate was 0.12. Appraisers should not use the secondary data from the samples, but watch the fluctuations in these rates and study their relationships over time to test the reasonableness of the relationships indicated by local data.

Computer Simulation Programs

The cost of acquiring small computer systems has declined and the availability of packaged real estate investment software has increased, so computer analysis of the discounted cash flows of investment real estate has become standard. Because shopping centers are primarily viewed as income streams and future cash flows can be forecast fairly reliably from the leases in place, most shopping center appraisals will include a computer-supported discounted cash flow analysis. It is beyond the scope of this text to guide the appraiser in the selection of computer hardware or software,

2. Some representative national and regional firms that publish newsletters are Cushman and Wakefield, Appraisal Division, *Real Estate Outlook*; Laventhol & Horwath Real Estate Appraisal Services, *Real Estate Investor Survey*; Valuation Network Inc., *Viewpoint '90-91*; and Pritchett, Ball & White, Inc., *Atlanta Real Estate Investors' Criteria Survey*.

but a few general considerations are warranted in selecting software for shopping center analysis. (A more detailed list from which these items were drawn is presented in the appendix to this chapter.[3])

- Does the program provide for different revenue types (e.g., base rental income, percentage rentals, and expense recoveries)?
- Does the software allow for a minimum holding period of at least 10 years?
- Is there sufficient flexibility to handle the growth of revenue and expense items—i.e., an opportunity to vary them for each year of the holding period?
- Will the program allow the analyst to specify a different market rent for each tenant as well as different rates of growth in market rents for different kinds of space?
- Will the program recompute expense stops for new leases throughout the holding period?
- Will the program compute cash flows on a monthly basis as well as an annual basis? Does the supporting documentation give examples of output formats?
- How well does the program handle different growth rates in each expense category? Is it able to vary the rate each year?
- Are there provisions for stepped increases in revenues and expenses
   —as dollar amounts (total or per square foot)
   —per the Consumer Price Index
   —for variable increases within the base lease term
   —for variable rates for each year of the holding
      period or during option terms?
- Are there provisions for free rent concessions, which are usually specified in months?

---

3. This list is derived from an excellent overview of DCF software by James R. Burbach, MAI, "What to Look for in Discounted Cash Flow Software, "*The Appraisal Journal* (April 1990), 196-201.

- Does the software have the ability to calculate tenant improvement costs either in annual dollars or at a rate per square foot, and to differentiate rates between new tenants and renewal tenants?

- Can the software calculate leasing commission costs either in dollars per square foot or as a percentage of the lease revenue over the lease term? Again, can the program differentiate between new tenants and renewal tenants?

- Does the software provide for a one-time charge or amortization of tenant improvement costs and leasing commissions over the lease period?

- For the reversionary calculation, can the software either include or exclude tenant improvement costs and leasing commissions from the net income to be capitalized?

Specific Shopping Center Software

Numerous sources and journals publish reviews and other information about software packages appropriate for shopping center appraisals. The Appraisal Institute publishes *The Quarterly Byte*, which provides reviews of software and covers computer-related issues of concern to appraisers.[4] Private user groups such as the Real Estate Analysts Microcomputer Users Group, or REMUG, in Berkeley, California offer appraisers opportunities to exchange information.[5] The spring issue of *Real Estate Finance* has for several years carried a real estate software report. This report identifies popular software and comments on its use. In the past few years the review has been prepared by the Software Testing Center at the University of Denver Real Estate Construction Management Department. The comments in the report are based on department testing and are offered as unbiased evaluations; however, the software is tested by students who are not professional testers.

The author's own survey of shopping center appraisers and lenders indicates that the most widely used programs include ProJect, which is sometimes linked with Dynamis for after-tax analysis and financial struc-

---

4. For subscription information, call the Appraisal Institute at (312) 335-4100.

5. For membership and subscription information, call REMUG at (818) 785-5416.

ture testing, and Center.[6] The University of Denver's Software Testing Center report for Spring 1990 reviewed programs in the following categories: analysis, appraisal, development and construction, mortgage servicing, and property management and marketing. Included in the review were the ARGUS software, Dynamis, PlanEASe, RealVal2, and RE-FINE:TWO, among others. The Spring 1989 report reviewed ARGUS, LYNS, ATV2, and others. Neither issue included Center. The report included publishers' names and addresses, the price of the canned routine, and whether demonstration disks were available.

Additional directory and evaluation information is available from the following sources:

- *Real Estate Software Sourcebook, 1988-1989*, Federal Research Press, 210 Lincoln Street, Boston, MA 02111-2491.

- *Construction Computer Applications Directory*, Construction Industry Press, 58 Paul Drive, Suite F, San Rafael, CA 94903.

- *Guide to Real Estate Software*, Real Estate Solutions, Inc., Klingle Road, N.W., Washington, D.C. 20005.

- *Microcomputer Applications in Real Estate*, American Real Estate Society, c/o Craig Stanley, California State University, Sacramento, CA 95819.

- *Mortgage Banking Software*, Mortgage Banking Association, 1125 15th Street, N.W., Washington, D.C. 20005.

- *Real Estate Software*, Texas Real Estate Research Center, Texas A&M University, College Station, TX 77843.[7]

From published reviews and random interviews with shopping center specialists, it appears that the emerging dominant software package for regional centers is ProJect. As of this writing, many leading life insurance companies have specified that this packaged computer program be used

---

6. Users of the computer programs described in this book should be aware that the Appraisal Institute has not developed, reviewed, or approved them. Therefore, the Appraisal Institute takes no responsibility and assumes no liability for any damage that might result from their use. Users of these programs must verify their accuracy and assume all responsibility for their proper use.

7. This list is reprinted from Glenn R. Mueller, "Real Estate Software Report, 1990," *Real Estate Finance* (Spring 1990), 21.

for appraisals and analyses submitted to them. ProJect is a detailed, sophisticated, multilease (or lease-by-lease) analytical computer program. This program meets all performance criteria listed in the preceding section, but it is considered difficult to learn and use. In the author's experience, to attain and maintain competence with ProJect an appraiser would need to use it on a regular basis.

Sample Computer-Supported Discounted Cash Flow Analysis

The computer output from one popular packaged program is presented in Table 8.1. The program used by this appraiser was ProJect. Certain details have been disguised to preserve confidentiality. The analyst used the program to test a preliminary property value of $1,000,000 for various yields (or discount rates) starting at 0.10 and rising in increments of 0.005 to a top discount rate of 0.12. A terminal capitalization rate of 0.11 was applied to the income forecast for Year 12 to estimate the probable resale price (or property reversion) at the end of Year 11. Various revenue and expense items were reported on a unit basis to facilitate comparison with other data. The excerpted report indicates that an internal rate of return of 0.102, or 10.2%, could result from the forecasted cash flows.

Appraising the Problem Property

The current business environment has caused many real estate problems. Overbuilding in some markets has resulted from excessive capital investment and been aggravated by income tax incentives. The lack of demand for space experienced in recessionary periods has caused further distress. Deregulation of the thrift industry and bank capital shortfalls have contributed to many real estate problems.

Other problems with shopping center development can result from strictly physical factors such as environmental hazards, inadequate ingress and egress, poor visibility and signage, and insufficient construction quality. Many problems are caused by developers: excessive leverage, ineffective control of construction costs, naive financial projections, poor business management, and fraudulent actions.

As a result of these problems, many properties do not have sufficient cash flow to meet operating expenses and debt service. Consequently, the

Table 8.1 Sample Computer-Supported DCF Analysis for a Shopping Plaza

GLA 13,783 sq. ft.
Terminal cap rate 11.0%
Discount floor 10.0%

Price $1,000,000
Sale expense 2.0%
Discount step 0.5%

	Year 1 1992	Year 2 1993	Year 3 1994	Year 4 1995	Year 5 1996	Year 6 1997	Year 7 1998	Year 8 1999	Year 9 2000	Year 10 2001	Year 11 2002	Year 12 2003
Gross potential income												
Cleaners	$10,416	$12,310	$13,343	$10,982	$13,644	$14,326	$12,259	$15,233	$15,995	$13,539	$16,511	$17,336
Hair dresser	$12,000	$12,000	$15,000	$15,750	$13,136	$16,260	$17,073	$14,638	$18,153	$19,061	$16,214	$19,675
Bookstore	$12,917	$14,880	$15,624	$16,405	$13,550	$16,937	$17,784	$14,833	$18,360	$19,278	$16,528	$20,497
Takeout food	$22,036	$22,000	$16,812	$16,112	$16,918	$14,608	$17,462	$18,335	$17,574	$17,418	$19,872	$20,866
Mail service	$14,900	$14,158	$11,557	$13,185	$13,844	$11,490	$14,293	$15,007	$12,842	$15,958	$16,755	$14,182
Dentist	$8,010	$9,225	$9,686	$8,239	$9,998	$10,498	$9,019	$10,836	$11,378	$9,873	$11,743	$12,330
Physical therapist	$33,600	$30,600	$32,130	$33,737	$27,865	$34,831	$36,572	$30,503	$37,756	$39,644	$33,990	$42,152
Retail merchant	$8,680	$15,314	$16,080	$13,610	$16,599	$17,428	$14,899	$17,990	$18,889	$16,309	$19,496	$20,471
Office tenant	$2,700	$10,935	$11,482	$9,914	$11,851	$12,443	$11,927	$11,821	$13,487	$14,161	$11,753	$14,620
Free rent	($8,061)	($4,880)	($4,753)	($7,524)	($11,889)	($3,745)	($8,668)	($14,152)	($2,584)	($7,481)	($19,336)	($2,824)
Total gross potential rental income	$117,198	$136,542	$136,961	$130,410	$125,516	$145,076	$142,620	$135,044	$161,850	$157,760	$143,526	$179,305
Per sq. ft.	$8.50	$9.91	$9.94	$9.46	$9.11	$10.53	$10.35	$9.80	$11.74	$11.45	$10.41	$13.01
Tenant recoveries												
Real estate taxes	$4,229	$4,719	$4,853	$4,935	$5,066	$5,236	$5,394	$5,534	$5,813	$5,797	$6,042	$6,448
Insurance	$630	$702	$723	$734	$754	$780	$803	$823	$866	$862	$898	$959
Common area maintenance	$5,425	$6,057	$6,226	$6,334	$6,502	$6,721	$6,920	$7,102	$7,460	$7,439	$7,753	$8,273
Management	$2,904	$3,331	$3,250	$3,094	$3,308	$3,462	$3,355	$3,640	$3,895	$3,574	$3,954	$4,413
Total tenant recoveries	$13,188	$14,809	$15,052	$15,097	$15,630	$16,199	$16,472	$17,099	$18,034	$17,672	$18,647	$20,093
Per sq. ft.	$0.96	$1.07	$1.09	$1.10	$1.13	$1.18	$1.20	$1.24	$1.31	$1.28	$1.35	$1.46

Table 8.1 Sample Computer-Supported DCF Analysis for a Shopping Plaza (continued)

	Year 1 1992	Year 2 1993	Year 3 1994	Year 4 1995	Year 5 1996	Year 6 1997	Year 7 1998	Year 8 1999	Year 9 2000	Year 10 2001	Year 11 2002	Year 12 2003
Total gross potential income	$130,386	$151,351	$152,013	$145,507	$141,146	$161,275	$159,092	$152,143	$179,884	$175,432	$162,173	$199,398
Per sq. ft.	$9.46	$10.98	$11.03	$10.58	$10.24	$11.70	$11.54	$11.04	$13.05	$12.73	$11.77	$14.47
Credit loss	($2,114)	($2,532)	($2,710)	($2,531)	($2,425)	($2,911)	($2,799)	($2,611)	($3,185)	($3,161)	($2,775)	($3,497)
Misc. income & credit loss	($2,114)	($2,532)	($2,710)	($2,531)	($2,425)	($2,911)	($2,799)	($2,611)	($3,185)	($3,161)	($2,775)	($3,497)
Effective gross income	$128,272	$148,819	$149,303	$142,976	$138,721	$158,364	$156,293	$149,532	$176,699	$172,271	$159,398	$195,901
Per sq. ft.	$9.31	$10.80	$10.83	$10.37	$10.06	$11.49	$11.34	$10.85	$12.82	$12.50	$11.56	$14.21
Expenses												
Real estate taxes	$9,432	$9,715	$10,007	$10,307	$10,616	$10,935	$11,263	$11,600	$11,948	$12,307	$12,676	$13,056
Insurance	$1,403	$1,446	$1,489	$1,534	$1,580	$1,627	$1,676	$1,726	$1,778	$1,831	$1,886	$1,943
Management	$5,131	$5,953	$5,972	$5,719	$5,549	$6,335	$6,252	$5,981	$7,068	$6,891	$6,376	$7,836
Common area maintenance	$10,526	$10,842	$11,167	$11,502	$11,847	$12,202	$12,568	$12,945	$13,334	$13,734	$14,146	$14,570
Full service utilities	$5,535	$5,701	$5,872	$6,048	$6,230	$6,417	$6,609	$6,808	$7,012	$7,222	$7,439	$7,662
Full service janitor	$3,460	$3,563	$3,670	$3,780	$3,894	$4,011	$4,131	$4,255	$4,382	$4,514	$4,649	$4,789
Replacement reserves	$1,403	$1,446	$1,489	$1,534	$1,580	$1,627	$1,676	$1,726	$1,778	$1,831	$1,886	$1,943
Total expenses	$36,890	$38,666	$39,666	$40,424	$41,296	$43,154	$44,175	$45,041	$47,300	$48,330	$49,058	$51,799
Per sq. ft.	$2.68	$2.81	$2.88	$2.93	$3.00	$3.13	$3.21	$3.27	$3.43	$3.51	$3.56	$3.76
NOI before nonoperating expenses	$91,382	$110,153	$109,637	$102,552	$97,425	$115,210	$112,118	$104,491	$129,399	$123,941	$110,340	$144,102
Per sq. ft.	$6.63	$7.99	$7.95	$7.44	$7.07	$8.36	$8.13	$7.58	$9.39	$8.99	$8.01	$10.46

Table 8.1 Sample Computer-Supported DCF Analysis for a Shopping Plaza (continued)

	Year 1 1992	Year 2 1993	Year 3 1994	Year 4 1995	Year 5 1996	Year 6 1997	Year 7 1998	Year 8 1999	Year 9 2000	Year 10 2001	Year 11 2002	Year 12 2003
Nonoperating expenses												
Commissions	$3,940	$2,551	$3,394	$4,273	$6,294	$6,641	$6,661	$6,814	$7,367	$7,272	$7,406	$8,203
Capital improvements	$9,000	$0	$0	$0	$0	$0	$0	$0	$0	$0	$0	$0
Alterations	$17,056	$7,613	$7,528	$15,559	$20,496	$8,468	$12,921	$27,982	$4,355	$15,431	$36,741	$4,899
Total nonoperating expenses	$29,996	$10,164	$10,922	$19,832	$26,790	$15,109	$19,582	$34,796	$11,722	$22,703	$44,147	$13,102
Per sq. ft.	$2.18	$0.74	$0.79	$1.44	$1.94	$1.10	$1.42	$2.52	$0.85	$1.65	$3.20	$0.95
NOI after nonoperating expenses	$61,386	$99,989	$98,715	$82,720	$70,635	$100,101	$92,536	$69,695	$117,677	$101,238	$66,193	$131,000
Per sq. ft.	$4.45	$7.25	$7.16	$6.00	$5.12	$7.26	$6.71	$5.06	$8.54	$7.35	$4.80	$9.50
Market value @ end of Year 11 capitalizing Year 12 at 11.0%						$1,310,018						
Sale expenses						$26,200						
Net sale proceeds						$1,283,818						
Cash flows per year	$61,386	$99,989	$98,715	$82,720	$70,635	$100,101	$92,536	$69,695	$117,677	$101,238	$1,350,011	

PV of cash flows in Years 1-11 discounted at:		$/Sq. Ft.		PV of cash flows in Years 2-11 discounted at:		$/Sq. Ft
10.0%	$1,012,000	$73.42		10.0%	$1,051,000	$76.25
10.5%	$977,000	$70.88		10.5%	$1,018,000	$73.86
11.0%	$943,000	$68.42		11.0%	$986,000	$71.54
11.5%	$912,000	$66.17		11.5%	$955,000	$69.29
12.0%	$881,000	$63.92		12.0%	$926,000	$67.18

Internal rate of return based on a price of $1,000,000

IRR 10.2%

Second year overall rate 10.0%

developers and owners must default on their obligations. In recent years, real estate valuations have been used by lenders to set workout or foreclosure strategies and by bankruptcy courts to determine equity values.

In many ways the appraisal of a problem property is the same as the valuation of a healthy property. In either case the purpose of the appraisal is carefully specified; the date of the valuation is stated; the rights being appraised are identified; thoughtful market (area) analysis is performed to review the important forces affecting demand and supply in the submarket for the subject property; properly focused trade area (neighborhood) analysis is conducted to profile demand and supply conditions and transaction terms in the immediate submarket; and all of the decision processes of likely market participants must be understood and replicated. One primary difference in appraising a problem property, however, is that the input data for the appraisal are much less reliable and, consequently, the reliability of the resulting value estimate may be substantially reduced or completely lacking.

Unfortunately, appraisers do not always state the confidence levels associated with their forecasts. In popular practice an appraiser usually provides a point estimate of market value with no quantitative nor qualitative analysis of its reliability. For many years it has been suggested that standard deviations or ranges be used to let the user of the report know how much to depend on the numerical answer. Most appraisal users may not know how to evaluate this additional information, however, and might be confounded by it. Nevertheless, current economic conditions in real estate markets may make it necessary to embrace all available techniques to minimize financial uncertainty.

Sometimes analysts attempt to capture the impact of a risk merely by making an explicit assumption and effectively eliminating any alternatives. For example, the valuation of a regional mall may be predicated on the assumption that the anchor will stay in operation, even though there is a chance that it may close. The report may offer no analysis about that possibility.

It may be instructive to examine how purchasers of shopping centers behave. For a 150,000-sq.-ft. center with 40% vacancies, an investor may offer a price that represents the present value of the "income in place," and consider any potential growth as a return on his managerial and entrepreneurial efforts. This rationale could be employed when trade area analysis shows little hope for demographic or purchasing power growth. In essence this investor is assuming that the property has already achieved its stabilized effective gross income. In another situation the buyer may find reason to anticipate growth, if trade analysis indicates favorable demographics and good merchandising.

A regional mall with an anchor that has closed or is in bankruptcy presents a different kind of problem. In this case the investor is likely to evaluate the possibility of procuring a substitute anchor tenant to occupy the space and replace the generating energy of the previous anchor. The investor will also consider how the whole center would be affected if the space were redesigned for smaller tenants. If neither of these plans is feasible and no other long-term use is likely, many institutional investors would pass over the property. In such a case the investment opportunity is substantially more complicated than a pricing issue.

Simple, traditional methods for dealing with risk or uncertainty include the use of increased capitalization rates or discount rates, which are used subjectively to incorporate a risk dimension into the analysis. No professional literature is available to guide the appraiser in determining how much of a risk premium is appropriate for this purpose.

Computer technology gives appraisers a tool for testing alternative assumptions and their impact on a variety of property measures. By simulating a large number of detailed assumptions about an investment property, analysts can ask "What if. . . ?" questions to understand the dynamics of a property more fully and better estimate its value. A partial equilibrium analysis can be performed by changing one input variable at a time (e.g., the vacancy rate) to observe the sensitivity of yield or value to that variable. When an input variable is shown to be critical to the output, it can be subjected to field investigation, which is more rigorous and expensive.

Another type of financial modeling is the use of best case and worse case scenarios to pinpoint the most probable scenario and elucidate the full range of likely events. Each of these simulation runs is termed deterministic because each leads to a single answer.

When computer cash flow modeling is combined with probability theory, the analyst can run a program, or *density model*, a large number of times. Each run draws a probability estimate from a random number generator and extends the best/worse/most probable case triad. With this technique, a large number of yield or value estimates can be described with statistical variability indications.

Although popular in academic circles, such stochastic models have been criticized by practitioners. Appraisers agree that they cannot obtain sufficient data to determine probability distributions for vacancies, expense growth rates, rental growth rates, or other input variables. Moreover, early users of these techniques did not account for interactions among some of the input variables. Thus a probability model might draw a high growth rate from the probability distribution for rental growth rates and simultaneously select a low growth rate for operating expense growth; this might be an unlikely combination in an inflationary environment where both rents and expenses would increase at comparatively high rates.

Despite experimentation with probabilistic simulation and the subsequent development of popular software such as @Risk for use with spreadsheet applications, computer simulation technology has not been easily accepted by practitioners. A lack of basic information on probability theory has probably contributed to their distrust.

As computer technology becomes increasingly available and affordable, more small appraisal firms are using computer modeling. One very popular, expensive modeling package for multitenant properties such as shopping centers and office towers includes probabilistic modeling. In modeling lease expirations with the ProJect routine, the user is asked to estimate the probability of a particular tenant renewing the lease as well as the probability of resulting tenant improvement expenses and commission payments. Practitioners have become accustomed to making such estimates in their computer programs. Perhaps they are comforted by the law of offsetting errors, which indicates that an error in the likelihood of one tenant's renewing can be offset by an opposite error in the estimate made for another tenant. As they become more familiar and confident with computer programs, practitioners are probably ready to reconsider probabilistic simulation and combine random number generators with PC-based spreadsheet simulators. The @Risk program is an adjunct to popular spreadsheets which provides an array of probability distributions that a user can incorporate into discounted cash flow modeling.

Appraisers still need to deal with the lack of available input data for estimating the likelihood of various alternative outcomes. They know they will not be able to obtain large samples of closely related data pertaining to market sales, rates of return, or other necessary inputs. Many have learned to work confidently with very small data sets based on a few good comparable sales; others rely on experts to help them develop inputs for simulation models.

For example, one of the worst things that can happen to a regional mall is for an anchor tenant to close or, in the language of the trade, "go dark." This has such an adverse effect on the tenant mix and the draw of center that the property may fail. An equally bad situation is created when the anchor tenant continues to make rental payments, so as not to default under the terms of the lease, but ceases its operations. Such events are impossible to forecast with the implied reliability of most market value appraisals. The mere uncertainty that an anchor may go bankrupt, as so many retailers have, or withdraw when the operating agreement expires, may cause a mall to drop out of the category of investment-grade properties of interest to large investing institutions. If these potential buyers are lost, there are no analogues from which to infer and develop a value indication. In effect the value becomes imponderable, but it is not practical to prepare an appraisal report indicating that the value cannot be determined. As a result, the practitioner is likely to try to derive a point estimate of value based on a set of clearly stated assumptions. However, the effect of each of these clearly stated assumptions is deterministic; the client really has received an imponderable value estimate, but has not been forced to face it.

An alternative approach to such an appraisal might be to report that a small panel of experts believe that the anchor will withdraw from the subject mall. If five such experts could be interviewed and persuaded to offer odds or probabilities along with their opinions, the appraiser could reconcile these judgments into a single probability estimate or perhaps construct a distribution from them. Providing this estimate with a recapitulation of the interview comments to the client could add a very useful dimension to the appraisal analysis.

The decision-making process just described is called a *delphi method*, and it is a standard part of college business courses. Sometimes the panelists are told the opinions of the other experts and allowed to revise their expectations or forecasts accordingly.

Where would an appraiser find such experts in the appraisal of a shopping center? The possibilities might include

- The mall manager who has been regularly involved in discussions with the anchor manager
- The manager of a competitive anchor
- Credit-reporting sources that have been tracking the finances of the anchor or its parent company
- Securities analysts who have been following the retailing industry and possibly tracking the anchor company's stock (Company and industry reports are accessible to analysts on CD ROM disks, which are now available in public and university libraries.)

A final value estimate could be developed by weighting the expected outcomes. Assume that the appraiser has carefully analyzed the operating results of the shopping center if the anchor remains and recent trends continue as well as the likely business results if the anchor departs. The appraiser has carefully read all of the mall leases to see which of the mall tenants have the right to withdraw or reduce their rents to percentage rates only if the anchor leaves. The new level of sales without the anchor's drawing power has also been estimated, perhaps with the help of expert witness panels. The appraiser estimates that the value of the center with the anchor is $10 million; without it the value is $5 million. The odds of the anchor failing are 40%, and the chances of succeeding at least during the investment ownership period projected in the appraisal report are 60%. With this information, a value of $7 million can be calculated as follows:

$$.40 \times \$10 \text{ million} = \$4 \text{ million}$$
$$.60 \times \$5 \text{ million} = \$3 \text{ million}$$
$$\text{Total} \qquad \$7 \text{ million}$$

A calculation such as this is standard fare in elementary probability courses. This simplified example fails to do justice to the technique; it is obviously wrong in either case. The center will be worth either $10 million or $5 million, but in neither case will it be worth $7 million. In this simple example this is a very serious flaw, but in a practical application a larger number of conditions would be analyzed with a wider range of possible inputs. The final output would be expressed in such a way that a sophisticated reader could interpret it and judge the reliability of the estimate. Figure 8.2 illustrates a sample probability distribution of values.[8]

In addition to forecasting value distributions, this method can be used to generate a probability distribution for net operating incomes. A graphics package could be used to plot the incomes and a figure resembling the traditional bell-shaped curve might be produced. Then the level of debt service could be plotted, and the proportion of the values falling under the income curve but above the debt service curve would provide an estimate of the risk (in terms of percentage probability) that the property will fail to cover the required debt service.[9]

Summary

Established decision theory can suggest ways to deal with uncertainty in a logical, documented manner which is, of course, the objective of appraisal reporting. While many appraisers have not yet embraced these techniques, the failure of some traditional analytical methods and the prevalence of problem properties may lead to a rethinking of the valuation process and greater interest in this experimental technique.

Chapter 8 Appendix: Selecting Computer Simulation Programs

The complete list of selection criteria presented by James R. Burbach is set forth below.[10]

- Is the software limited to a specific property type or can it analyze various real estate classifications and multiuse properties?

---

8. A discussion of this technique using the PlanEASe software with a case example and illustrative graphics appears in Kenneth J. Gain, "Appraising By Probability Analysis," *The Appraisal Journal* (January 1990). A review of PlanEASe by Kenneth Gain appears with a sample graphic in *The Quarterly Byte*, vol. 7, no. 2, 12–14, published by the Appraisal Institute.

9. Professor Julian Diaz III of Georgia State University suggested this idea.

10. James R. Burbach, MAI, "What to Look for in Discounted Cash Flow Software," *The Appraisal Journal* (April 1990), 196-201.

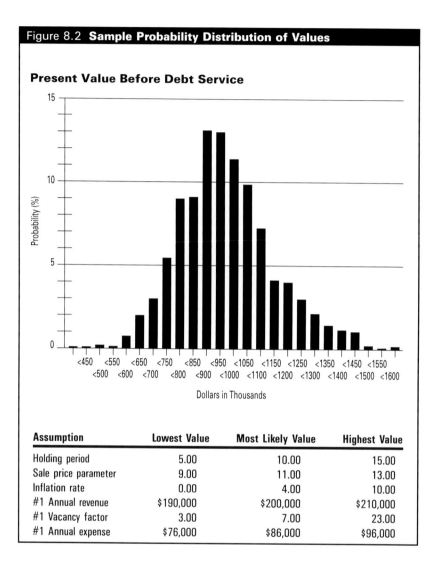

Figure 8.2 **Sample Probability Distribution of Values**

Present Value Before Debt Service

Assumption	Lowest Value	Most Likely Value	Highest Value
Holding period	5.00	10.00	15.00
Sale price parameter	9.00	11.00	13.00
Inflation rate	0.00	4.00	10.00
#1 Annual revenue	$190,000	$200,000	$210,000
#1 Vacancy factor	3.00	7.00	23.00
#1 Annual expense	$76,000	$86,000	$96,000

- Can the analyst download completed analyses into a spreadsheet program for further manipulation?
- Does the program provide for different revenue types (base rental income, percentage rentals, and expense recoveries)?
- Does the software permit at least a ten-year minimum holding period?

- Is there sufficient flexibility in treating the growth of revenue and expense items — such as an opportunity to vary them for each year of the holding period?
- Will the program allow specification of a different market rent for each tenant as well as different growth rates in market rents for different kinds of space?
- Can the program adjust variable expenses to reflect the occupancy in the building?
- Is it possible to create a custom expense code that permits the pass-through of certain expenses for some tenants and a different set of expenses for other tenants?
- Will it recompute expense stops for new leases throughout the holding period?
- Will the program compute cash flows on a monthly basis as well as an annual basis? Does the supporting documentation give examples of output formats?
- Is data analyzed on the basis of the calendar or fiscal year or both? The mix of uses in the same property analysis is another important factor to consider. Some programs, for example, require separation of retail from office uses in the discounted cash flow.
- What is the largest number of portfolios, properties, or leases that can be input?
- How flexible is the program in changing titles for revenue/expense categories?
- What is the capability for different growth rates in each expense category, including the ability to vary the rate each year?
- What about the ability to input base expenses either as a dollar amount or a percentage of revenue?
- Can the program input lease income on either an annual, monthly, or per square foot basis?
- Are there provisions for stepped increases in revenues and expenses:
  —as dollar amounts (total or per square foot)
  —per Consumer Price Index

—for variable increases within base lease term

—for variable rates for each year of the holding period or during option terms

- Are there provisions for free rent concessions, which are usually specified in months?

- Does the software have the ability to calculate tenant improvement costs either by annual dollars or a rate per square foot, and to differentiate rates between new tenants and renewal tenants?

- Can the software calculate leasing commission costs either by dollars per square foot or as a percentage of the lease revenue over the lease term? Again, can the program differentiate between new tenants and renewal tenants?

- Does the software provide for a one-time charge or amortization of tenant improvement costs and leasing commissions over the lease period?

- For the reversionary calculation, does the software have the ability to include or exclude tenant improvement costs and leasing commissions from the net income to be capitalized?

- What about flexibility in the treatment of lease types, such as

—gross or full service (all expenses paid by landlord)

—expense stop (tenant pays expenses over specified base for a specific year or dollar amount per square foot)

—net lease (tenant pays all expenses)

- Can future lease terms be variable for different tenants, along with different vacancy assumptions for the individual spaces between new leases terms?

- Can the software handle percentage clauses based on retail sales volumes?

- Can the software vary the length of the holding period, from at least one to ten years?

- Can the reversionary value be based on the capitalization of the net income in the last year of the holding period, the following year's net income, or is there an option for either year?

- Is there a provision for sales and closing costs upon sale of the property in the last year of the holding period?
- Is there a provision for capital expense items for each year of the holding period and for ground rent payments for each year of the holding period.
- The software should be able to handle various aspects of after-tax analysis, including
  —depreciation schedules
  —debt service treatment for principal and interest payments
  —capital gains (if tax laws change again)
  —consideration of investor tax brackets
- It may be necessary to have a vendor who, for an annual service fee, will ensure that the program reflects current tax laws.
- Can the program provide a printout of the
  —detailed annual cash flow analysis for the property
  —individual tenant rent and expense escalations, vacancy, new lease terms, commissions, and refit costs
  —tenant directory or rent roll
  —pro forma operating statement
  —summary of assumptions used
- Can the program handle lease changes in the initial lease term and future option terms?
- Does the program perform present value and internal rate of return analyses, before and after tax?

Western Canadian mall   *K. Vreeland / H. Armstrong Roberts*

Chapter Nine

ALLOCATION PROBLEMS: BUSINESS VALUE, ASSESSMENTS, AND APPRAISING ANCHORS

Introduction

The appraisal of shopping centers is dynamic and many issues are unsettled. Three related problem areas are

1. Identification of the business enterprise value (*BEV*) associated with a shopping mall,

2. Correct procedures for shopping center assessment

3. Appraisal and assessment procedures for anchor stores and their sites

These general appraisal problems seem to be of greatest concern to taxpayers and assessors; they most often arise in the valuation of regional and superregional malls. All three problem areas concern the allocation of value among various components. Without well-established procedures for appraisers, these issues are being considered in court arguments and decisions. The discussion presented here is more descriptive than prescriptive and attempts to sensitize practitioners to these controversial topics.

Business Enterprise Theory

A current debate in shopping center valuations is whether to recognize going-concern value, or business enterprise value (*BEV*), in a center and how to measure it. To prove that there is a business value component over and above conventional real estate (or real property) value, market followers point to the low capitalization rates exhibited in many shopping center sales and to sale prices that exceed replacement costs. Such evidence is usually associated with superregional and regional malls.

If some of the value in a shopping center is business value, and it is included in local property tax assessments, double taxation may result when this value is taxed again in paying federal and state income taxes. Another concern is that mortgage lenders, because of regulation or company policy, do not lend on intangibles. They need to have an accurate estimate of the collateral subject to their lien and to separate out business intangibles that would not, or might not, continue under other ownership.

The issue is significant. Some mall owner-operators and anchor retailers contend that local property taxes are unfairly levied on non-realty business value; when these charges are passed through to the mall tenants, their operating expenses are increased unfairly and their competitiveness may be threatened. If these taxpayers are given relief, however, local communities must face a substantial loss in revenue or shift the tax burden to other taxpayers.

Some of the arguments against recognizing business value have been summarized by Arthur E. Gimmy:

- Mall land prices uniquely make up the difference between sales price and the depreciated replacement cost of the buildings and other improvements because the sites are monopolistic and unrelated to surrounding retail site prices.
- Appraisers and investors have traditionally not recognized shopping malls as businesses.
- Mall businesses have not been sold, exchanged or valued outside of a tax appeal assignment.
- Mall management does not conduct itself in a manner separate from a specialized real estate management team, is unlicensed, and doesn't consider itself as a taxable revenue entity.

- Malls are really only comprised of a large group of individual businesses and as such are only a means for these businesses to succeed and contribute to the economic health of the community.[1]

After reviewing research literature in business and economics and assessment case law, William Kinnard and Jeffrey Fisher have both concluded that a business value component does indeed exist.[2] They and others have cited many uses commonly thought to be combined with business value, including hotels, resorts, nursing homes, and private hospitals.[3] These properties are characterized by a high degree of business managerial ability and entrepreneurial effort, which contribute to the viability of the business and the value of the real estate.

The value of an asset derives from its productivity, with a fair market rate of return allocated to each of the agents of production. Traditionally these agents have included land, labor, and capital, with land frequently presumed to represent the residual. Kinnard and Fisher argue that a fourth agent, entrepreneurship, needs to be recognized and accorded a return, and that entrepreneurship, not the land, is the residual agent.

There are elements of entrepreneurship in the creation of a shopping center, throughout its construction, and subsequently in its operation. First the labor is allocated a market return through the payment of salaries and wages; then the invested capital receives its mortgage interest or equity cash flows; third, the land is afforded a fair market return (at market value for generic retail land) and, finally, any remaining income to the shopping center enterprise is considered to be a return for the entrepreneurship of the owner-operator. Kinnard and Fisher stress that entrepreneurship is especially significant in a seasoned center that has been successfully promoted and leased over several years. The capitalized

1. Arthur E. Gimmy, MAI, "Conflict at the Mall: The Tax Reduction Solution," *Appraisal Views*, a quarterly newsletter published by Schultz, Carr, Bissette, & Atwater/VNI.

2. William N. Kinnard, Jr., "Valuing the Real Estate of Regional Shopping Centers Independently of Operating Business Value Components: A Review of Recent Research," a paper prepared for AIREA annual meeting, Chicago, May 3, 1990, and Jeffrey D. Fisher and

William N. Kinnard, Jr., "The Business Value Component of Operating Properties: The Example of Shopping Malls," a paper presented at the 1989 National Conference of the International Association of Assessing Officers, Fort Worth, Texas, September 20, 1989.

3. Jeffrey D. Fisher, "Mall and Department Store Valuation," a working paper prepared for the Center for Real Estate Studies, Indiana University, March 1989.

present value of the residual income stream creates an intangible business or enterprise value that should not be imputed to the land.

Kinnard asserts, "It has long been held that any excess of contract rental over market rental is an intangible."[4] Jeffrey Fisher and George Lentz have observed that shopping center management is able to renew tenants at above-market rates because those tenants believe in the additional enterprise value of the center, its operation, and the synergistic image it presents to customers.[5]

Various authorities mandate the recognition and separation of non-real property value. Standards Rule 1-2 of the Uniform Standards of Professional Appraisal Practice states

> In developing a real property appraisal, an appraiser must observe the following specific appraisal guidelines:
> . . . . . (e) Identify and consider the effect on value of any personal property, trade fixtures or intangible items that are not real property but are included in the appraisal.

The Uniform Standards have been adopted by six key federal agencies to implement Title XI of the Financial Institutions Reform, Recovery and Enforcement Act of 1989 for appraisals "used in connection with certain real estate related financial transactions entered into or regulated by these agencies."[6]

Business enterprise value can easily be confused with shopping center real estate value when the comparable data to be analyzed are not properly defined. As Kinnard points out, the data set for comparable sites should include retail sites in general; to consider only shopping center land is a de facto classification or bias.[7] The operating ratios used in the income approach should be derived from data on a range of retail competitors, which are published by the International Council of Shopping Centers and the Urban Land Institute, not just from data on large malls. Otherwise, business value will be difficult to recognize.

4. Kinnard, 7.
5. Jeffrey D. Fisher and George H. Lentz, "Measuring Business Value in Shopping Malls," a paper published by the School of Business, Indiana University, Bloomington, September 1989.
6. *Federal Register*, vol. 55, no. 251, December 31, 1990, page 53610.
7. Kinnard, 11

In gathering sales data, appraisers must understand that the market for shopping centers is regional or national; it is not limited to the competitive retail trade area. Local assessors often have difficulty assessing shopping centers because they do not have enough data within their jurisdictions and lack sufficient resources to investigate elsewhere. When a comparable sale involves a particularly capable investor or operator, it may be appropriate to make an adjustment in the sales comparison approach to reflect such an atypical transaction.

Overestimating the economic life of a shopping center was discussed in Chapter 6. Considering the 12- to 15-year economic lives of many center improvements, rather than their longer physical life expectancies, will lower the value of the real estate as estimated with the cost approach. The amount by which the observed sale price exceeds the cost-based value estimate is business value. Effective age differences must also be considered in making adjustments to comparable sales in the sales comparison approach.

Kinnard reminds us that an assignment to estimate market value implies typical buyers, sellers, and operators. A center that is built and operated by a nationally recognized developer-owner such as The Rouse Company or Melvin Simon has greater desirability and thus greater value. This added value may be more appropriately considered business use value rather than market value.[8]

Other property types have recognized business value. There seems to be little debate that properties such as hotels, motels, and various kinds of congregate health care facilities have a business value component. An expert in the valuation of hotels and motels, Stephen Rushmore, MAI, writes:

> . . . lodging facilities are more than land, bricks and mortar. They are retail-oriented, labor-intensive businesses necessitating a high level of managerial expertise. In addition, hostelries require a significant investment in personal property (furniture, fixtures, and

8. Ibid.

equipment) that has a relatively short useful life and is subject to rapid depreciation and obsolescence.[9]

Rushmore states that it is important to separate the value of the business and the personalty from the real estate value to produce fair real property valuations for property tax assessment purposes.

In an earlier publication, Rushmore acknowledges that separating the business value of a hotel from its real estate value is a controversial topic because it is difficult to distinguish between business income and real estate returns. Sometimes, he indicates, the separation is not made:

> In an appraisal assignment in which the market value encompasses the entire property, the business is part of the "going concern" value and is not separated from the real estate. However, some insurance laws, condemnation proceedings, and property tax assessments require a "pure" real estate value, which necessitates treating business value as a separate entity.[10]

The work of Kinnard and Fisher has attracted other thinkers. Mark Kenney has offered an *enhanced property rights* concept with the following comments:

1. What is being appraised is real property, as a bundle of legal rights, and not just real estate in a physical sense.
2. The value created through agglomeration economics in a successful regional mall is created by the use of operating agreements as distinguished from a mall operator.
3. This operating agreement runs with the land and is part of the property rights. The agreement expands the property rights of all the parcels in the mall thereby enhancing them and the value.
4. The synergy of businesses is not independent of the land. The result is a relationship that produces a value increment over

---

9. Stephen Rushmore, MAI, and Karen E. Rubin, "The Valuation of Hotels and Motels for Assessment Purposes," *The Appraisal Journal* (April 1984), 270–288.

10. Stephen Rushmore, MAI, *Hotels, Motels and Restaurants: Valuations and Market Studies* (Chicago: American Institute of Real Estate Appraisers, 1983), 105.

and above the physical real estate, but not beyond the real property rights owned by the mall owner.

5. The management expertise which is required is compensated through fees that are expensed out of the rental income stream and thereby extracted from both income and value.

6. Hotel properties and their associated business values are not good analogues for shopping malls. Hotel management contracts don't run with the land; hotel rooms are marketed by chain operators who capitalize on national name recognition and a corporate sameness and dependability, while malls strive for individuality and cater to locational convenience; and the management company provides services to mall tenants rather than to final consumers with whom a business relationship would be developed.[11]

Kenney is willing to recognize a business enterprise value in two cases: 1) when extraordinary management enables a center to generate demonstrably higher rental incomes than comparable properties under average management, and 2) when a percentage rental clause generates rental income that exceeds market rates of rental income, thus creating a business relationship between the tenant and the owner. Some appraisers have wondered whether to allocate this income to the realty or personalty. Others question whether the business value created is attributable to the mall or the retail business.

J. D. Brown has explored another characteristic of business value or, as he calls it, *going-concern value*. He has written that this component of value can probably be transferred to another site and remain intact. In the case of a nationally famous fast-food outlet, for example, the value could be transferred.[12] A regional shopping mall seems to fall at the opposite extreme. Because of its site-specific, monopolistic penetration of the demographics and the exclusive commitments of the anchors, an alternative site in the submarket is probably precluded. A regional shopping center is in-

11. Mark T. Kenney, "Does Shopping Mall Development Create Business Value?" *The Appraisal Journal* (July 1991), 303-313.

12. James D. Brown, MAI, "Going Concern Value in the Congregate Care Industry and R 41C," *The Appraisal Journal* (April 1987), 286-291.

extricably linked to its site, so the business enterprise value is a nontangible component of real property value.

Brown argues that the consideration of business value could depend in part on the use of the appraisal.

> If the purpose is to allocate the purchase price for tax depreciation purposes, it may be proper to include intangible assets as part of the improvements. However, if the appraisal is to be made for ad valorem tax assessment purposes, it may be proper to exclude intangible assets from the value conclusion, since ad valorem taxes may be assessed only against tangible real property.[13]

More work needs to be done on this topic. Until agreement is reached, each individual appraiser must determine the appropriate treatment of business enterprise value according to the Appraisal Standards Boards interpretations of the Uniform Standards of Professional Appraisal Practice.

Methodology for Business Enterprise Valuation

For those who decide that business value needs to be recognized, the next question is, "How?" One analogue for the valuation of business enterprise value in shopping centers is the valuation of this component in fitness and racquet sports facilities. Arthur Gimmy suggests that business value is the difference between the property value estimates produced by the cost approach and the income approach.[14] Alternatively, if a property has been appraised using both the cost approach and the sales comparison approach and the value indicated by the sales comparison approach is based on real estate alone, then an average of these two estimates might be compared to the value derived using the income capitalization approach. Either way, the excess indicated by the income capitalization approach can be assigned to the business value. See Figure 9.1 for an illustration of how such a methodology could be applied to a shopping center.

---

13. Brown, 288-289.

14. Arthur E. Gimmy, MAI, and Brain B. Woodworth, *Fitness, Racquet Sports, and Spa Projects:* *A Guide to Appraisal, Market Analysis, Development, and Financing* (Chicago: American Institute of Real Estate Appraisers, 1989), 147.

Figure 9.1	**Sample Calculation of Business Enterprise Value by Extraction**	
Total market value of subject property (as indicated by the income and/or sales comparison approaches)		$10,900,000
Less real property value		
Land (by cost approach)	$1,500,000	
Building and site improvements (by cost approach)	$7,500,000	
Total		−$9,000,000
Indicated business enterprise value		$1,900,000

Kinnard agrees with this proposed methodology:

Reproduction cost new plus the indicated market value of the land as a site for a regional shopping center does appear to serve as an effective upper limit to market value of the real estate, *provided* developers overhead and profit are appropriately included as the measure of entrepreneurial profit in the cost new estimate.[15]

To estimate the value of a hotel property, exclusive of personalty and business value, Stephen Rushmore employs a residual income approach. He reduces the projected net operating income by specific amounts attributable to the value of the business and other personalty. The amount of income allocated to business income is estimated by multiplying the total business revenue by a market-derived management fee rate. Management fees for hotels typically range from 2% to 8% depending on whether the subject property is an independent or a chain and on other variables. Use of this procedure is supported by historical accounts of hotels owned by entirely passive investors, who contracted the operation to skilled merchandisers and managers at negotiated fees.

Net operating income is further reduced for the return on and of personal property by applying an income rate to its value. To develop this in-

---

15. Kinnard, 26-27.

come rate, the return of the capital invested in the personal property is estimated based on straight-line amortization of the replacement cost of all the personalty and an appropriate rate of return on the capital invested is added. Finally, the remaining income is capitalized into a value estimate for the real estate (see Figure 9.2).

Figure 9.2 **Sample Estimation of Business Enterprise Value by Residual Income Allocation**		
Net operating income to subject property		$1,000,000
Less return on hotel business		
0.05 × $10,000,000 business revenue	$500,000	
Less return on personal property		
0.11 × $500,000	$55,000	
Less return of capital in personal property with estimated remaining economic life of 10 years		
1/10 × $500,000	$50,000	
Total		−605,000
Income allocated to hotel real property		$395,000
Capitalized at indicated market rate for real property only		
$395,000/0.105		$3,761,900

Income to the personal property can also be estimated as a percentage of total revenue. This procedure is based on hotel management contracts, which require that a certain percentage of total revenues be set aside as reserves for replacement. Industry norms call for reserves equal to 1% to 3.5% of total revenue, depending on the circumstances.

The two methods described above are residual approaches which establish the preferential return needed to provide both a return on and a return of the capital invested in waning personalty as well as a market-based income for the business value. The remaining stabilized net operating income is attributed to the real property and is capitalized to derive a market value.

Can these hotel valuation methods be applied to value the business enterprise associated with a shopping center? After reviewing earlier shopping center literature, especially the work of Kinnard and Fisher, it might be argued that a shopping center often has a shorter economic life than a hotel and must be more frequently renewed and revitalized to remain competitive. The cost and sales comparison approaches cannot easily be dismissed because they probably do figure into the thinking of shopping center investors, although this remains to be determined in a general context and in individual appraisal assignments. A shopping center's stabilized net operating income could be allocated among various contributing components. Allocating a percentage of hotel income to the management function is facilitated by the market-negotiated management rates used in the hotel management industry. There are similar management contracts for shopping centers. Management fees for shopping centers range from 3% to 5% of total revenues (excluding utility revenues) plus leasing commissions. Of course, local rates would have to be determined through property analysis. If the subject property is operated under such a management contract, however, the income and presumed business enterprise value would have already been removed. The appraiser need only segregate the income and value when they have been intermingled.

If a residual process were to be used in a shopping center appraisal, it is likely the shopping center real estate value would first have to be estimated with the most reliable approach and accorded a market return; then the residual income could be allocated to business value and capitalized at an appropriate rate based on returns to the businesses, as distinguished from returns to the real estate.

In this context using the value derived through the income approach appears redundant and a value estimate derived through sales comparison would not separate the realty and intangible components. Only the depreciated reproduction cost of the improvements plus the market value of the site in a retail use offers a value indication that represents the land and building components without business enterprise value. For this reason, appraisers should not overlook the cost approach in the appraisal of shopping centers. In fact, an appraiser who does not apply the cost approach will probably not consider whether some of the value should be allocated to business enterprise value. Further analysis raises a question as to whether all of the shopping center management fee is really a return to the business value. Certainly it is part of the business manager's obligation to care for the real estate. This is not a perfect way of allocating economic productivity between real assets and intangibles.

Another method of allocating hotel value is discussed by Rushmore. Using this approach the value of the entire property is estimated by dividing an overall capitalization rate into the property's net operating income after a reserve is deducted for the replacement of furniture, fixtures, and equipment.[16] Then a market rental is allocated to the leased fee estate by multiplying the total property revenue by a competitive market rate or occupancy cost rate. In Rushmore's example the rate happens to be 0.16 of the total revenue, but no discussion is provided on how the rate is derived from the market. The value of the business is treated as the residual. To use this technique to allocate shopping center value to the business enterprise component, the appraiser would have to identify the relationship between total shopping center rental collections from the retail merchants and an equivalent, leased fee rental paid for the use and control of the land and buildings. No evidence is available to support such a relationship.

Nevertheless, it may be observed that small income properties are frequently managed by contract managers. For example, medium-sized apartment properties are often managed by professional management firms that charge a fee equal to 5% or 6% of annual rents. If Rushmore's first technique of reducing the property income by the management fee could be applied to an apartment property, the land and buildings could represent part of the total property value and the residual value could be identified as business enterprise value, compensation for screening and servicing the apartment tenants. Although investment in multi-family housing may entail certain political risks and management challenges, there is little discussion of allocating apartment property values between real estate and business value for assessment or any other purposes, except possibly to recognize a business value for subsidized housing.

As a third method, Rushmore indicates that the business value of a hotel can be identified by estimating the management fee as the product of a typical 4% management fee rate and total revenue; this estimated management fee is then capitalized by the overall rate for the property. This is

16. Rushmore, *Hotels, Motels and Restaurants*, 105.

similar to the two hotel valuation methods described previously except that the property's overall rate is used to capitalize the business income. This procedure is used to adjust the observed price of a comparable sale in a tax assessment dispute to justify differences between that sale and the subject property.[17]

James Brown has suggested two techniques for estimating going-concern value in appraising congregate care facilities. The first is a cost-based allocation identifying going-concern value as the amount by which the value derived by the income capitalization or sales comparison approach (whichever is more reliable) exceeds the depreciated replacement cost of the improvements. The second method is based on income capitalization rates. To use this method Brown suggests defining and gathering data on two types of capitalization rates R_1 and R_2.

> R_1 is the overall rate for similar passive real estate investments which do not include personal property or business enterprise value. These investments might be properties in different uses that have similar physical and investment characteristics.
>
> R_2 is the overall capitalization rate applicable to the subject property and similar properties that do include business enterprise value.

The ratio of R_1 to R_2 suggests how total value should be allocated between tangible real property and business value.

In his nursing home example, Brown finds an overall capitalization rate of .12 applicable to the subject property and rates of approximately .10 appropriate for apartment buildings of similar age, condition, and value. He attributes the higher rate for the property with business value to its greater risk, which derives from the fact that the intangible business value is more easily dissipated than tangible real property. With a total property value of $10,900,000, the amount allocated to real, tangible property would be

17. Stephen Rushmore, MAI, and Thomas Arasi, "Adjusting Comparable Sales for Hotel Assessment Appeals," *The Appraisal Journal* (July 1986), 356-366.

$$.10/.12 \times \$10,900,000 =$$
$$.8333333 \times \$10,900,000 = \$9,083,333$$

The value of intangibles and non-real property would be estimated as $10,900,000–$9,083,333, or $1,816,667. These figures would be rounded. In the case of a nursing home, value would also be assigned to furniture, fixtures, and equipment based on their estimated replacement cost and value in use.

A problem arises in applying Brown's approach to shopping centers because a successful mall, where business enterprise value is most likely to be an issue, may be so attractive to investors that it will probably be sold at a lower capitalization rate than comparable substitute investments.

In summary, the various methods discussed here reflect two distinct approaches to estimating business value. These approaches might be termed the *differentiated cash flow method* and the *business-value-as-residual method.* Ideally sufficient data would be available to employ both methods and their results could be reconciled to derive a reliable allocation of total property value between real estate and business enterprise value.

Fisher and Lentz have suggested a differentiated cash flow approach specifically applicable to shopping centers. Through empirical research they have observed that renewal rents are frequently higher than the rents new tenants are charged for the same type of space.[18] They ascribe this difference to business value because the renewing tenant is willing to pay a premium to retain his location in an established and presumably successful environment, not just a particular geographic location. They indicate that the premium paid by the renewing tenant is only part of the value attributable to business value and such premiums reflect a marginal increase in business value. Arguably, some business value is also present in the base rentals paid by new tenants. It is possible that this business value rental premium can be isolated by carefully comparing shopping center rents to rental rates for similar retail properties that are not in shopping centers. In this way the premium for the shopping center location might be

18. Fisher and Lentz.

identified. Capitalizing this premium at a defendable capitalization rate might provide further evidence of business value in the mall.

Estimating an Assessed Value Without the Tax Expense

When an appraiser estimates the value of a shopping center for property tax purposes, it is common practice to complete one round of analysis without including the property taxes in the operating expenses. Then a value can be estimated before property taxes by capitalizing the net operating income before property taxes with a capitalization rate that includes the effective property tax rate in that jurisdiction.

For example, assume the effective gross income minus operating expenses (excluding property taxes) is $500,000 and that the normal cap rate is 8%. Further assume that the jurisdiction has a mandated property-tax-assessment-to-market-value ratio of 40% and a mill rate of property taxes to assessed value of .035. Multiplying the tax rate by the assessment ratio produces the following contribution to the capitalization rate:

$$.035 \times .40 = .014$$

The pre-property tax capitalization rate would be

$$.08 + .014 = .094$$

Experimentation will demonstrate that this capitalization rate can be used to produce a value prior to property taxes, which when subjected to the assessment ratio will produce an assessed value. This assessed value times the mill rate will equal the property tax. That property tax subtracted from the *NOI* will produce an *NOI* which, when capitalized at .08, equals the same value. The proof follows:

Assumed market cap rate	.080
Plus effective cap rate for property taxes	
(.40×.035)	.014
Estimated pre-property tax value	.094
($500,000/.094)	$5,319,149

Property tax assessed value	
(.40×$5,319,149)	$2,127,660
Estimated property tax assessment × tax rate	
($2,127,660 × .035 = $74,468)	
Reconstructed *NOI* after property taxes	
Pre-property tax *NOI*	$500,000
Less estimated property taxes	−74,468
Net operating income	$425,532
Property value estimate ($425,532/.08)	$5,319,149

With this procedure the appraiser can estimate what the value of a mall should be if the property taxes are fairly levied on an assessed value based on that same appraised value. This procedure provides a direct solution to value without circular logic. The method assumes that the property tax assessor agrees with the appraiser's estimate. If the assessor is not in agreement and is unwilling to alter the assessment, this procedure would not be appropriate. Furthermore, this method should not be applied when the property taxes are passed through to tenants under the terms of their leases unless the additional revenues from the recoveries is included in the analysis.

Other Shopping Center Property Tax Assessment Problems

Government officials responsible for determining property tax assessments and collecting tax revenues have heard many arguments about shopping centers.[19] Some individuals argue that shopping centers should be partially exempt from taxes because of the civic and community benefits they generate—i.e., the fountains and park-like amenities built at investors' expense but enjoyed by the public. Others argue that shopping center operators provide for themselves many services that the city does not have to provide, including trash collection, police protection, traffic control, street and parking lot maintenance, street lighting, and snow removal.

---

19. This section draws on David D. Roberts, "Appraisals of Shopping Centers For Tax Assessment Purposes," *Assessors* Journal (July 1968), 10-17 and James F. Gossett, "Assessment Law Notes; The Myriad Problems of Shopping Center Assessment," *The Journal of State Taxation* (Summer 1985).

There are disadvantages affecting shopping centers that other kinds of real estate are not burdened with. David Roberts lists the following:

- Losses are likely to be incurred for many years before the center stabilizes its tenant mix and enjoys profits.
- Tenant leases and operating agreements control the expansion of the shopping center and its parking.
- Exclusive use provisions in tenant leases limit the operator's ability to lease freely to new tenants.
- The shopping center operator is frequently called on to assist merchant tenants in their promotional activities.
- Tenant leases may stabilize the income from tenants as well as many of their expenses, but the owner bears the risk of unforeseen, extraordinary expenses.

Assessors often divide the valuation of a shopping center into two parts. First they value the anchor store with its land and parking, and then they value the mall, which includes the *GLA* of mall shops and all interior and exterior common areas.[20]

A number of court cases have indicated that replacement cost minus accumulated depreciation is the preferred approach for assessment purposes. Arizona has legislated this approach. The value estimate that results from calculating the cost of reproduction minus depreciation has been used to set the upper limit of value for assessment purposes.

Application of the income approach has been accepted in some jurisdictions and is required in others. It has been found to be premature in some cases due to the need to wait for business results from the property in question. Some assessors object to the income approach because changes in economic outlooks and capital market interest rates can produce values that fluctuate too much for assessment purposes. A court has rejected the sole use of the income approach in a case in which a building was used by the owner, bore his name, and generated no rental income. One court decision sanctioned the assessor's use of two different capitali-

20. Vern Tessier, CPA, "The Valuation of Regional and Super-Regional Malls," *Assessment Digest* (Sept./Oct. 1991), 2-13.

zation rates, with the lower one reflecting the lower risk associated with the rental income from an anchor tenant.

Many cases have addressed the definition of income. Arguments have arisen over whether the income approach should consider actual contract rents or economic rents. Some have argued that if the valuation assignment is to estimate the market value of the fee simple estate, then market rents should be used as though the property is unencumbered by leases; if the assignment is to value the actual leased fee estate (or encumbered fee), then the contract rental rate is relevant. While court decisions differ, James Gossett concludes that most of the decisions have favored economic rents over actual contract rents.[21] The reasoning behind this choice is that all interests in the real estate are to be valued, not just the lessor's. These interests include benefits derived by tenants from leases that have been negotiated at below-market (or owner-subsidized) rentals.

Litigation has focused on whether the income considered should include the percentage of sales rental provided in the lease. Robert Beebe reports that this item has been treated both ways.[22] Also disputed is the landlord's income from ancillary services such as utility service sold to tenants, storage lockers, and kiosks. These incomes have all been included at some time.

Attempts to capture all real estate value in the assessment process have frustrated tenants, who may be required under the terms of their leases to complete the construction of walls, partitions, ceilings, and fixtures, but are not able to deduct from their taxable income the property tax associated with the asset. Concurrently, landlords have argued that to include these tenant expenditures as part of the fee interest in the replacement cost approach is to unfairly overtax the fee.

One important property tax assessment case that appears in shopping center appraisal literature is *Lawrence Associates* v. *Lawrence Township*, which includes the following findings:

21. Gossett, 217-227.

22. Robert L. Beebe, "The Assessor and the Shopping Center: Valuation Issues and Problems," a paper presented at the International Association of Assessing Officers Eighth Annual Legal Seminar, San Francisco, October 1988.

- Economic rent could be imputed to office space within a shopping mall that was used by the owner, not rented to tenants, because the space could have generated income.

- Percentage rentals received by the shopping center operator could rightfully be considered part of the economic rent for the property.

- Taxable assessed value could be based in part on an income approach which included the sale by the mall owner of electricity, hot and chilled water, and trash removal services; the rental of storage lockers; and public telephone space rental. Other income derived from the rental of baby strollers and a series of special events was not to be considered.

- Entrepreneurial profit could be included in the replacement cost approach and be based on a percentage of the cost of the building and the site improvements.

- A sales comparison approach to site valuation could include land sale comparables in the immediate vicinity of the subject shopping center, even though their value may have been enhanced by the construction of the subject mall.

- The court preferred that an income capitalization approach be applied to derive property values when assessment dates followed the commencement of mall operations, but preferred values based on reproduction cost when valuation dates preceded the opening.[23]

James Gossett reports:

> The court held that in spite of lease agreements to the contrary, real property included all building improvements, machinery, equipment, or fixtures on the land, and that real estate must generally be assessed as a whole. The court said that government should therefore assess all real estate, including tenant improvements, to the shopping center owner and if the tenant and owner

---

23. *Lawrence Associates* v *Lawrence Township*, 5 N.J.,
    Tax Court 481, 497.

consider improvements as personal property, they could arrange for separate compensation between themselves.[24]

This conclusion has been drawn in several cases.

There is some debate about how to assess tenant finishes such as partitioning, wiring, lighting, and display cases. Most courts treat them as items to be separately valued and taxed,[25] but appraisers should study leases to allocate responsibilities and determine the future dominion of such property.

A number of courts have permitted the assessment of shopping center properties as a whole despite arguments from taxpayers that different ownership interests mandate separate approaches with lower per-unit valuations for some of the subparcels.

Valuing Anchor Stores and Their Sites

One of the current controversies in shopping center appraisal is how to forecast a value for the anchor store and site. When comparable sales are unavailable, property tax assessors and others have estimated depreciated replacement costs. In the process they have tended to infer a land price from sales of surrounding retail sites. Frequently these sites are outparcels that are not truly comparable. (Problems of comparability were discussed in the land valuation section.) The prices of these sites often exceed the observable transaction prices of sites more similar to the subject. In one market, for example, outparcels sell for $10 to $12 per square foot, while sites being purchased for mall development sell for approximately $5 per square foot. If an analyst were to attempt a residual land valuation after allocating some of the imputed market rental as a return, at market capitalization rates, on the previously estimated depreciated replacement cost, little or no income would remain as a return to the land.

This problem has been studied by Michael McElveen and Barry Diskin, who gathered data on site sales for a number of department stores in the Southeast.[26] They found that often the mall developer not only sold the

24. Extensive examination of the arguments and issues raised here is beyond the scope of this text. Assessors and appraisers who wish to obtain further information are directed to the Gossett article for specific citations.

25. Beebe.

26. Michael A. McElveen, MAI, and Barry A. Diskin, PhD, SRPA, "Valuation of Anchor Department Stores," *Assessment Digest* (Sept./Oct. 1990), 14-21.

site for a lower price than was reflected in nearby transactions, but the mall developer also contributed heavily to the department store construction costs and provided other site improvements. In addition to acquiring the site and building the anchor store, the tenant also signed the operating agreement, thus becoming part of a larger co-operative retailing venture.

An operating agreement commits the tenant to a limited, unitary business use of the site for a long period of time and may give the mall operator the right of first refusal at the time of an attempted sale. (As explained earlier, it may also constrain the highest and best use of the site to use as a department store, rather than a bank, fast-food restaurant, or other use typical of outparcels.) Thus, effective shares of ownership are transferred to all the other tenants in the mall. This is what Kenney calls the *enhancement effect*. According to McElveen and Diskin, this reduced bundle of rights is not comparable to the greater bundle of rights held by owners of nearby sites that are not similarly encumbered. These nearby sales are poor comparables because they do not have the same highest and best use.

Why do department store sites sell for less than apparently similar retail land in the vicinity? In addition to the differences in the defined bundle of rights, it seems that the department store is bringing something else of great value to the center — its presence. The anchor's ability to draw customers and thereby enhance the sales of the other tenants and their leasehold estates is a nonmonetary benefit. The challenge for the appraiser and the property tax assessor seems to be whether to convert this into a monetary payment and, if so, how. If the definition of value is limited to "payment in cash or terms equivalent to cash," can this contribution to the center's synergism be measured? Kinnard has speculated that when the identity of a particular anchor tenant is critical to the success of a venture, the situation may fail to include a typical market user as cited in the definition of market value. The value may instead be a value in use.

Comparatively low anchor store values can be a function of comparatively low rental rates. For example, anchors routinely pay rent of $3 to $5 per square foot, while mall stores are paying $10 to $15 per square foot.[27] Anchor stores, particularly department stores, warrant lower rental rates because they take large blocks of space for longer periods of time than most mall tenants, and they generally have superior credit ratings. Therefore they present significantly less risk for the owner.

There are some additional considerations. It is generally known that anchor department stores advertise more than other mall tenants. There is often a tradeoff between the payment of rent and advertising outlays. If most of the department store's merchandise is also available for sale in the other mall stores, and most merchants cannot escape from price competition, it follows that anchor stores that pay more for advertising have less capacity to pay rent.

In a sense, advertising and rent are related in the anchor store's occupancy costs. Although no specific data were found to confirm this supposition, it does offer one explanation for anchor stores' lower rental rates. Their reduced capacity to pay occupancy costs on a rental rate basis could translate into lower capitalized values when one of the store buildings is sold. Furthermore, the market for used department store buildings appears to be limited to a few similar retailers. A sale may be especially difficult to arrange if the location and demographics have apparently not worked well for the seller.

Data for appraising department store sites are available, but difficult to obtain. Some improved sales are of stores that were purchased in leveraged buyouts. The value of such a store might be the historical book value as carried by the seller or a portion of the greater value of the business. Often such transactions include non-real estate items such as fixtures and equipment. Freestanding department stores that are not part of a larger center are poor comparables because they represent a larger bundle of rights if they are not subject to a similar operating agreement. In general, the market data are flawed, require extensive verification, and are frequently derived from transactions that are not arms-length indicators of market activity, as specified by our idealistic definitions of market value.

---

27. *Dollars & Cents of Shopping Centers* has information on department store occupancy costs. See pages 84 and 85 of the 1990 edition.

Gregory Lafakis and other writers suggest that most states direct that the fee simple estate be assessed using market rents.[28] Anchor department store tenants protest that the actual contracts governing their payment obligations and the property rights they enjoy usually set a lower contract rate, which should be considered. Court decisions are inconsistent.

The question remains: How should anchor sites and anchor store properties be valued? To value the site, writers have considered the sales comparison approach, after making careful adjustments for the property rights conveyed, and the land residual approach. For the anchor store property they have suggested the use of the sales comparison approach, again with careful adjustments for the property rights conveyed, and the income approach. Since the market of buyers and sellers for department stores is national (or perhaps international), the search for and selection of comparable sales should be extensive.

In arguing their property tax cases, some anchors develop an estimate of market rental rates by multiplying the store's forecasted sales by an implied or "attributed" occupancy cost of 3%. Then expenses for maintenance, insurance, and reserves are subtracted from this estimate to derive a net income. Net income is then capitalized at 10% to derive a value estimate. One observer has objected to this method, arguing that forecasting rents as a function of sales, which varying among different stores and over time, makes the property tax too sensitive to the ability of the tenant merchandiser. "The property tax should tax property, not people."[29]

In a thoughtful and well-documented paper about department store assessments, Gaylord Wood indicates that the problem in assessing anchors and shopping centers is that the symbiotic relationship between the center's developer/manager and the tenants results in a unified economic entity that generates income and creates value. All the parts are essential and none can be appropriately valued separately. Nevertheless, property tax law assigns parcel identification to individual parts or owners.

For valuing anchors Wood chooses the allocation method, which is commonly applied to public utility properties that lie in several jurisdictions and to telephone companies, airlines, and pipelines.

---

28. Gregory J. Lafakis, "Valuation Concepts and Issues and the Taxpayer's Responsibilities Concerning Regional Shopping Centers," a paper presented at the International Association of Assessing Officers Eighth Annual Legal Seminar, San Francisco, October 1988.

29. Gaylord A. Wood, Jr., "Assessment of Department Stores Associated with Regional Malls," a paper presented at the International Association of Assessing Officers Eighth Annual Legal Seminar, San Francisco, October 1988.

No one part of the system has more than salvage value without all of the pieces being in place as part of an operating economic property. Under unitary appraisal, the "system" is appraised as one economic unit. The appraisal activity necessarily ceases at the system level.[30]

The total system's value is allocated to various jurisdictions or locations according to a multifactor formula which considers use or productivity factors, property factors, and economic factors. In the case of airlines or utilities, use or productivity factors might include air miles, ton miles, passengers boarded, or kilowatts produced. Property factors could include miles of track, plant capacity, the number of substations, or the number of employees. Economic factors might refer to the number of customers and sales volume. Wood asserts that the courts will generally uphold plausible methods. The allocation method can be applied to a unitary asset in the hands of multiple owners or an asset in several locations or jurisdictions. Wood concludes, "This way ensures equity among the participants in the shopping center venture."

Summary

Some problem areas for shopping center appraisers, assessors, and others are: 1) separating out business enterprise value, 2) establishing shopping center assessments for property tax purposes, and 3) estimating a value for the anchor store and site — especially for property tax purposes. These issues have not been settled and more discussion is needed. Some writers report that tax equity may be preserved by establishing unitary values for the tax parcels and allowing those involved to negotiate the allocation of taxes.

---

30. Ibid.

APPENDIX

Many appraisers continually develop data collection forms to train their personnel and improve the quality of their data gathering. Others find their operations so unique that standard forms are not practical. Some sample forms are included in this appendix to help you decide for yourself and get started. Of course, additional forms can be developed for many purposes.

Pre-Appraisal Data Request

If possible, the client should supply the following items:

- Last three years' operating budgets
- Detailed history of income and expenses, tenant turnover, gross sales percentage rental income, parking garage income and expenses
- A current rent roll, lease abstracts, and leases (both master leases and subleases); copies of all side agreements (if applicable); copies of all letters of intent; copies of service contracts
- Copies of the most recent property tax bills; copy of title insurance policy
- Information on hazard insurance coverage, premiums, and terms; name, address, and phone number of insurance agent
- Market surveys performed in-house; customer profile (local/tourist/conventioneers breakdown), demographics and number of visitors; frequency, expenditures, and time of travel
- Any prior appraisals, market studies, feasibility studies, computer templates (e.g., ProJect, Lotus); occupancy history
- "As-built" property survey; photographs, including aerials
- Building plans and specifications summary; name, address, and phone number of architect
- Ownership history, including warranty deed
- Cost summary of site work
- Cost summaries of existing buildings and budgets of proposed buildings
- Environmental studies
- Marketing brochures and pre-leasing plans and summaries; information on current leasing strategies—free rent, tenant improvements, fixture allowance, other concessions; floor plans/leasing plans
- Data on other sales and leasing activity in the subject's vicinity
- Name, address, and phone number of local property contact
- Schedule of recent and planned capital expenditures and replacements

Data Organization Forms

HISTORY

Current owner (partnership name, principals): _____
_____

County: _____ Book: _____ Page: _____

Grantor: _____

Recorded price/terms: _____
_____

Condition/state of development at time of sale: _____
_____

(If owned less than 3 years, repeat next section as necessary)
Previous grantor: _____

Date acquired: _____

County: _____ Book: _____ Page: _____

Grantor: _____

Recorded price/terms: _____
_____

Condition/state of development at time of sale: _____
_____

(If property is under contract)
Buyer: _____

Seller: _____

Contract date: _____ Contract price: _____

Terms: _____

Comments: _____

Construction begins: _____ Construction ends: _____

Leasing commences: _____ Pre-leasing: _____

Present occupancy: _____ Trend: _____

Renovations: _____ Approx. $ spent: _____

Comments: (construction problems, leasing history, occupancy, etc.) _____
_____
_____

By: _____ Date: _____

ZONING

Jurisdiction: _____   Legal description: _____

_____   _____

Contact: _____   District: _____

Section: _____   Parcel no.: _____

Current zoning: _____

Recent changes and date: _____

Likelihood of change: _____

General attitude regarding growth: _____

_____

_____

Permitted uses: _____

_____

Permitted density: _____

Actual density: _____

Requirements:

Parking: _____   Open area: _____

Side setback: _____   Back setback: _____

Front setback: _____   Other: _____

Floodplain/environmental: _____

Restrictions: _____

Site plan approved?   Y   N   Date: _____

What remains to be done for approval? _____

Conforming use?   Y   N

What is required to make conforming? _____

Approval process: _____

_____

Comments: _____

By: _____   Date: _____

TAX INFORMATION FORM

Name: _____   Assessor contact: _____

Owner: _____   Phone: _____

Parcel no.: _____   Taxing district: _____

Size: _____   Millage rate: _____

NRA GLA GBA

Assessment ratio: _____

Methodology of valuation: _____

_____

_____

Construction details: _____

_____

_____

Status on January 1 of tax year: _____

	Full Market Value	Assessed Value	Taxes	
			Total	Per Sq. Ft.
Land				
Improvements				
Other				
Total				

Other assessments:

Sanitation: _____   Date of last revaluation: _____

Other: _____   Date of next revaluation: _____

Valuation trend: _____

Originator: _____   Date: _____

LAND SALE NO.

Verification Name: _____   Phone: _____

Relation: _____   Date: _____
(Buyer, seller, broker, etc.)

Location: _____
_____

Grantor: _____

Grantee: _____

Date of sale: _____ Size (acres): _____ Price/acre: _____

Sale price: $ _____ Size (sq. ft.): _____ Price/sq. ft.: _____

Allowable density: _____ Price/FAR: _____

Terms of sale: _____
_____

Time on market: _____ Contract date: _____
Offers: _____

Zoning: _____

Current/proposed use: _____
_____

Frontage: _____ ft. _____
_____ ft. _____
_____ ft. _____

Utilities available: Water   Sewer   Electric   Gas   Storm Sewer   Telephone
_____

Topography: _____
_____

Comments: (restrictions, floodplain, visibility, identity, access, surroundings, buyer
motivation.) _____
_____
_____
_____
_____
_____
_____

Originator: _____   Date: _____

RETAIL

Comparable Lease Information

	Anchor	Size	Rent

Name: _____   _____

Location: _____   _____

Ownership: _____

Contact: _____   Phone: _____

Construction: (exterior, canopies, landscaping, visibility, parking, access, condition, etc.) _____

Total project size: _____   Land size: _____

Retail space: _____   Year built: _____

Rental   credit $_____ /sq.ft.   Escalators   Y   N   min: _____

rates: retail $_____ /sq.ft.   How _____   max: _____

Market rate for subject: $_____ /sq.ft.

% rent _____ breakpoint: _____

Finish provided: _____   Lease term: _____

_____   Options: _____

Concessions: (free rent, rent abatement, tenant finish, cash, etc.)

_____

Average bay sizes: _____   Configuration: _____

Competition: _____

Current occupancy: _____   Opening date: _____

Occupancy at opening: _____   Absorption rate: _____

Date of stabilization: _____   (pre-lease included ?)

Stabilized occupancy for market: _____

Landlord			**Tenant**		

Expenses:	Base		Admin.	Base/Current Amount
Real estate taxes	_____ _____	+	_____	_____
Insurance	_____ _____	+	_____	_____
CAM	_____ _____	+	_____	_____
Management	_____ _____	+	_____	_____
Total	_____ _____	+	_____	_____

Commissions: _____ % leases cash out   over term _____

Any sales ? _____

Comments: (trade area, merchant attitude, etc.) _____

_____

_____

Originator: _____   Date: _____

RETAIL LEASE ABSTRACT

Tenant name: _____ Bay no. _____

Sublease: _____

Size: _____ sq.ft. Lease year: _____ to _____

Rental structure

    Base rental rate

    Total annual: $_____ Monthly: $_____ Per sq.ft.: $_____

Lease commencement	Amendments
Term begins: _____	1 _____
Term ends: _____	2 _____
Years: _____	3 _____
Months: _____	
Options: Y N	Number · term _____
Escalations: Y N	When: _____
How: CPI _____	Cap min. _____ max. _____ %
Stated _____	

Initial term	Annual Amount	$/Sq. Ft.	% Rent	Sq. Ft. Breakpoint
Yr. 1 ___ to ___	___	___	___	___
Yr. 2 ___ to ___	___	___	___	___
Yr. 3 ___ to ___	___	___	___	___
Yr. 4 ___ to ___	___	___	___	___
Yr. 5 ___ to ___	___	___	___	___

Options	Annual Amount	$/Sq. Ft.	% Rent	Sq. Ft. Breakpoint	Market Rent at Rollover	Exercise Option
Yr. 1 ___ to ___	___	___	___	___		Y N
Yr. 2 ___ to ___	___	___	___	___		Y N
Yr. 3 ___ to ___	___	___	___	___		Y N
Yr. 4 ___ to ___	___	___	___	___		Y N
Yr. 5 ___ to ___	___	___	___	___		Y N

Expense contributions:	Landlord	Tenant	Admin.	Max. Amount
Real estate taxes	___	___	___	___
Insurance	___	___	___	___
CAM	___	___	___	___
Property mngt.	___	___	___	___
Structural & exterior repairs and maintenance	___	___	___	___
Other _____	___	___	___	___

CAM definition: _____

Commissions: cash out over term none   Concessions: _____ none

    Initial _____   Free rent _____

    Options _____   Tenant improvements _____

Exclusives: _____

Comments: _____

Originator: _____ Date: _____

Shopping Center Sale No. _____

Verification name: _____ Phone: _____

Relation: _____ Date: _____
(buyer, seller, broker, etc.)

Name: _____

Location: _____

Grantor: _____

Grantee: _____

Date of sale: _____ Sale price: $ _____ Sale price/sq. ft. _____

Terms of sale: _____
_____

Total project size: _____ Retail space: _____

Land size: _____ Year built: _____

Improvements: _____

Anchor: _____ _____ sq. ft. $ _____ / sq. ft.

Tenants: _____ _____ sq. ft. $ _____ / sq. ft.

_____ _____ sq. ft. $ _____ / sq. ft.

Occupancy   Current   Increasing
at sale: _____ occupancy: _____ Decreasing

Retail   Master Y N   Anticipated
rents: $_____ / sq. ft. lease: _____% vacancy: _____

Potential gross income: _____

Effective gross income: _____ *EGI*/sq. ft. _____ *EGIM*: _____

Expenses: _____ *EXP*/sq. ft. _____ *OER*: _____

Net income: _____ *NOI*/sq. ft. _____ *OAR*: _____

Debt service: _____ Are expenses net of reimbursements? _____

                                Did expenses include reserves? $ _____

Purchase   *OAR* _____ % _____

Criteria: *IRR* _____ % _____

            Other _____ _____

Comments: _____
_____
_____
_____

Originator: _____ Date: _____

Comparable Sales Adjustment Worksheet

Subject is: _____   C:Comparable;   S:Superior or +:Superior;   I:Inferior or –:Inferior.

Name: _____

Sale No.	Conditions of Sale	Market Conditions	Location	Physical Characteristics			Zoning	Topo-Contour		Natural Site		Overall Comparability	$/Unit	$/Acre
Financing				Frontage	Size	Utilities		Grade		Amenities		+		
				Visibility	Shape							C		
				Access	Site Utility			Drainage				–		

Name: _____

Sale No.	Conditions of Sale	Market Conditions	Location	Physical Characteristics			Zoning	Topo-Contour		Natural Site		Overall Comparability	$/Unit	$/Acre
Financing				Frontage	Size	Utilities		Grade		Amenities		+		
				Visibility	Shape							C		
				Access	Site Utility			Drainage				–		

Name: _____

Sale No.	Conditions of Sale	Market Conditions	Location	Physical Characteristics			Zoning	Topo-Contour		Natural Site		Overall Comparability	$/Unit	$/Acre
Financing				Frontage	Size	Utilities		Grade		Amenities		+		
				Visibility	Shape							C		
				Access	Site Utility			Drainage				–		

Appraisal Review Checklist

Factual Data Summary	Effective Date	Value Estimated
1. Date appraisal was prepared	_____	_____
2. Market value "as is"	_____	_____
* 3. Prospective market value upon completion	_____	_____
* 4. Prospective market value upon stabilized occupancy	_____	_____

Identification of Property and Value Definition	Adequate Yes	Inadequate No	N/A
5. Was the correct legal description used?			
6. Were the real property rights correctly identified?			
7. Were any non-realty rights correctly identified?			
8. Were any special provisions contained in the instrument that created the appraised estate properly described?			
9. Was the correct market value definition used?			
10. Was an appropriate summary of salient facts and conclusions supplied?			

Identification of Economic and Environmental Factors			
11. Relevance and adequacy of regional and city economic data			
12. Relevance and adequacy of neighborhood analysis			
13. Were emerging trends in land usage properly addressed?			
14. Were the availability, cost, and adequacy of public utilities addressed?			
15. Was the analysis of ad valorem taxes properly developed and were the ad valorem taxes for the subject identified?			

* Required for all reports involving proposed construction, change of use, partially completed improvements, and rehabilitation work.

Appraisal Review Checklist

	Adequate Yes	Inadequate No	N/A
16. Was an appropriate analysis of the legal restrictions on use other than zoning supplied?			
17. Description of shape and size of site			
18. Description of topographical features			
19. Description of zoning restrictions affecting site			
20. Description of drainage and existence of floodplain condition			
21. Was a site sketch or survey included?			
22. Analysis of functional adequacy of site			
23. Description of ingress and egress			
24. Relationship to adjoining properties			
25. Description of nuisances and hazards			
26. Analysis of soil and subsoil conditions			

Physical Description of Improvements

27. Were adequate photographs of the improvements included?			
28. Was a sketch or improvement plan with dimensions included?			
29. Was the description of construction components appropriate?			
30. Was the description of the quality of construction adequate?			
31. Was the description of the current condition of the improvements adequate?			
32. Was an appropriate analysis of the adequacy of design, layout, etc., included?			
33. Was the physical age of the improvements supplied?			
34. Was the effective age of the improvements supplied?			
35. Was the remaining economic life of the improvements supplied?			
36. Was the description of the utility of improvements appropriate?			

Appraisal Review Checklist

	Adequate Yes	Inadequate No	N/A
37. Was an appropriate description of the improvements' compatibility with surrounding uses provided?			
*38. Were the specific plans and specifications for any proposed work identified?			
39. Was the adequacy of the site improvements for the proposed use addressed?			
40. Was an appropriate description of the equipment, fixtures, and chattel property supplied?			

Highest and Best Use Analysis

	Adequate Yes	Inadequate No	N/A
41. Was the highest and best use of the site as if vacant analyzed?			
42. Was the highest and best use of the property as improved or as proposed to be improved analyzed?			
43. Was the highest and best use identified for the site and the overall property consistent with the purpose of the appraisal?			
44. Were the legally permitted uses properly evaluated?			
45. Were the physically possible uses properly evaluated?			
46. Were supply and demand factors properly considered in the evaluation of the marketable title?			
47. Did the concluded highest and best use(s) represent the optimal combination of legal, physical, and marketable uses?			
*48. Did the appraiser evaluate the economic feasibility of the highest and best use?			
*49. Was the timing of any proposed use or change in use properly considered in the report?			

Cost Approach Analysis and Conclusions

	Adequate Yes	Inadequate No	N/A
50. If the cost approach was excluded, was proper justification supplied?			

* Required for all reports involving proposed construction, change of use, partially completed improvements, and rehabilitation work.

Appraisal Review Checklist

	Adequate Yes	Inadequate No	N/A
51. Did the report include photographs of the land or site comparable sales?			
52. Did the report include a sales/subject property locational map?			
53. Was the site valued as if vacant and available for its highest and best use?			
54. Was the site value based on sales with a highest and best use comparable to the subject site?			
55. Was the site value based on sales that were physically and economically comparable to the subject property?			
56. Were all sales properly adjusted for cash equivalency?			
57. Were the comparable data adequate and properly analyzed?			
58. Was the reproduction cost estimate properly documented and supported?			
59. If replacement cost was used, were the elements of functional obsolescence eliminated properly described?			
60. Were all costs of production included and consistent with the effective date(s) of valuation or condition of the improvement?			
61. Were all losses due to physical deterioration and functional and economic obsolescence properly supported?			
62. Was the contributory value of the site improvements properly documented?			
63. Was the as is condition appropriately developed and reported?			
*64. If required by the assignment letter, were the values as of completion and as of stabilized occupancy appropriately developed and reported?			

Sales Comparison Approach
Analysis and Conclusions

	Adequate Yes	Inadequate No	N/A
65. If the sales comparison approach was excluded, was proper justification supplied?			

* Required for all reports involving proposed construction, change of use, partially completed improvements, and rehabilitation work.

Appraisal Review Checklist

	Adequate Yes	Inadequate No	N/A
66. Did the analysis demonstrate that the comparable sales were physically and economically similar to the subject?			
67. Was the highest and best use of the sales similar to the highest and best use of the subject property?			
68. Were all sales properly adjusted for cash equivalency?			
69. Were the sales properly compared to the subject?			
70. Were the comparable data adequate and properly analyzed?			
71. Were all adjustments for differences supported with market data or a logical analysis?			
72. Did the report include photographs of the comparables?			
73. Did the report include a sales/subject property locational map?			
74. Was the as is value appropriately developed and reported?			
*75. If required by the assignment letter, were the values as of completion and as of stabilized occupancy appropriately developed and reported?			
76. Was the value estimate(s) consistent with the data presented?			

Income Approach Analysis and Conclusions

	Adequate Yes	Inadequate No	N/A
77. If the income approach was excluded, was proper justification supplied?			
78. Did the report include a comparable/ subject property locational map?			
79. Did the report include the required comparable photographs?			
80. Was the actual income and expense history of the subject supplied?			

* Required for all reports involving proposed construction, change of use, partially completed improvements, and rehabilitation work.

Appraisal Review Checklist			
	Adequate Yes	Inadequate No	N/A
81. Were all existing leases properly reviewed and described?			
82. Were the comparable rentals properly described and compared to the subject property?			
83. Did the comparables reflect uses comparable to the highest and best use of the subject property?			
84. Were any adjustments applied to the comparables supported with market data or a logical analysis?			
85. Were all sales properly adjusted for cash equivalency?			
86. Were the comparable data adequate and properly analyzed?			
87. Did the report establish whether the existing leases were at market rates and terms?			
88. Was a summary of the historical financial performances of the subject property supplied in the appraisal?			
89. Was the expense forecast properly supported with comparable financial data?			
90. Were replacement reserves properly handled?			
91. Was the reconstructed operating statement properly related to the property's historical data?			
92. Were all appropriate deductions and discounts applied or accounted for in the analysis?			
93. Was the appraiser's selection of the capitalization or discounted cash flow technique supported with market data?			
94. Was each element of the capitalization or discounted cash flow technique applied supported with market data?			
95. Were non-realty components of value properly separated from the real estate interests?			
96. Was the impact of existing leases or other legal limitations properly considered if the fee simple estate was being valued?			
97. Was the as is value appropriately developed and reported?			

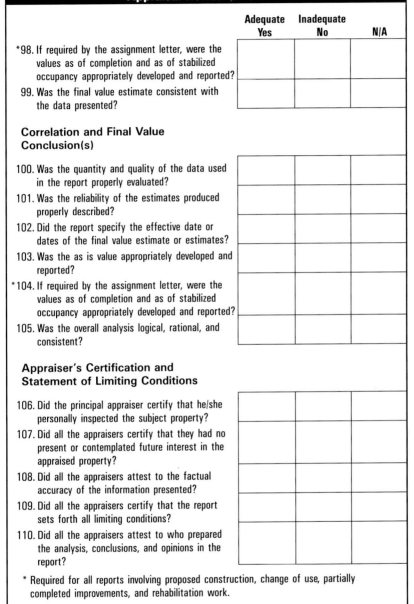

Appraisal Review Checklist

	Adequate Yes	Inadequate No	N/A
*98. If required by the assignment letter, were the values as of completion and as of stabilized occupancy appropriately developed and reported?			
99. Was the final value estimate consistent with the data presented?			

Correlation and Final Value Conclusion(s)

	Adequate Yes	Inadequate No	N/A
100. Was the quantity and quality of the data used in the report properly evaluated?			
101. Was the reliability of the estimates produced properly described?			
102. Did the report specify the effective date or dates of the final value estimate or estimates?			
103. Was the as is value appropriately developed and reported?			
*104. If required by the assignment letter, were the values as of completion and as of stabilized occupancy appropriately developed and reported?			
105. Was the overall analysis logical, rational, and consistent?			

Appraiser's Certification and Statement of Limiting Conditions

	Adequate Yes	Inadequate No	N/A
106. Did the principal appraiser certify that he/she personally inspected the subject property?			
107. Did all the appraisers certify that they had no present or contemplated future interest in the appraised property?			
108. Did all the appraisers attest to the factual accuracy of the information presented?			
109. Did all the appraisers certify that the report sets forth all limiting conditions?			
110. Did all the appraisers attest to who prepared the analysis, conclusions, and opinions in the report?			

* Required for all reports involving proposed construction, change of use, partially completed improvements, and rehabilitation work.

Appraisal Review Checklist

	Adequate Yes	Inadequate No	N/A
111. Was the certification signed by all the appraisers who prepared the appraisal?			
112. Did the report set forth all pertinent limiting conditions in one location?			
113. Were the limiting conditions appropriate to the valuation problem?			

Overall Report Rating

	Adequate Yes	Inadequate No	N/A
114. Does the appraisal comply with the client's written appraisal policies?			
115. Does the report comply with the requirements of the assignment specified in the engagement letter?			
116. Was the level of detail contained in the appraisal commensurate with the complexity of the valuation problem and property type?			
117. Did the appraisal contain sufficient information to support the value estimate(s)?			
118. Were any significant appraisal deficiencies noted which might affect the reported value estimates?			
119. Did the appraiser estimate a blended mortgage/equity discount rate for our internal use?			
120. Did the appraiser estimate the time it will take to transact a sale and closing to a single purchaser at the appraised value?			

Reviewer's Comments

_____

_____

_____

_____

_____

_____

_____

Note. The reviewer's comments should be numbered to correspond to the numbering scheme used in the Appraisal Review Checklist.

Tenant Classifications and Code Numbers

	SIC Code	Tenant Class		SIC Code	Tenant Class
General Merchandise			Cafeteria	5812	C-03
Department store	5311	A-01	Fast food/carryout	5812	C-04
Junior department store	5311	A-02	Cocktail lounge	5813	C-05
Variety store	5311	A-03	Doughnut shop	5812	C-06
Discount department store	5311	A-04	Ice cream parlor	5812	C-07
Showroom/catalog store	5399	A-05	Pretzel shop	5812	C-09
			Cookie shop	5812	C-10
Food					
Supermarket	5411	B-01	**Clothing**		
Convenience market	5411	B-02	Ladies' specialty	5631	D-01
Meat, poultry and fish	5423	B-03	Ladies' ready-to-wear	5621	D-02
Specialty food	5499	B-04	Bridal shop	5621	D-03
Delicatessen	5411	B-05	Maternity	5621	D-04
Bakery	5463	B-06	Hosiery	5631	D-05
Candy and nuts	5441	B-07	Children's wear	5641	D-07
Dairy products	5451	B-08	Menswear	5611	D-08
Health food	5499	B-09	Family wear	5651	D-09
			Unisex/jean shop	5699	D-11
Food Service			Leather shop	5699	D-12
Restaurant without liquor	5812	C-01	Uniform shop	5699	D-13
Restaurant with liquor	5812	C-02	Special apparel — unisex	5699	D-14

Tenant Classifications and Code Numbers (continued)

	SIC Code	Tenant Class		SIC Code	Tenant Class
Shoes			Records and tapes	5733	G-04
Family shoes	5611	E-01	Musical instruments	5733	G-05
Ladies' shoes	5661	E-02	Gourmet cookware	5719	G-06
Men's and boys' shoes	5611	E-03	Computer/calculator (retail)	5999	G-07
Children's shoes	5661	E-04			
Athletic footwear	5661/5941	E-05	**Building Materials/Garden**		
			Paint and wallpaper	5231	H-02
Home Furnishings			Hardware	5251	H-03
Furniture	5712	F-01	Home improvements	5211	H-04
Lamps	5719	F-02			
Floor coverings	5713	F-03	**Automotive Supplies/Service Station**		
Curtains and drapes	5714	F-04	Automotive (TBA)	5531	K-01
China and glassware	5719	F-06	Service station	5541	K-03
Fireplace equipment	5719	F-07			
Bath shop	5719	F-08	**Hobby/Special Interest**		
Contemporary home accessories	5719	F-09	Sporting goods—general	5941	M-01
Cutlery	5719	F-10	Hobby	5945	M-02
			Art gallery	5999	M-03
Home Appliances/Music			Cameras	5946	M-04
Appliances	5722	G-01	Toys	5945	M-05
Radio, video, stereo	5732	G-02	Bike shop	5941	M-06
Sewing machines	5722	G-03	Arts and crafts	5999	M-07
			Coin shop	5999	M-08

Tenant Classifications and Code Numbers (continued)

	SIC Code	Tenant Class
Outfitters	5941	M-09
Game store	5945	M-10
Gifts/Specialty		
Imports	5999	N-01
Luggage and leather	5948	N-02
Cards and gifts	5947	N-03
Candle	5999	N-04
Books and stationery	5942/3	N-05
Decorative accessories (including hardware and collectible gifts)	5947/5719	N-06
Jewelry and Cosmetics		
Credit jewelry	5944	P-01
Costume jewelry	5999	P-02
Jewelry	5944	P-03
Cosmetics	5999	P-04
Liquor		
Liquor and wine	5921	Q-01
Wine and cheese	5921/5451	Q-02

	SIC Code	Tenant Class
Drugs		
Super drug (over 10,000 square feet)	5912	R-01
Drugs	5912	R-02
Other Retail		
Fabric shop	5949	S-01
Tobacco	5993	S-02
Pet shop	5999	S-03
Flowers	5992	S-04
Plant store	5992	S-05
Other retail	5999	S-06
Telephone store	5999	S-07
Eyeglasses – optician	5999/8042	S-08
Personal Services		
Beauty	7231	T-01
Barber	7241	T-02
Shoe repair	7251	T-03
Cleaner and dyers	7212	T-04
Laundry	7212	T-05

Tenant Classifications and Code Numbers (continued)

	SIC Code	Tenant Class		SIC Code	Tenant Class
Health spa/figure salon	7299	T-06	**Financial**		
Photographer	7221	T-07	Banks	602	X-01
Formal wear/rental	7299	T-08	Savings and loan	612	X-02
Interior decorator	7399	T-09	Finance company	6145	X-03
Travel agent	4722	T-10	Brokerage	6211	X-05
Key shop	7699	T-11	Insurance	6411	X-06
Unisex hair	7231/8299	T-12	Real estate	6531	X-07
Film processing	7395	T-13	Automatic teller machine	6059	X-08
Photocopy/fast print	7332	T-14			
			Offices (other than financial)		
Recreation/Community			Optometrist	8042	Y-01
Post office	7399	W-01	Medical and dental	8011/8021/8031	Y-02
Music studio and dance	7911/8299	W-02	Legal	8111	Y-03
Bowling alley	7933	W-03	Accounting	8931	Y-04
Cinemas	7832	W-04	Employment agency	7361	Y-06
Ice/roller skating	7999	W-05	Other offices	—	Y-07
Community hall	—	W-06			
Arcade, amusement	7993	W-07	**Other**		
Day care and nursery	8351	W-08	Vacant space	—	Z-01
			Miscellaneous income	—	Z-02
			Warehouse	—	Z-03

(Tenant class numbers not in sequence indicate classificaitons not repeated from previous *Dollars & Cents of Shopping Centers* studies.)

Source: SIC codes are from *The Standard Industrial Classification Manual* (Washington, D.C. U.S. Office of Management and Budget). Tenant classes are from *Dollars & Cents of Shopping Centers: 1984* (Washington, D.C. Urban Land Institute, 1984).

GLOSSARY

absorption rate. The rate at which properties for sale or lease have been or are expected to be successfully sold or leased in a given market area; usually applied in forecasting sales or leasing activity.

access. 1. The means or way by which a property is approached (access to the site). 2. The means or method of entrance into or upon a property (access onto the site).

accessibility. 1. The relative degree of effort (time and cost) by which a site can be reached; indicates ease of entrance upon a property. 2. A location factor which will identify the most probable and profitable use of a site in terms of ease and convenience.

"act of God" clause. A lease provision that allows for extra construction time in the event of extraordinary difficulties that the landlord cannot control; it may be an escape clause for the tenant if construction is not begun or completed by a specified date.

amenities. The tangible and intangible benefits associated with a property's lot, onsite improvements (e.g., design, size, quality) and offsite improvements (e.g., schools, recreational facilities, location).

analogue approach. A process in which existing, successful properties similar to the subject property are found and comparisons are made based on customer profiles and the physical, financial, and locational features of the sites.

anchor tenant. The major store within a shopping center that attracts or generates traffic for the facility, e.g., a supermarket in a neighborhood shopping center, a major chain or department store in a regional shopping center.

Applebaum's customer spotting model. A procedure in which primary data obtained through onsite consumer interviews are used to define a retail establishment's primary and secondary trade areas and identify the penetration rate in the trade area.

base rent. The minimum rent stipulated in a lease.

belt highway. An arterial highway that carries traffic partially or entirely around an urban area and is connected with the city by principal streets or highways.

breakpoint. In a lease the sales threshold at which percentage rental payments commence; it may be computed by dividing the decimal percentage rate into the base rent.

built-to-suit lease. An arrangement in which the developer builds or finances the construction of the improvements according to the tenant's needs and then leases the combined land and improvements back to the user.

business enterprise value (BEV). An intangible element of value created in the construction and operation of a shopping center; generally not considered part of the real property value, but as a return on entrepreneurship.

business valuation. An appraisal of a business, usually performed to determine the present and future monetary rewards of complete or partial ownership rights in the business.

buying power index (BPI). A measure of demand in the local area relative to a benchmark value. One such index, the Survey of Buying Power, uses the United States as a benchmark in the following formula:

$BPI = 0.5$ (local area's percentage of income)

$+ 0.3$ (local area's percentage of U.S. retail sales)

$+ 0.2$ (local area's percentage of U.S. population)

Another form of *BPI* could use a single region or a state as the benchmark value.

CAM. *See* common area maintenance.

capture rate. The share of the market obtained by the subject. *See also* market share.

capture rate analysis. A type of analysis based on the assumption that retail centers attract expenditure levels relative to their size and location. Thus a center is more likely to attract a shopper if it is larger, is located nearer the shopper's residence than other centers, or both.

central business district (CBD). The core or downtown area of a city where the major retail, financial, governmental, professional, recreational, and service activities of the community are concentrated.

central place theory. A theory that cities are created in response to the service needs of surrounding rural areas and that the location of urban settlements can be understood by studying the functions they perform for these outlying areas.

closed period. A time during which a loan may not be pre-paid; may deprive the owner of a source of cash flow from refinancing.

clustering. *See* cumulative attraction.

common area. The area within a property that is not designed for sale or rental, but is available for common use by all owners, tenants, and their guests, e.g., parking and its appurtenances, malls, sidewalks, landscaped areas, recreational areas, public toilets, truck and service facilities.

common area charges. Income that is collected from owners or tenants to pay for the operation and maintenance of common areas.

common area maintenance (CAM). The expense of operating and maintaining common areas. *See also* common area.

community shopping center. A shopping center of 100,000 to 300,000 square feet that usually contains one junior department store, a variety or discount department store, a supermarket, and specialty stores.

comparison goods. Merchandise offered by department stores, apparel stores, furniture stores, and other stores in sufficient variety to give consumers a broad choice of merchandise.

competitive analysis. *See* survey of the competition.

competitive area. The physical space or geographic area in which the competition for a subject property operates; the area where economic and demographic changes can affect the subject's revenues, expenses, and value.

competitive differential. The process in which the special features that give one property a competitive edge over another are identified using data from a survey of the competition.

concentric zone theory. A theory of urban growth developed in the 1920s by Ernest W. Burgess which states that predominant land uses tend to be positioned in a series of concentric, circular zones around a city's central business district.

consolidated metropolitan statistical area (CMSA). A large geographic area that consists of two or more primary metropolitan statistical areas (PMSAs); designated under standards set in 1980 by the Federal Committee on MSAs.

Consumer Price Index (CPI). A measurement of the cost of living determined by the U.S. Bureau of Labor Statistics.

convenience goods. Commodities purchased frequently and without extensive comparison of style, price, or quality.

convenience (or low-order) products. Nondurable commodities that are needed immediately, relatively inexpensive, and purchased frequently (i.e., daily, weekly, monthly) at the most convenient location without extensive comparison of style, price, and quality. Because the consumer purchases these goods often, the quality of products and their prices are well known.

convenience shopping center. A center in which most retailers sell daily necessities.

Converse's modification. An enhanced version of Reilly's model of retail gravitation used to determine the geographic trade area boundaries of a retail establishment; allows the analyst to estimate the distance from the site where that site's influence is equal to that of its competitors. *See also* Reilly's model of retail gravitation.

corner influence. The value effect of a location at or near the intersection of two streets; the increment of value resulting from such a location.

covenant. A promise between two or more parties, incorporated in a trust indenture or other formal instrument, to perform certain acts or to refrain from performing certain acts.

cross-easements. Reciprocal easements created by contract; an easement is granted in favor of the premises.

cumulative attraction. A situation that results when retail establishments locate next to each other so that each establishment can benefit from the increased volume of potential customers drawn to the cluster of retail establishments; also called *clustering*.

customer spotting model or technique. *See* Applebaum's customer spotting model.

data. The information pertinent to a specific assignment; may be divided into two classes: general (relating to the economic and demographic background, the region, the city, and the neighborhood) and specific (relating to the subject property and comparable properties in the market).

debt coverage ratio *(DCR)*. The ratio of net operating income to annual debt service $(DCR=NOI/I_M)$; also called *debt service coverage ratio (DSCR.)*

department store type merchandise (DSTM). General merchandise, apparel, furniture, and other goods as defined by the Department of Commerce's Census of Retail Trade; also called *GAFO*.

disaggregation. Differentiation of the subject property from other properties by subclassification into smaller groups with differing physical and locational characteristics.

discount rate. A rate of return commensurate with perceived risk and used to convert future payments or receipts into present value.

discount shopping center. A community center that is anchored by a discount department store and is smaller than a regional mall.

drawing power. The relative ability of one retail establishment to attract and retain customers' patronage.

DSTM. *See* department store type merchandise.

due diligence. A thorough investigation undertaken by sophisticated investors before they purchase major assets. The process is conducted by a team of experts in accounting, finance, appraisal, engineering, property management, and law.

due-on-sale clause. A clause in a mortgage that allows the lender to call in the remaining balance for immediate payment upon conveyance of the lease; may limit value in a sale that could be facilitated by a loan assumption.

economic base. The economic activity of a community that enables it to attract income from outside its borders.

economic base analysis. A technique that uses the relationship between basic and nonbasic employment to predict population, income, or other variables that affect real estate values or land utilization.

effective rent. Rental rate net of financial concessions such as periods of no rent during a lease term; may be calculated on a discounted basis, reflecting the time value of money, or on a simple straight-line basis.

efficiency ratio. 1. In appraising, the ratio between a building's net rentable area, i.e., the space used and occupied exclusively by tenants, and its gross area, which includes the building's core. 2. In economics, the ratio between the ends produced, or output, and the means used, or input. 3. In land economics, the ratio between the value of the product flowing from the site and the expense of the labor and capital that produced it; refers to the average amount of net product, e.g., rent returned per unit of labor and capital applied.

elastic. In economics, describes the responsiveness of prices to changes in the supply or demand for a good.

Ellwood's modification. A variation of Reilly's retail gravitation model in which travel time is substituted for distance and the square footage of retail space is substituted for population in the equation.

employment base. The number of gainfully employed persons in a community or city.

employment density. The ratio between the number of employees actually working the largest, regular daily shift at a plant site and the land area of the site.

equity capitalization rate (R_E). An income rate that reflects the relationship between a single year's pre-tax cash flow expectancy, or an annual average of several years' pre-tax cash flow expectancies, and the equity investment; used in direct capitalization to convert pre-tax cash flow into an equity value indication. Also called *equity dividend rate, cash on cash rate,* or *cash flow rate* $(R_E = \text{pre-tax cash flow/equity})$.

escalation clause. A clause in an agreement that provides for the adjustment of a price or rent based on some event or index, e.g., a provision to increase rent if operating expenses increase.

escalation income. Income that is generated from an escalation clause in a lease.

escape clause. The provision that permits tenant cancellation of a lease under circumstances that would not ordinarily be considered justification for lease cancellation.

excess land. The part of a parcel that is not needed in the present use. The land must be usable (or salable) in terms of shape, topography, and other characteristics.

excess rent. The amount by which contract rent exceeds market rent at the time of the appraisal; created by a lease favorable to the landlord (lessor) and may reflect a locational advantage, unusual management, unknowledgeable parties, or a lease execution in a earlier, stronger rental market. Due to the higher risk inherent in the receipt of excess rent, it may be calculated separately and capitalized at a higher rate in the income capitalization approach.

exclusive use clause. A provision in a lease that prohibits the landlord from leasing other space in the shopping center to competitors.

exculpatory clause. A provision in an agreement that limits one party's recourse against the other party in the event of default; e.g., a nonrecourse mortgage limits recovery to the property itself.

expense stop. A clause in a lease that limits the landlord's expense obligation because the lessee assumes any expenses above an established level.

facade. The principal, exterior face of a structure; usually the front face or front elevation of a building.

fashion shopping center. A concentration of apparel shops, boutiques, and custom quality shops that carry special merchandise, usually high-quality, high-priced goods.

festival shopping center. A type of specialty shopping center designed to provide a special experience. It is characterized by a high percentage of *GLA* devoted to specialty restaurants and food vendors with an emphasis on ethnic authenticity, unique offerings, impulse and specialty retail goods, and a strong entertainment theme, e.g., Faneuil Hall Marketplace in Boston, South Street Seaport in Manhattan.

flat rental. A specified level of rent that continues throughout the lease term; also called *level payment rental*.

gap analysis. A comparison of demand and supply data to uncover any present or future excess demand or excess supply in a market; identification of unmet demand or supply shortages. *See also* market gap analysis and spatial gap analysis.

generative business. A retail operation that has such strong market appeal that it is a primary destination for customers in a specific location. Department stores, well-known specialty stores, supermarkets, and other anchor stores are examples of this type of business.

going-concern value. The value created by a proven property operation; it is considered as a separate entity to be valued with an established business; also called *going value*.

goodwill. A salable business asset based on reputation, not physical assets.

gross building area (GBA). The total floor area of a building, excluding unenclosed areas, measured from the exterior of the walls; the most common standard of measurement, especially for determining the size of industrial buildings.

gross leasable area (GLA). The total floor area designed for the occupancy and exclusive use of tenants, including basements and mezzanines; the standard of measurement commonly used for determining the size of shopping centers.

gross lease. A lease in which the landlord receives stipulated rent and is obligated to pay all or most of the operating expenses of the real estate.

hard goods. A class of merchandise composed primarily of durable items such as hardware, machines, heavy appliances, electrical and plumbing fixtures, and farming machinery and supplies; sometimes referred to as *hardlines*.

holdover tenant. A tenant who remains in possession of the leased real estate after the lease has expired; in many states, the lease is automatically renewed if the lessor accepts a rent payment after the expiration of the lease.

Huff's probability formulation. An extension and modification of Reilly's model of retail gravitation which establishes the probability that a consumer located at a given point of origin will travel to shop at a specific shopping center or in a retail district.

hypermarket. A horizontally integrated community center with typical retail establishments operated by a single owner under one roof. Such a center has centralized checkout for all goods and enjoys a quasi-monopoly position.

impulse good. A product that is purchased without a prior decision to shop for it.

income participation. The right of the mortgagee to share some portion of the future income generated by the property, usually over the term of the mortgage.

index lease. A lease that provides for periodic rent adjustments based on the change in a specific index, e.g., the cost of living index.

in-line store. A store that is contiguous with its neighbors, in contrast to a freestanding store.

intangible assets. 1. Nonphysical items of personal property, e.g., franchises, trademarks, patents, copyrights, goodwill. 2. Deferred items such as a development or organizational expense.

intercept locations. The competitive locations that are first encountered and first seen by potential users of the subject site; because of their favorable exposure, these stores may divert activity or capture part of the market being sought by the subject site.

internal rate of return *(IRR)*. A measure of investment performance; the rate of return on capital that is generated or capable of being generated within an investment or portfolio over a period of ownership; similar to the equity yield rate; often used to measure profitability after income taxes, i.e, the after-tax equity yield rate; the rate of discount that equates the present value of the benefits to the present value of the capital outlays.

joint and several obligation. A situation in which each signing party is liable for his or her share of a debt or obligation plus the shares of all other signing parties; as distinguished from several obligation, in which each signatory is responsible only for his or her liabilities.

junior department store. A store that can be classified between a full-line department store and a variety store in terms of its size and selection of merchandise.

kick-out clause. A lease clause that allows a retailer to cancel a long-term lease of five or ten years after the first, second, or third year if sales have not achieved a specified threshold. One variant allows the tenant to cancel its lease if the landlord is unable to replace a departing anchor tenant within a specified period.

landlord. The owner of real property that is leased to another.

landlord burden clause. A clause in a lease that specifies a lower stop for common area maintenance (CAM) expenses to be paid by anchor tenants, shifting a greater portion of expenses to either other mall tenants (typically) or the owner.

law of retail gravitation. *See* Reilly's model of retail gravitation, Huff's probability formulation, Converse's modification, and Ellwood's modification.

leasehold improvements. Improvements or additions to leased property that have been made by the lessee.

lease rollover. The expiration of a lease and the subsequent re-leasing of the space.

lessee. One who has the right to use or occupy a property under a lease agreement; the leaseholder or tenant.

lessor. One who holds property title and conveys the right to use and occupy the property under a lease agreement; the leased fee owner or landlord.

letter of credit. A letter issued by a financial institution that certifies that the person named can draw on the institution or that the institution will honor his or her credit up to a certain limit.

linkage. 1. The movement over space necessary to maintain spatial relationships. A householder must commute to work; a shopper must travel to the store. The act of moving can only be accomplished when transfer costs are incurred by the individual who has undertaken the move. 2. Time and distance relationships between a particular use (e.g., residential) and supporting facilities such as schools, shopping centers, and employment sites. These uses are interrelated and must be provided through public or private market action. Transfer costs can be regarded as linkages with other parcels of real estate.

local economic analysis. Study of the fundamental determinants of the demand for and supply of all real estate in the market. The analysis considers the factors basic to the demand for all types of real estate in a local economy—i.e., population, households, employment, and income. Past trends and forecasts of these basic demand determinants are made for a defined geographic area. The supply-side factors to be considered include the amount of land available for specific land uses, construction costs, and the local infrastructure. Economic base analysis and input-output analysis are two techniques used to describe the local economy.

location. The time-distance relationships, or linkages, between a property or neighborhood and all other possible origins and destinations of people going to or coming from the property or neighborhood.

major tenant. The store that generates the greatest amount of customer patronage to a shopping center. Sometimes referred to as the *key tenant* or the *anchor*, the major tenant is strong enough to stand alone and is effective in attracting patronage from beyond the primary trade area. Department stores, junior department stores, large variety stores, and supermarkets generally function as major tenants in regional, intermediate, and neighborhood shopping center developments. *See also* anchor tenant.

mall. 1. Originally, a shaded walk. 2. An area designed for pedestrian use only. 3. A large shopping center, usually a regional shopping center.

mall tenants. The non-anchor tenants in a shopping center; also referred to as *tenants of shop space* or *local tenants*.

marketability study. A microeconomic study that examines the marketability of a given property or class of properties to determine a specific highest and best use, test development proposals, or project an appropriate tenant mix.

market analysis. The identification and study of a pertinent market.

market area. A geographic area or political jurisdiction in which alternative, similar properties effectively compete with the subject property in the minds of probable, potential purchasers and users.

market disaggregation. The process of dividing a market into smaller, more homogeneous submarkets based on product characteristics. *See also* disaggregation.

market gap analysis. An analysis undertaken to determine whether there is or will be unmet or unfilled demand in the market. *See also* gap analysis.

market rent. The rental income that a property would most probably command in the open market.

market segmentation. The process by which submarkets within a larger market are identified and analyzed.

market share. The portion of a trade area's potential—e.g., retail sales to be generated, office space to be absorbed—that can be attributed to a proposed facility; based on the property's known market strength and position relative to competitive facilities.

mean. A measure of central tendency. The sum of the values of a set divided by the number of values. *See also* median and mode.

median. A measure of central tendency. The value of the middle item in an uneven number of items arranged or arrayed according to size; the arithmetic average of the two central items in an even number of items similarly arranged; a positional average that is not affected by the size of extreme values.

mode. A measure of central tendency. The most frequent, or typical, value in an array of numbers; a positional average that is not affected by extreme values. It is the most descriptive average and easily identified when the number of items is small; however, if the sample is too small, none of the values may be repeated and no mode exists.

neighborhood shopping center. A center offering convenience goods (foods, drugs, and sundries) and personal services (laundry and dry cleaning, barbering, and shoe repair) to satisfy the day-to-day living needs of the immediate neighborhood. A supermarket is typically the anchor tenant of a neighborhood center, which may have a gross leasable area of 30,000 to 100,000 square feet.

net lease. A lease in which the tenant pays all property charges in addition to the stipulated rent.

net operating balance. A term used to describe *net operating income* in *Dollars & Cents of Shopping Centers*.

net sales area. The area in a department or retail store that is available for the sale of merchandise, excluding storage and equipment areas, rest rooms, etc.; the actual floor area used for merchandising.

occupancy costs. The total costs incurred by the tenant for occupying space, including total rent and expense reimbursements to the landlord and any other charges for which the tenant is responsible.

off-price shopping center. A center with retail stores that sell brand-name goods at 20% to 70% below department store prices. Off-price stores generally offer better-quality merchandise than discount stores and appeal to middle-income and upper-middle-income consumers.

operating agreement. A document containing commitments from the anchors and the center operator to maintain the site in a specified use; also called a *reciprocal easement*.

operating expense ratio *(OER)*. The ratio of total operating expenses to effective gross income; the complement of the net income ratio.

outlet shopping center. A collection of factory outlet stores.

outparcels. Portions of the shopping center site located at its periphery and generally along major traffic thoroughfares; popular locations for banks, fast-food restaurants, and auto service stores.

overage rent. The percentage rent paid over and above the guaranteed minimum rent.

overall capitalization rate *(R_o)*. An income rate for a total real property interest that reflects the relationship between a single year's net operating income expectancy, or an annual average of several years' income expectancies, and the total price or value; used to convert net operating income into an indication of overall property value ($R_o = NOI/V$).

pad. The land beneath a condominium unit or a store in a shopping center.

parking ratio. The number of available parking spaces per rentable area, residential unit, hotel room, restaurant seat, etc.; a standard of comparison that indicates the relationship between the number of parking spaces and the economic or physical unit of comparison.

percentage lease. A lease in which the rent, or some portion of it, represents a specified percentage of the volume of business, productivity, or use achieved by the tenant.

percentage rent. Rental income received in accordance with the terms of a percentage clause in a lease; typically derived from retail store tenants based on a certain percentage of their retail sales.

point-of-view oriented. A retailing strategy that offers greater service and unique merchandise in an expensive environment designed to draw shopper traffic.

power center. A large community center with more than 250,000 square feet of space anchored by three or more anchor tenants that occupy 60% to 90% of the gross leasable area.

primary trade area. The geographic area around a retail facility from which approximately 60% to 70% of its customers come. The geographic radius and driving time identified with the primary trading area will vary with the type of facility.

radius clause. A lease provision that promises a major tenant that no other property within a specified radius owned by the shopping center owner will contain that same use.

regional shopping center. A center that offers general merchandise, apparel, furniture, and home furnishings in depth and variety, as well as a range of services and recreational facilities. Its orientation is the provision of shopping goods, with substantially less emphasis on convenience goods. A regional shopping center is built around one or two full-line department stores of generally not less than 100,000 square feet each. A typical regional center has 400,000 to 750,000 square feet of gross leasable area.

Reilly's model of retail gravitation. An analytical theory that holds that ". . . under normal conditions two cities draw retail trade from a smaller, intermediate city or town in direct proportion to some power of the population of these two larger cities and in an inverse proportion to some power of the distance of each of the cities from the smaller, intermediate city. In any particular case, the exponents used in connection with population or distance are dependent upon the particular combination of retail circumstances involved in that case. Typically, however, two cities draw trade from a smaller, intermediate city or town approximately in direct proportion to the first power of the population of these two larger cities and in an inverse proportion to the square of the distance of each of the larger cities from the smaller, intermediate city."

relative per capita sales *(RPCS)*. A measure of relative sales potential for a given product or retail category calculated using the following formula:

$RPCA$ = local per capita sales/U.S. per capita sales

State or regional sales figures can be used as the benchmark instead of U.S. per capita sales.

rent abatement clause. A lease clause that may allow a major tenant to offset some or all of its percentage rent payments against its prorated share of some expense item such as taxes; also called an *offset clause*.

rent roll. A report that is prepared regularly, usually each month, and indicates the rent-paying status of each tenant.

rent-up period. The period of time over which the initial leasing of a rental property is conducted; may begin before or after construction and last until stabilized occupancy is achieved.

residual analysis. *See* vacuum technique.

retail clusters. *See* cumulative attraction.

sales area. Rentable area minus storage space. Because the proportion of rentable store area devoted to sales varies among store types and individual stores, calculations of sales or rent are more uniform if they are based on total store area.

secondary location. A location that is near or adjacent to the prime location; a second-best location; gains enhancement from proximity to the prime location.

secondary trade area. The portion of a trade area that provides additional support for a shopping center, beyond that supplied by the primary trade area. Secondary trade area patronage of the shopping center is primarily generated by the comparison shopping stores in the center, while convenience shopping is usually done at neighborhood centers close to home.

share-of-the-market analysis. An analytical technique which assumes that strong stores that are capably and aggressively merchandised will obtain their representative share of the total market in that category despite the existence of competing units. Stores that have an identifiable name and appeal to shoppers, such as department stores, are likely to attract a certain share of total business under normal operating conditions.

shopping center. A tract of land, under individual or joint real estate ownership or control, improved with a coordinated group of retail buildings with a variety of stores and free parking. *See also* community shopping center; neighborhood shopping center; regional shopping center; superregional shopping center.

shopping goods. Goods sold by variety, department, and general merchandise stores—e.g., clothing, furniture, appliances.

soft goods. Nondurable merchandise such as wearing apparel, linen and towels, bedding, and yard goods; also known as *softlines*.

spatial gap analysis. An analysis undertaken to determine if there is unsatisfied, unfilled, or unmet demand that the proposed site could satisfy. *See also* gap analysis.

specialty goods. Goods which shoppers take more care and spend greater effort to purchase.

specialty shopping center. A nontraditional shopping center characterized by the absence of the traditional anchor tenant and the existence of a unique feature, mix of tenants, or theme.

stabilized income. An estimate of the economic productivity of the real estate for one representative year of the income forecast.

stabilized occupancy. The optimum range of long-term occupancy, which an income-producing real estate project is expected to achieve under competent management after exposure for leasing in the open market for a reasonable period of time at terms and conditions comparable to competitive offerings.

stop clause. A lease provision that sets an upper limit on an expense to be paid by the landlord; the tenant pays amounts above that ceiling.

strip shopping center. A line of stores often tied together with a canopy over the sidewalk that runs along the storefronts.

subjective distance. Consumer perceptions about distance and travel time from one site to another. Consumers' perceptions of distance or travel time may differ from the actual figures. Pleasant circumstances can make the subjective distance shorter than the actual distance or travel time while unpleasant circumstances have the opposite effect.

subjective probability. A decision maker's evaluation of the relative likelihood of unknown events.

sublease. An agreement in which the lessee in a prior lease conveys the right of use and occupancy of a property to another, the sublessee.

supermarket. A large retail store built on one level and stocked with goods that are conveniently and conspicuously displayed so that customers may make their selections without the help of a clerk; usually sells food products and household supplies that are paid for at a checkout counter.

superregional shopping center. A center that offers an extensive variety of general merchandise, apparel, furniture, and home furnishings as well as a range of services and recreational facilities. A superregional center is built around at least three major department stores of not less than 100,000 square feet each. A typical superregional center has 800,000 or more square feet of gross leasable area, but most newly constructed centers have more than 1,000,000 square feet of *GLA*.

supplemental agreement. A document used in conjunction with an operating agreement that contains additional important agreements and is typically not recorded. The supplemental agreement states the price of the anchor's land parcel and any reimbursement the anchor makes for site improvements.

survey of the competition. Identification of the properties in the market or trade area that have similar characteristics and attract the same potential buyers or space users.

suscipient business. A retail establishment that draws its market appeal from an independent source, such as a major public transportation facility, which attracts customers into an area where the retail operation can position itself to offer its goods or services. This type of business is parasitic; it depends on an external source and is subject to the peculiarities of that particular market. For example, a retail business may depend on the captive market within an office center and close on Saturday when most employees do not come to work.

targeting analysis. Study of the demographics and other characteristics of a population to see who they are and what can be sold to them.

tax shelter. A reduction in federal and state income tax liability created by making deductions from taxable income for depreciation and other outlays relating to certain assets.

tenant improvement allowances. Payments made by the landlord to or for the tenant to help finish the space and thus induce the tenant to enter into a lease.

trade area. The geographic area from which sustaining patronage for a shopping center is obtained; its extent depends on the shopping center itself, its accessibility, the presence of physical barriers, the location of competing facilities, the limitations of driving time and distance, and other factors.

traffic. The movement of people and vehicles along a way or past a point; the people and vehicles that move along the way.

traffic count. The number of people and/or vehicles moving past a location during a specified period of time. Traffic counts may be used to determine the volume of vehicular traffic past a proposed service station site or the number of pedestrians passing a retail location as a measure of potential sales volume. Traffic counts may also identify the composition of the traffic—i.e., the numbers of men and women, the number of private automobiles as opposed to trucks and buses. They can reflect traffic conditions on certain days of the week or year and at certain hours of the day.

traffic density. The number of vehicles occupying a specific length of a roadway at a given instant; usually expressed in vehicles per mile.

traffic survey. A survey conducted to obtain information relating to traffic such as its quantity and composition, the drivers' origins and destinations, the purpose of trips, and means of transportation; usually relates to a specific time and day of the week.

transfer costs. The costs incurred by users of a site to travel to and from that site to other destinations such as homes, schools, and doctors; include monetary costs for fuel, maintenance, repair, tolls, and parking as well as nonmonetary costs such as the value of time spent in transport.

utility area. The portion of space in a retail establishment devoted to the provision of essential building services such as heating and refuse disposal. *See also* sales area.

vacuum technique. A procedure used to establish the amount of unrealized retail potential within a trade area. The trade area of the site is identified on the basis of driving times, adjusted for natural boundaries. The amount of retail business potential within the trade area is calculated based on population, income, and expenditure data. The floor areas of stores in the trade area are measured and multiplied by national sales averages to arrive at the existing sales volume. The existing sales volume is subtracted from the sales potential, and the remainder, or vacuum, is the potential available to the new store or shopping center. The vacuum technique is applied primarily to outlying shopping centers and is also known as *residual analysis* or the *residual technique*.

value- or commodity-oriented retailer. A retailer who offers depth of inventory and selection in a modest shopping environment. Value-oriented retailers such as Toys R Us and Home Depot may have limited drawing power for the rest of the center.

visibility analysis. A process examining property elements that provide potential site users with information about the activities and conditions available on the site and affect their decision to continue to use it. Such a study concentrates specifically on the visibility of all the site's principal and supporting uses, specific activities and points that require more visibility, signs and information about such activities, and access conditions and internal site connections.

visitation rate. In retail trade analysis, the frequency of customer trips to the property on a weekly, monthly, or other basis.

warehouse club. A store of 100,000 to 120,000 square feet in a nontraditional location that sells brand-name merchandise at deeply discounted prices. Customers pay an annual membership fee and must bag or box their own purchases. Warehouse clubs make high profits by selling a limited selection of goods at very low prices with little advertising.

yield rate *(Y)*. A measure of investment return that is applied to a series of incomes to obtain the present value of each; examples are the interest rate, the discount rate, the internal rate of return *(IRR)*, and the equity yield rate *(Y_E)*.

BIBLIOGRAPHY

Books and Reports

Alexander, Alan A., et al. *Managing the Shopping Center*. Chicago: Institute of Real Estate Management, 1987.

American Institute of Real Estate Appraisers. *Case Studies in Shopping Center Valuation*. Chicago: American Institute of Real Estate Appraisers, 1964.

Applebaum, William. *Case Studies in Shopping Center Development and Operation*. New York: International Council of Shopping Centers, 1974.

Appraisal Institute. *The Appraisal of Real Estate*, 10th ed. Chicago: Appraisal Institute, 1992.

Atlanta Regional Commission. *Atlanta Region Shopping Center Survey: Research Report*. Atlanta: Atlanta Regional Commission, 1987.

Bell, Curtis. *Shopping Center Development Guide*. Washington D.C.: National Association of Home Builders, 1975.

Berry, Brian and J.B. Parr. *Market Centers and Retail Location: Theory and Applications*. Englewood Cliffs, N. J.: Prentice-Hall Inc., 1988.

Born, Waldo L. and Karla D. Svoboda. *Special Report: Real Estate Market Research Publications*. College Station: Real Estate Center, Texas A&M University, November 1987.

Brueggeman, William B., Jeffrey D. Fisher, and Leo D. Stone. *Real Estate Finance*, 8th ed. Homewood, Illinois: Richard D. Irwin & Company, 1989.

Carn, Neil G., Joseph Rabianski, Ronald Racster, and Maury Seldin. *Real Estate Market Analysis Techniques and Applications*. Englewood Cliffs, N.J.: Prentice-Hall, 1988.

Carpenter, Horace. *Shopping Center Management: Principles and Practices*. New York: International Council of Shopping Centers, 1978.

Casazza, John. *Shopping Center Development Handbook*, 2d ed. Washington, D.C.: Urban Land Institute, 1986.

Clapp, John. *Handbook for Real Estate Market Analysis*. Englewood Cliffs, N.J.: Prentice-Hall, 1987.

Cummings, Jack. *Complete Guide to Real Estate Financing*. Englewood Cliffs, N.J.: Prentice-Hall, 1978.

Downtown Research and Development Center. *A New Concept, The Downtown Shopping Center*. Alexander A. Laurence, ed. New York: Downtown Research and Development Center, 1975.

——.*Downtown Mall Annual and Urban Design Report*. New York: Downtown Research and Development Center, 1977-1978.

——.*Downtown Malls: Feasibility and Development*. New York: Downtown Research and Development Center, 1974.

Friedman, Edith J. *Encyclopedia of Real Estate Appraising*, 3d ed. Englewood Cliffs, N.J.: Prentice-Hall, 1978.

Friedman, Jack P., Waldo Born, and Arthur L. Wright. *Developing and Managing a Freestanding Store*. College Station: Real Estate Center, Texas A&M University, 1989.

Garrett, Robert L., et al. *The Valuation of Shopping Centers*. Chicago: American Institute of Real Estate Appraisers, 1976.

Goldstucker, Jac, et al. *New Developments in Retail Trading Area Analysis and Site Selection*. Atlanta: Georgia Business Publishing Division, College of Business Administration, Georgia State University, 1978.

Hines, Mary Alice. *Income-Property Development, Financing, and Investment*. Lexington, Mass.: Lexington Books, 1983.

——.*Shopping Center Development and Investment*. New York: Wiley, 1983.

Institute of Real Estate Management. *Income/Expense Analysis, Shopping Centers*, 1991 ed. Chicago: Institute of Real Estate Management, 1991.

Kinnard, William N., Jr. "Valuing the Real Estate of Regional Shopping Centers Independently of Operation Business Value Components: A Review of Recent Research." A paper prepared for AIREA Annual Meeting, Chicago, May 1990.

Lion, Edgar. *Shopping Centers: Planning, Development, and Administration*. New York: Wiley, 1976.

Martin, Peter G. *Shopping Center Management*. London: E. & F.N. Spon, 1982.

Rams, Edwin. *Analysis and Valuation of Retail Locations*. Reston, Va.: Reston Publishing Company, Inc., a Prentice-Hall company, 1976.

Robinson, Peter C. *Complete Guide to Appraising Commercial and Industrial Properties*. Englewood Cliffs, N.J.: Prentice-Hall, 1977.

————.*How to Appraise Commercial Properties*. Englewood Cliffs, N.J.: Prentice-Hall, 1977.

Roca, Ruben, ed. *Market Research for Shopping Centers*. New York: International Council of Shopping Centers, 1980

Sternlieb, G. and J. Hughes. *Shopping Centers, USA*. Piscataway, N. J.: Center for Urban Policy Research, Rutgers University, 1981.

Thompson, John S. *Site Selection*. New York: Chain Store Publishing Co.

Urban Land Institute. *Dollars & Cents of Shopping Centers, 1990*. Washington, D.C.: Urban Land Institute, 1990.

————.*Shopping Center Development Handbook*, 2d ed. Washington, D.C.: Urban Land Institute, 1985.

Vernor, James D. *Readings in Market Research for Real Estate*. Chicago: American Institute of Real Estate Appraisers, 1985.

Wulfe, E.D. "Shopping Centers" in *Texas Real Estate Investment Guide*. College Station: Real Estate Center, Texas A&M University, 1990.

Articles

On shopping center valuation

Burbach, James R., MAI. "What to Look for in Discounted Cash Flow Software." *The Appraisal Journal* (April 1990): 196-201.

Gelbtuch, Howard C., MAI. "Shopping Centers Are a Business Too." *The Appraisal Journal* (January 1989): 57-64.

International Council of Shopping Centers. *Shopping Centers Today*, published monthly. New York.

Johnston, Rod P. "Appraising Income-Producing Properties: Another Way." *The Appraisal Journal* (January 1985): 27-40.

Martin, Vernon, III. "Reviewing Discounted Cash Flow Analysis." *The Appraisal Journal* (January 1990).

Mueller, Glenn R. "Real Estate Software Report, 1990." *Real Estate Finance* (Spring 1990): 21.

Ordway, Alexander, and Mark E. Eakin. "Developing a Visibility Index to Classify Shopping Centers." *The Appraisal Journal* (April 1988): 233-242.

Scrirens, Robert H. "Reviewing a Regional Shopping Center Appraisal Report." *Appraisal Review and Mortgage Underwriting Journal* (Winter 1989): 57-61.

Sorenson, Richard C., MAI. "Interviewing Techniques for Appraisers." *The Appraisal Journal* (October 1988): 531-535.

———."Checklist for Confirming Sales." *The Appraisal Journal*, (April 1986): 274-281.

Tessier, Vern, CPA. "The Valuation of Regional and Super-Regional Malls." *Assessment Digest* (Sept/Oct. 1991): 2-13.

Trippi, Robert R. and Robert J. Spiegel. "Computer Assisted Appraisal of the Regional Shopping Mall." *The Real Estate Appraiser and Analyst* (September/October 1978): 24.

On shopping center finance

Crawford, William P. "Out-Parcel Leasing Strategies Part of Total Financing Picture" from *ANDREWSREPORT*, vol. 5, no. 3, 1991: 1, 3.

"Financing Comes From a Variety of Sources." *Chain Store Age Executive* (February 1988): 14A-17.

Forman, Ellen. "Edwin Goodman's Investing Puts Profits Before Glamour." *Daily News Record*, October 13, 1988: 7.

Gruen, Nina J. "Retailing Fundamentals, Problems, and Solutions." *Urban Land* (July 1990): 26.

"Neighborhood Shopping Centers in Strong Demand." *National Real Estate Investor* (May 1988): 28-30.

Nichol, Fran. "The Southeast: Lenders, Investors Cautious About Starting New Space." *National Real Estate Investor* (May 1988): 62-65.

"Regional Malls Are Continuing as Favored Investment." *National Real Estate Investor* (May 1988): 32-34.

"Taking a Chance on Hitting It Big; Retailing Lures Venture Capitalists as Other Industries Strike Out." *Chain Store Age Executive* (March 1986): 45-47.

Turchiano, Francesca. "The Unmalling of America." *American Demographics* (April 1990): 37.

On shopping center management

Bean, James C., Charles E. Noon, et al. "Selecting Tenants in a Shopping Mall." *Interfaces* (March-April 1988): 1-9.

Campbell, Boyd. "A Comeback for a Mall." *New York Times*, November 27, 1988: 26.

"Greenbriar Knows Its Neighbors; Atlanta Mall Pioneers Trend, Catering to Growing Ethnic Market." *Chain Store Age Executive* (December 1988): 56-61.

Greenspan, Jodi. "Solving the Tenant Mix Puzzle in Your Shopping Center." *Journal of Property Management* (July-August 1987): 27- 31.

Hinsche, Gary. "Reviving a Shopping Center To Attract Customers." *Journal of Property Management* (Sept-Oct 1987): 14-16.

Klokis, Holly. "Leasing Issues: Developers Speak Out." *Chain Store Age Executive* (November 1987): 37-40.

Kovach, Jerry. "Compensating Shopping Center Managers." *Real Estate Review* (Summer 1986): 28-31.

Newman, Jeffrey H. "The Default and Remedies Clause of the Commercial Lease." *Real Estate Review* (Summer 1989): 37.

"Rights of Assignment and Subletting; Keys That Unlock Future Value." *Real Estate Review* (Spring 1989): 27-31.

"Shopping Centers (The Real Estate Markets in 1988 - Coming Into Focus)." *Journal of Property Management* (March-April 1988): 29- 31.

Silverman, Robert A. "Pitfalls in Shopping Center Use and Exclusive Use Clauses." *Real Estate Review* (Summer 1990): 60-62.

Switzer, Michael H. "Using Due Diligence in Shopping Center Purchasing." *Real Estate Review* (Fall 1986): 88-92.

"Turn Good Into Better: Get Involved; Concerned Mall Managers Keep Centers Operating at Peak Efficiency." *Chain Store Age Executive* (October 1986): 33-36.

On shopping center construction

Fletcher, June. "Shopping Centers." *Builder* (May 1986): 158-165.

Wilderman, Milton A. "Creative Site Planning: A Competitive Tool." *Progressive Grocer* (November 1987): 16-18.

On shopping center report preparation

Atkins, Merle E. "Real Estate Appraisals Fact or Fiction." *The National Mall Monitor* (July/August 1987): 45-46.

Graaskamp, James A. *The Appraisal of 25 N. Pinckney: A Demonstration Case for Contemporary Appraisal Methods.* Madison, Wis.: Landmark Research Inc., 1977.

Pardue, William P., Jr. "Writing Effective Appraisal Reports." *The Appraisal Journal* (January 1990): 16-22.

Society of Real Estate Appraisers. *A Guide To Narrative Demonstration Appraisal Reporting.* Chicago: Society of Real Estate Appraisers, 1976.

On shopping center taxation

Beebe, Robert L. "The Assessor and the Shopping Center: Valuation Issues and Problems." A paper presented at the International Association of Assessing Officers Eighth Annual Legal Seminar, San Francisco, October 1988.

Gimmy, Arthur E., MAI. "Conflict at the Mall: The Tax Reduction Solution." *Appraisal Views.* Newsletter of Schultz, Carr, Bissette, and Atwater/VNI, vol. 3, no. 2, Atlanta.

James F. Gossett, "Assessment Law Notes; The Myriad Problems of Shopping Center Assessment." *The Journal of State Taxation* (Summer 1985); *Assessment Law Notes*: 217-227.

Lafakis, Gregory J. "Valuation Concepts and Issues and the Taxpayer's Responsibilities Concerning Regional Shopping Centers." A paper presented at the International Association of Assessing Officers Eighth Annual Legal Seminar, San Francisco, October 1988.

McElveen, Michael A., MAI, and Barry A. Diskin, Ph.D., SRPA. "Valuation of Anchor Department Stores," unpublished manuscript, September 1989.

Roberts, David D. "Appraisals of Shopping Center for Tax Assessment Purposes." *Assessors Journal* (July 1968): 10-17.

Rushmore, Stephen, MAI, and Arasi, Thomas. "Adjusting Comparable Sales for Hotel Assessment Appeals." *The Appraisal Journal* (July 1986): 356-366.

On shopping center business value

Rushmore, Stephen, MAI, and Karen E. Rubin. "The Valuation of Hotels and Motels for Assessment Purposes." *The Appraisal Journal* (April 1984): 270-288.

On retailing

Gruen, Nina J. "Retailing Fundamentals, Problems, and Solutions." *Urban Land* (July 1990): 26.

Mangan, Daryl T. "Consolidation of the Shopping Center Industry." *Urban Land* (June 1990): 30-31.

Turchiano, Francesca. "The Unmalling of America." *American Demographics* (April 1990): 37.

INDEX